Jesus said that everyone who understands the kingdom of Heaven is like the head of a household, who can bring forth from his storeroom treasures old and new.

For twelve years HLI has brought forth from its warehouse tons of the best pro-life/family educational treasures -- from timeless papal teaching such as <u>Humanae Vitae</u> to powerful new videos. Then we have sent them to the very ends of the earth.

None of this would be possible without your prayers, gifts and encouragement, dear friend. I thank God and His Mother daily for you, and for all you do to extend the Reign of Christ from pole to pole.

May He shower His choicest blessings upon you and your dear ones forever!

With deepest gratitude,
Rev. Paul Marx, O.S.B.

The Warehouse Priest

Father Paul Marx, OSB, PhD

Foreword by Gianna Jessen, Age 16
Saline Abortion Survivor

iv

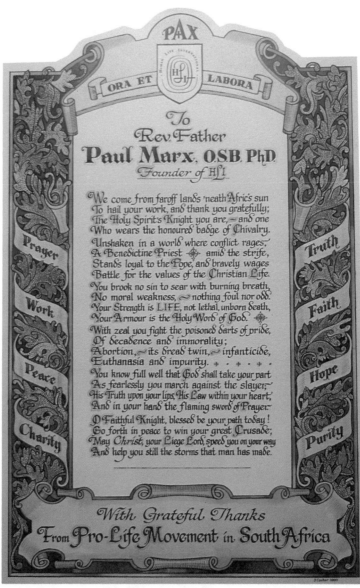

Dr. Claude Newbury of HLI-South Africa read and presented this magnificent hand-illuminated tribute to Fr. Paul Marx before 750 souls at the banquet during HLI's World Conference in Houston. The touching poem, composed and rendered in the Benedictine style by Joyce Coulter, brought tears to many eyes.

vi

HUMAN LIFE INTERNATIONAL
7845 Airpark Road, Suite E
Gaithersburg, Maryland 20879 USA
301/670-7884
FAX 301/869-7363

HLI-CANADA
P.O. Box 7400, Station V
Vanier, Ontario K1L 8E4 CANADA
613/745-9405
FAX 613/745-9868

Dedication

To His Holiness Pope Paul VI, Bishop of Rome, Vicar of Jesus Christ, Successor of St. Peter, Prince of the Apostles, Supreme Pontiff of the Universal Church and Defender of Life and Love, I joyfully dedicate this book.

For your obedience to the Will of God, we remember you.

For your courage in promulgating Humanae Vitae, we honor you.

For your fidelity to the eternal truths enshrined in that great encyclical, we thank you.

"Those who instruct many unto justice will shine like the stars for all eternity" (Dan. 12:3). With the Blessed Virgin Mary, your holy predecessors and all the angels and saints, may you intercede for us poor sinners as we labor to restore God's vineyard.

Rev. Paul Marx, OSB

Twenty-fifth Anniversary of **Humanae Vitae**

25 July 1993 was the 25th anniversary of *Humanae Vitae*, the most controversial encyclical of the century. Many of the events chronicled in this book are woven around this encyclical. One of the distinctive marks of HLI is its insistence upon getting to the root cause of abortion throughout the world. We know for a fact that abortion is the ultimate abuse of sex, but that this begins with the original abuse, which is promiscuity and contraception. If pro-life groups choose to ignore this connection, then they are only dealing with symptoms and not basic causes. Their efforts are doomed to frustration.

Fr. Paul Marx was one of the first pro-life leaders to make this connection. Now the task is to get the message out to the world, and to help people of good faith to see that if abortion is the problem, then *Humanae Vitae is the solution*. This means that our moral guides and spiritual leaders must teach *HV* from the pulpit and in bishops' pastorals. It means that doctors and nurses must understand the devastating effect of their prescribing contraceptives, and doing or making referrals for sterilization. It means that parents and catechists must understand that they cannot teach youth the virtue of chastity if they themselves dissent from God's moral order. This book narrates the ongoing pilgrimage of a man God has raised up to lead the battle against abortion and the abuse of children, women, marriages and family life.

Fr. Matthew Habiger, OSB

TABLE OF CONTENTS

FOREWORD

The Washington, D.C., area is full of important people doing important things. To a teenager like me it can appear as a place where people leap tall buildings in a single bound yet still have time on landing to make a noticed appearance at the Hard Rock Cafe and other "cool" places.

Washington, through the eyes of youth, is a kaleidoscope of lies and dares, mystery and intrigue, power, hope, compromise and disappointment. It was founded on Truth, but has become lost to deception. What was once morally wrong is now politically correct. Washington no longer lives up to its historic promise nor to the lofty quotes of its famous statesmen. It thrives on controversy and headlines.

Washington weighs matters—and now human beings—in terms of convenience or inconvenience. Which label applies depends on who is putting the value on the one in question. To the opportunist, the value is only the temporary usefulness of the person. To the power-seeker, the value is found in the strengths stolen from human stepping stones. I'm not too young to know about this stuff. I'm not too young to feel it. Neither are my peers.

People ask me time after time what teenagers are looking for. Maybe the question should be, "What are teenagers seeing?" What we are looking for is honesty, straight messages, acknowledgement of our value, indication that we have intelligence and, unfortunately, **permission** to be moral. What we are seeing is dishonesty, mixed messages, indifference to our value as a person, a move toward educational brainwashing and encouragement to be *immoral*. What we are getting are non-credible leaders. What we want are upstanding mentors.

There are such mentors tucked away in the environs of Washington. They are unshifting teachers, standing firm in their moral and spiritual convictions. They slip around behind the scenes, moving things in a Heavenly direction. These people speak rather softly, yet are sometimes heard with a thunder. So it is with Father Paul Marx, who has become both a friend and a mentor to me and who lives unpretentiously in a warehouse in the shadow of this great city.

I have had the chance to see Father Marx up close. My Mom and I traveled with Father and other HLI staff on a mission for the unborn in Ireland. I know secret stuff about him—like how much he loves candy; that he's not grumpy early in the morning; how every day he reads all the newspapers he can collect and cuts out, then memorizes, the important facts relating to the protection of life.

I know with what effort he hikes up the hills to see beautiful sights like the Cliffs of Moher. Despite the harsh wind and pounding Irish rain he waited for me, and despite his own infirmity, he gave me a tug to help pull me up the difficult path that climbs high above the sea near Galway Bay.

I do not stand in awe of Father Marx because he has chosen a life of poverty and chastity. Nor does my admiration for him come because of his choice of the priesthood; for as an evangelical Christian I do not completely understand that choice. What I see is the faithfulness of a man who has not compromised his calling. I see a man who has counted the cost and has still chosen to walk the dusty path he has been told to follow. I have been given, in the example of Father Marx, a portrait of humbleness, a perfect picture of love for mankind, and a visual testimony of a man who allows God to whisper in his ear, then listens and obeys.

Father Marx must know the Scripture, "If God is for me, who can be against me?" because he walks in places most would fear to go. He tells the truth about life, conception, contraception and biblical living. He takes the risk; he is not ashamed of the Gospel. He is pro-life, pro-family, pro-God, pro-Church and pro-Gospel. He believes in the potential of all people, even people like me who have physical disabilities that others say dictate a poor quality of life. I do not believe there is such a life type to Father Marx; he sees all life as valuable and full of promise.

There was a story my Mom read to me when I was a little girl. It was about a boy named Johnny Appleseed. Father Marx is a Johnny Appleseed. He sprinkles seeds of truth around the world. Little seeds of truth about abortion, euthanasia, contraception, sterilization, population control and the true value of people as given by God. Many people don't like these little seeds, but Father Marx keeps sprinkling them about and they are growing into trees that bear fruit that is being reaped and harvested; plants that are cultivated and replanted. The seeds are growing in the fertile soil despite attempts of many people who want to bury them in fallow ground.

The Apostle Paul says in Philippians 4 (NIV) "I know what it is to be in need, and I know what it is to have plenty. I have learned the secret of being content in any and every situation, whether well fed or hungry, whether living in plenty or in want. I can do everything through Him who gives me strength." Unless we have walked in need and in plenty, we cannot begin to imagine what either would be like.

I didn't used to understand the poverty choice Father Marx has made or how he is content to live in a small space in a plain warehouse. This Scripture has allowed me to understand it. It is by this choice that he can travel the world and understand how others must live. It is by having little that he has much.

Jesus tells us that He is preparing a place for us, and in this place there are many mansions. Father Marx, the humble, wise Warehouse Priest, will no doubt have a mansion of gold, filled with little angelic ones just waiting to greet him on the day he enters into the glory of Heaven.

I do not see Father Marx through eyes that notice a difference in theological or Church doctrine—or through eyes that see a man well-seasoned by 73 years on a troubled earth. I see him through my Father's wonderful eyes of love and respect—and I thank you, Father Marx, for being a good, faithful servant who has a heart of gladness. But most of all, I thank you for being a strong hand that continues to reach down and gently help me up the path, lightening my burden as I make my long, steep climb.

With love,

Gianna Jessen
San Clemente, California

INTRODUCTION

"The Pope always buries his undertakers." As we draw near the year 2000, it is interesting to note that some things never change. For example, self-important worldings have been digging graves for the papacy for 2,000 years now.

The Roman emperors martyred dozens of St. Peter's successors. Attila planned to sack Pope Leo's Rome. Moslem armies tried for centuries to destroy the pope's dominion.

In our own times, Stalin asked Churchill, "How many divisions does the pope have?" Hitler and Himmler actually plotted to hang Pope Pius XII.

Napoleon mocked his captive, Pope Pius VII, asking, "Does he think that he can twist the arms from my soldiers' hands?" His atheistic Grand Army suffered just such an end on the frozen plains of Christian Russia.

Late in the 18th century, Frederick II of Prussia dismissed Pius VI as an "old man in Rome," one "whose stupid ceremonies would soon die out." Seventy years later, John Henry Newman told an audience of Anglo-Catholics in London, "The 'old man,' the pope, is found in his own place as before, saying Mass over the tomb of the Apostle."

The Chair of St. Peter has survived persecutions, wars, revolutions, plagues, plots, heresies, anti-popes and even bad popes. You would think our present-day dissenters would realize it will survive *them*, too.

You would think they would suspect that Pope Paul VI was right 25 years ago when he issued *Humanae Vitae*, renewing the Church's ancient and constant teaching against contraception. You would think they would admit they were wrong when they survey the flood of fornication, adultery, abortion, fetal "harvesting," sterilization, divorce, venereal disease, AIDS, discord and apostasy that they loosed upon humanity.

But the mark of the true heretic has always been

obstinacy. Puffed up with pride, most of the dissenters will go to their graves insisting that they are right and the Church is 2,000 years wrong.

Meanwhile, it is up to you and me to pray for them, give them a good example, debate them and offer them fraternal correction. Alas, reproving the false teachers must be a large part of HLI's work.

This is because defending and advancing the teachings of the Vicar of Christ on love and life is at the core of our missionary efforts.

As you read through this account of HLI's recent campaigns, you will see HLI proclaiming the Church's teachings on contraception and abortion as His Holiness does... correcting the theo-rebels as he does...opposing the rich countries' exportation of sin as he does...defending the rights of Catholic parents as he does...evangelizing the former Soviet bloc as he does...looking at "the big picture" as he does...praising loyal bishops as he does...resisting the radical Catholic feminists as he does...promoting the new *Catechism* as he does...all while crisscrossing the globe as he does.

Of course, we are persecuted in return, as Jesus warned us—no, promised us—in St. John's Gospel. Planned Barrenhood tries to block our projects, UN bureaucrats shut doors in our face, most of the media ignore us, our staff receives threats, chancery bureaucrats thwart us and even a few bishops criticize us. But the more you try to imitate St. Peter, the more you must expect such treatment.

Pope Paul VI was an example. He kept faith with his predecessors in the Petrine office by upholding fearlessly the truth about God's plan for love and life. And so, like Jesus, he met with contradiction, incredulity, ridicule, misunderstanding, hatred, betrayal and abandonment.

On 26 January 1973, four days after the U.S. Supreme Court stripped preborn Americans of all legal protection, I spoke for several minutes with this Pontiff. "Never give up," he ordered me. "You are a courageous fighter."

"Never give up"—that is all that we in the pro-life/family movement need to do, because, as every good Christian knows, it is only a matter of time before God's truth about love and life sweeps away the lies, confusion and delusions of the dissenters and the worldlings.

"Never give up"—whether that blessed day comes soon or a century from now.

"Never give up"—because all discouragement comes from Satan, who was a liar and a murderer from the beginning.

"Never give up"—because you have the example of Christ, the power of the Holy Spirit, the protection of St. Michael and all the angels, and the help of the Queen of Heaven and all the saints, including the Vicars of Christ in Paradise.

"All those who take part with Peter," Newman observed in 1853, "are on the winning side." Rest assured, my friend, that Peter will be standing firmly at the helm of his bark long after the Clintons, the Planned Barrenhooders, the TV anchormen, the "personally opposed" politicians, the Archbishop Weaklands, the Fr. McBriens, the Hans Küngs, the pro-abortion nuns, the "pick-and-choose" Catholics and the *National Catholic Reporter* have been relegated to footnotes in some dust-covered history book.

The Rock endures. The Rock *shall* endure. And you, by your prayers and support for HLI's work, are helping it to endure.

Peace and joy!

Rev. Paul Marx, OSB

The Philippines and Japan

No. 85   November 1991

I n **1974, Good Shepherd sister** Pilar Verzosa
and I founded Pro-Life Philippines. From time to time
I've returned to her country for speaking tours, but it
startled me recently to learn I hadn't been there since
1983. So I packed my bags again, and Father Matthew
Habiger and I headed for the airport.

HLI has maintained a constant flow of materials to
prolife/profamily leaders in this 7,000-island nation, the
only Catholic country in Asia. The Philippines have more
than 100 dioceses, but priests and even the many nuns are
far too few; parishes of 80,000-100,000 souls are common.
In one such parish in Manila, 250 baptisms took place last
Christmas and 350 babies were baptized on Holy
Childhood Sunday!

This year the Archdiocese of Manila ordained seven
priests; over the next five years, nineteen will be ordained
each year. New priestly and religious vocations are
many—so many, in fact, that women's religious communities faltering in Italy and Spain have established themselves here and have taken young novices back to Europe,
with highly questionable results because of cultural shock.
Cardinal Jaime Sin of Manila has rightly protested this
abuse.

ANTI–BABY FORCES TARGET CATHOLICS

More than 80 percent of all Filipinos are Catholic; considering the total situation, Mass attendance is fairly good.
There are many Catholic schools and institutions in Manila,
where one–fifth of the country's sixty million people live,
but 70 percent of all Filipino students attend public schools.
Planned Parenthood (PP), calling itself the Family Planning
Association (FPA), and other foreign depopulation agencies
have infiltrated the public–school system. They've imposed
a highly offensive sex-"education" program and, even worse,
diabolical antipopulation education.

The Filipinos suffered a series of natural disasters after the twenty–year political/economic disaster of Ferdinand and Imelda Marcos: floods, earthquakes, and the volcanic eruption of Mount Pinatubo, which has killed more than 400 people, destroyed almost 100,000 homes, wiped out the livelihoods of some 1.2 million people in about 213,000 families, and (not least) wrecked 3,500 classrooms.

Some twenty typhoons hit Manila every year! In fact, on the day we landed, a typhoon flooded much of the city, and a 4.0 earthquake hit, besides! Quakes happen repeatedly and always flood Manila, which lies below sea level and cannot afford proper storm drains and flood control. The huge, ashen mud slides from Mount Pinatubo are prolonging the misery.

Some 20 percent of the people are unemployed. The poverty is great, as the many slums attest pitifully. Half of all students in Manila cannot afford to attend the city's many colleges. Malnutrition takes a great toll. Making the economic situation worse is the centralization of the national government, retarding the proper development of the outlying islands' many and varied resources.

Cory Aquino's rule has been very disappointing, but the country never did have a stable, democratically functioning government. Corruption, the legacy of the Marcoses, is still extensive. The Communists, however, have suffered severe setbacks.

The Philippines have been victimized by multinational population-control forces.

The richly endowed but undeveloped Philippines provide a classic example of a country victimized by multinational population–control forces. The worst exploiters are the International Planned Parenthood Federation (IPPF), the World Bank, the U.S. Agency for International Development (USAID), the Upjohn Company of Kalamazoo, Michigan, and Johns Hopkins University. The World Bank and USAID have contributed $50 million to

FPA/PP. Thanks to these agencies, particularly to tax–subsidized Johns Hopkins, the public school texts are so laced with antibirth propaganda that every Filipino, it seems, believes there are too many people.

Schoolbooks show a family of well–dressed parents and one child enjoying lunch—and on the next page a shabbily dressed large family fighting over one fish. Right now Johns Hopkins is creating subliminal visual aids for TV, the press, and the schools to sell the idea that the small family is the happiest. The propaganda is truly diabolical. The wonderfully gentle and kind Filipinos are victimized totally.

"THE CHRISTIAN HOPE OF ASIA"

Still, they're fighting back to preserve their Catholic culture and their faith, benefiting from good episcopal leadership, especially that of Cardinal Sin. Last year the hierarchy produced the best national prolife pastoral letter I've ever seen, truly a masterpiece, called *Love Is Life*. After being deceived at first, the bishops for years have fought FPA's repeated attempts to involve them in immoral antibirth programs. Of course, as always and everywhere, they have too few resources to work with.

The prelates realize that it's of frightening importance that the Philippines remain Catholic. The country's emigrants bring Catholicism to many nations, not unlike the Irish of earlier days. You can meet Filipino priests and nuns almost everywhere.

Nearly one million Filipinos work in the Arab countries, and right now Filipinos are streaming back to Kuwait and Iraq. There are 80,000 Filipinos in Taiwan. The Japanese government has just contracted with the Philippine government for 200,000 Filipinos, who'll increase the size of the Catholic Church in Japan by almost 50 percent! Hong Kong claims 90,000 Catholic Filipinos. The USA has 23,000 Filipino doctors and more than 50,000 Filipina nurses, with many more to come.

When Pope John Paul II visited the Philippines, he told the people they were the Christian hope of Asia. He begged them to send missionaries to other Asian countries, something they've done very generously, considering their situation. The Filipinos are the natural apostles to other Asians, because they share their mentality.

H.L.I. AND BISHOPS SAVE BABIES

The bishops have totally supported our prolife efforts ever since 1974. At the invitation of Cardinal Sin, HLI will sponsor an International Asian Pacific Prolife Conference in Manila (January 31-February 2, 1992) to strengthen the prolife movement in the Philippines and neighboring nations. Before and after the meeting, Father Matthew and I will speak to key audiences throughout the country.

We also hope to set up more emergency pregnancy centers, of which there are only three in Metro Manila. Pregnant, unmarried Filipinas are easily persuaded not to abort. The three centers, which HLI friends support, save 90 percent of the babies! No other service in the world saves such a percentage. HLI was intimately involved in helping the Filipinos draft their post-Marcos 1987 constitution, which decrees, "The State recognizes the sanctity of family life and shall protect and strengthen the family as a basic social institution. It shall equally protect the life of the mother and the life of the unborn from conception..." (article II, section 12). We've been a part of several national Philippine prolife conventions, too.

Since 1974 we've shipped a constant stream of prolife materials—as many as we could afford—to the lively Filipino prolife movement, which enjoys the tireless leadership of Sister Pilar. It's impossible to exaggerate their needs.

Nor could I exaggerate the importance of saving the young, prolife Philippines. Cardinal Sin admits more than 500,000 abortions may be performed annually among 60 million people. (Their average completed family numbers 3.1 children, *versus* 1.9 in the USA.) The Filipinos, who hold a natural and deep respect for human life, would never kill their babies if we could give them the right information and help.

It's sickening to learn how your USAID tax dollars are used in the mountains to bribe highly paid "doctors" to abort babies with battery-operated suction machines. And then there's Upjohn, dispensing the abortifacient, injectible Depo-Provera—so dangerous to women that it's banned in the USA—without Philippine government approval. The "international contraceptive imperialists," as the Vatican has called them, stuff wombs with abortifacient IUDs, hand out abortifacient Pills, promote sterilization massively, and now are preparing to stick the abortifacient Norplant into women.

The godless population-controllers prove how important the Catholic Filipinos are by the amount of money they've poured in to destroy them. The angry international feminists, too, know how important the Filipinos are: some months ago they held one of their largest-ever meetings in Manila, drawing agitators from many countries. (Where do they get the funds? The devil must have lots of money.)

Several other groups have been working against the death pushers. One is the outstanding "Families for the Family." Among many other good things, members go into the schools to show that the Philippines aren't overpopulated and that the problems that exist are due to selfishness, injustice, and international intrigue. "Families for the Family" impressed me enormously. It's amazing what they do with so little to defend unborn babies, the family, the Church, and their nation. Your generosity will put more HLI weapons into their hands, as well as into those of other effective groups I don't have room to describe here. Please pray for them!

JAPAN'S MOTHERS WEEP FOR THEIR BABIES

On our way to address 5,000 souls at the First International Congress of Catholic Charismatic Servant Communities in Manila (July 26-28), Father Matthew and I dropped in on the great missionary Father Anthony Zimmerman, SVD, in Nagoya. We planned further international prolife activity and Natural Family Planning (NFP) promotion with him. Slightly smaller than California and only 15 percent arable, mountainous Japan is a fantastic country, perhaps the world's richest materially. She's

surely the most literate nation and one of the best educated, with an economy bursting at the seams with elec-
tronics, computers, and cars.

**The Japanese are ashamed of their
many abortions, thinking of them as a
painful necessity.**

In one way, the Japanese are also the poorest country:
abortion. They're ashamed of their many abortions, they
rarely talk about them, thinking of them as a painful
necessity.

Abortions have become common in Japanese culture,
but aborted mothers haven't forgotten their dead children,
whose humanity they never deny. Buddhist memorial services (*Mizuyo Kuyo*) for aborted babies have become a
major business in Japan. Mothers everywhere demand
such rites at temples.

The estimated total sum of money paid by mothers for
such rites per year now exceeds $350 million. The temples,
therefore, are reaping a spinoff profit from the abortion
industry. (The baby-killing business may be worth about
$1 billion annually to doctors and hospials.) There are
many temples where aborted mothers place hundreds of
little stone dolls (*mizuko*) to quiet the troubled spirits of
their children, sent "from dark to dark," as the Japanese
expression goes. The temple priests and alert laymen sense
that the sorrow of the mothers, and their wish to placate
the children, are keen enough to support high prices,
which help to soften the pain.

In 1948 the Japanese Diet (parliament) passed a law
allowing abortions for various reasons, which have led to
abortion-on-demand. It was known as the "Eugenics
Protection Act," part of an omnibus bill that was little discussed and pushed through at the end of a hurried session.
The same legislator who introduced the abortion bill also
submitted a bill for euthanasia three years later.

Since 1948, this sophisticated nation has killed at least
seventy million babies! Even today, there are an estimated
two million abortions annually—5,000 daily—for 123

million people. Two-thirds of the abortions are performed on married couples' babies, unlike those in Western countries. By the way, Japan outlawed saline abortions in the 1950s because they killed too many mothers.

PRESCHOOL SUICIDES AND A VANISHING WORK FORCE

The desire to get into a university and survive there creates enormous competition, which may explain why "only" an estimated 20,000-30,000 students obtain abortions each year: they have little time for fornication. Japanese parents prepare their little ones, even before kindergarten, to enter a university—preferably a public one. The kindergarten entrance fee is $750 in this most expensive country in the world, which boasts a per capita annual income of $23,400 (*versus* $19,800 in the USA). The number of college students committing suicide because of the pressure to get a prestigious education is appalling. Even little children have killed themselves to escape the pressure of having to get into the right preschool!

Last year the number of births fell to 1.2 million, down from 2 million fifteen years ago—the steepest drop of any industrial nation in history. One can foresee the pragmatic Japanese trying to tighten up on abortion, because the handwriting of the nation's demise is on the wall.

The birthrate is only 1.53 children per family in a married lifetime: the nation is aging fast. Today the labor shortage has precipitated a major national crisis. Unable to find workers, many companies have declared bankruptcy. In 30 years the work force will shrink by ten million; in 100 years, by fifty million. Retirement age is at 55-60 years, but the government wants to raise it to 65.

Women and elderly people are the only native source of additional labor. Both government and industry are offering outlandish financial incentives and schooling to produce more workers. One TV ad shows a boy playing with a puppy over the caption "For the child's sake, have one more." In desperation, the government recently appointed an unprecedented super-committee to find ways to improve family life and the birthrate.

The Justice Ministry estimates that 100,000-110,000 foreigners are working illegally in the country, about one-tenth of 1 percent of the population. This relatively homogeneous island nation resents immigrants, even though the Japanese are increasingly unwilling to do dirty, dangerous, or menial jobs at construction sites, restaurants, and machine shops.

Knowing what's happening in Europe and the USA, people bombard government and news offices with angry letters warning that Japan could be overrun by "swarms" and "torrents" of "cockroach-like refugees." According to Kanjo Nishio, a leading intellectual, "Japan is in danger of being swallowed by 2.5 billion Asians." Meanwhile, owners of businesses large and small are pressing for a relaxation of Japan's 22-year-old ban on the immigration of unskilled workers.

WHY JAPAN'S DOCTORS OPPOSE "MERCY" KILLING

Euthanasia has raised its ugly head and a small euthanasia society exists, but there's little talk about "mercy" killing. One reason: Japanese doctors manufacture their own drugs. By pumping medicines into their elderly patients, doctors make a fortune; therefore, they're reluctant to push euthanasia. By the way, the biennial meeting of the International Federation of Right to Die Societies (there are thirty-four) will meet in Tokyo in 1992. The Japanese enjoy the longest life expectancy on earth. They show a Confucian society's traditional respect for the elderly, but it's eroding because of the demographic disaster.

The Japanese Health Ministry (1974):
"All authentic studies...show that the
Pill is a bad medication."

In 1974 I asked the second in command in the Health Ministry why Japan had never approved the Pill. "All authentic studies from foreign countries," he explained, "show that the Pill is a bad medication." Japanese doctors don't promote the abortifacient IUD either, knowing it to cause infections. Nor do they push sterilization, the world's fastest-growing birth-"control" method, given the macho mentality of Japanese men.

Another reason the Pill was never permitted was the fear of encouraging fornication, of which there's little compared with Western countries. Considering the explosion of fornication that the Pill ignited in the West, the fear is justified.

Homosexuals are few. Japan has about 400 cases of AIDS and about 1,800 carriers of the AIDS virus, thanks in part to tourism. Since Japan's first AIDS case was diagnosed in 1985, the malady has killed 198 people.

Japan proves that condoms are no solution for abortion or AIDS. Here's the most educated and literate nation on earth, primarily (80 percent) using condoms for birth prevention, and still "needing" two million baby-killings annually as backup. Those U.S. sex educators who want to distribute condoms to teens are more than naive.

One reason there's comparatively little premarital sex, drug use, and alcohol abuse is that marriage partners are chosen by parents, who make a thorough investigation of the partner's past life. What's more, the Japanese have a close-knit family life, even though fathers and mothers recreate separately in groups, as do young people.

Marriage seems to be an arrangement of convenience. More than 40 percent of all wives work, and if they become pregnant it's their business to pay to "get rid of it." The pressure of jobs is enormous, with many people working until 10 p.m. After that, they may face two hours on the train home (many can't afford a house near the workplace). Then perhaps they can't find a seat, and the train is full of drunks singing and vomiting. Homes are small, almost like rabbit hutches—which is why the workaholic Japanese, living in a pressure cooker, rarely invite guests to their homes for a meal, taking them to restaurants instead.

Nevertheless, crowded Japan doesn't experience the crime rates and violence of Western countries. But massive corruption has surfaced recently in government and business. Bank irregularities, phony collateral, stock manipu-

lation, bribery, political favoritism, brokerage houses dealing with gangsters—these characterize today's fast-chang-
ing Japanese society. Pornography isn't much in evidence
but is readily available under the counter, even in cartoon
form; rape is a dominant theme.

A DECLINING CHURCH

The dominant religions are Buddhism and Shintoism, both
of which make for a kind of humanitarian order. There are
440,000 Catholics and about as many Protestants. Japan
has 1,800 priests and 5,000 nuns. Several thousand
Protestant sects have considerable success with the youth.
After the war, Japanese flocked into the Catholic Church;
the bishops asked for a native hierarchy to foster
Catholicism even more; the Holy See complied. Today I
find Japan's bishops rather dull and uncreative.

The evidence proves that the Church is actually going
backwards; baptisms have declined to 11.33 per 1,000. A
great obstacle to Japanese conversion to Catholicism,
besides their affluence, is Church teaching on contraception and abortion.

A tragedy is the bullheaded refusal of the bishops,
especially Tokyo's Archbishop Peter Seiichi Shirayanagi, to
teach and promote NFP to a people who aren't opposed to
it. In fact, the largest crowds of doctors, other professionals, and lay people I've ever seen at NFP conferences were
at those organized by Father Zimmerman in Tokyo.
Archbishop Shirayanagi's position is that priests shouldn't
talk about sex. Apparently, neither he nor most of his
priests have read Pope John Paul II's four volumes on the
subject.

When it comes to orthodoxy, Japanese seminary training leaves much to be desired. In 1978, Onkyo Eizo (Sound
and Image), on the campus of the Catholic University (and
seminary) of Nanzan (run by the Society of the Divine
Word), published *Ryoshin to Kyoikusha no Sei Kyoiku
Tokuhon* (*Handbook on Sex Education for Parents and
Teachers*). It contained, among other things, totally false
teaching on contraception. It quickly became a best seller,
and more than five years, and Rome's intervention, were

required to get it withdrawn.

The women of Japan occupy a rather repressed, subordinate role in family and society. The fledgling feminist movement is strong enough to tell the government, which is desperate about the low birthrate, that never again will women be "breeders," as Tojo's regime called on them to be in pre-World War II days. The motto then was "Give birth and build Japan."

The country maintains two excellent national TV channels, one devoted solely to educating the nation and the other providing current information on vital topics. Mother Teresa, a heroine in Japan, where she has a community in the slums, once spoke for thirty minutes to twenty million Japanese viewers.

RHYTHM, TEMPERATURE, AND NOW L'SOPHIA

Unfortunately, the Japanese imitate everything American, whether it's good or bad. For example, for twenty-four years, since 1967, Japan has organized contraceptive seminars for overseas visitors. In 1969 the Japanese, following the USA's example, began donating money to foreign depopulation programs. This year a dying Japan gave $58.8 million to the UNFPA.

PP, known as the Japanese Family Planning Association, plays a surprisingly subordinate role, except that it makes huge amounts of money selling condoms (peddled door-to-door, by the gross, to shy wives). According to government records, some 15 percent of all couples use the old Ogino rhythm calculations and 22 percent use the temperature method (with condoms?); if and when these fail, of course, the couples abort.

Ogino was the great, pioneering Japanese gynecological surgeon who, after measuring ovulatory blisters on the ova of many women on whom he operated, calculated that a woman ovulates between the twelfth and sixteenth days before the onset of her next menstrual period. This calculation became the basis of the rhythm method, a method actually as effective as the modern condom but now superseded by the ovulation and the sympto-thermic methods.

In fact, for the properly motivated couple, these methods are as effective a means of birth regulation as exists, short of sterilization.

The resourceful Japanese are again pioneering in NFP. A small electronic device known as "L'Sophia" helps women to detect ovulation and marks off their fertile times. In the past year more than 15,000 were sold across the world, and now 4,000 are being sold each month. L'Sophia will be demonstrated at our Eleventh World Conference on Love, Life and the Family in Ottawa next April 29-May 3.

Please pray for Japan, her babies and her Church!

Let the little children come unto me:
Fr. Matthew and Angela Cargiulo

Letters

The letters we excerpt in this book are representative of the thousands we receive every year.

God loves the small, the simple, the silent,
And He used humility,
Smallness, poverty, and helplessness
To prove to the world
That He loved the world.

Mother Teresa, MC

This brings you my prayer for all you have been doing for God, for life, and for family.

God love you for the love you have shared and the care you have given to the unborn through your writings by creating awareness among your readers of the preciousness of human life—especially that of the preborn, who are so helpless, so weak, so small, and so much in need of all the love, care, and nurture we can give.

In protecting the preborn so beautifully, by using the gifts God has given you, you and your staff have indeed made your own lives precious to God. May you continue to protect, promote, and build up life and uphold its sanctity.

God bless you.

Mother Teresa, MC
Calcutta, India

I should like to greet you and thank you for all you are doing for the voiceless children and for the young mothers who without support are often driven to do what they would rather not do.

I am a Dominican missionary sister in Zimbabwe, working at a mission hospital to which is attached a training school for young African women in nursing and

midwifery. Through the liberation war we have experienced a breakdown of moral standards of living.
Traditional values have to a great extent been lost.

Like all countries that advocate contraception, ours too
has movements that call for legalized abortion. In the face
of all this, we try to instill Christian values in our students.
I wonder whether you could give us some of your education
materials, including videos. Needless to say, we continue to
support your apostolate with our earnest prayers.

Sister Christiana, OP
St. Theresa's Hospital
Zimbabwe

I do not know how I should start this letter to you, over-
whelmed as I am for the gifts of leaflets, books, and even
V-cassettes you have sent to me. You are indeed the
Apostle of Life!

When I read the HLI reports about what's happening
here and there in the world, I sometimes wonder how some
people have become so stupid as to deny life. My simple
argument is: So, why are *they* alive? Why were they born?
Were their parents (especially mothers) stupid to bring
them into the world? Was, therefore, God stupid to give
them a human life?

Dear Father Marx, be glad. Many are converted by
your wonderful ministry. We are following you and pray
much for your continued success.

The Most Rev. James D. Sangu
Bishop of Mbeya,
Tanzania

Thanks be to the information drive from Human Life
International, the Catholic Church of Sri Lanka has been
awakened from a deep slumber. The Catholic newspapers
and other publications frequently carry articles against

abortion. On 24 December 1991 a teledrama against abortion was shown. Some churches in the coastal belt display banners and posters against abortion, homosexuality, and the spread of AIDS. More and more clergy and the laity are becoming aware of the dangers after reading HLI literature. The archbishop of Colombo and the bishops of Chilaw and Kurunegala sent me Christmas greetings and thanks for the prolife drive undertaken. The bishop of Galle too sent his best wishes.

You have expressed amazement that the seminarians ask for Church documents, etc., on abortion, as these should be available in Catholic libraries. Abortion, euthanasia, AIDS, etc., were not problems in this country till the recent past, and the Church here was reluctant to speak on these matters. Never were these problems discussed openly in this country. What happened in a bedroom and its consequences were treated as very private and secret.

Now our society is moving forward like a brakeless speed car! It is only now that the churches are discussing and equipping their libraries with books on these topics.

Bede N.A. Perera
Wennappuwa, Sri Lanka

In Japan, too, the government has started sex-ed (sexual propaganda). The commonsense public are worried, but the bishops remain silent: they are more concerned with bringing the Church nearer "the society."

Paul A. Sawada
Tokyo, Japan

While in the seminary I did a thesis on the legalization of abortion in Barbados and showed it to be a part of the international conspiracy to control and subjugate Third World countries like Barbados. Actually, the main reason I have delayed so long in writing to you is that a copy of that these was supposed to accompany this letter, but I will have to wait until I can get copies reprinted.

I am sorry that I was unable to attend last weekend's conference in Trinidad (November 1992). Father George Bardowell did, and he had the goodness to give me a copy of the program. I was flabbergasted! Had I known that this was to be the content of the conference, wild horses wouldn't have kept me away! From the way it was advertised I had the impression that it was to be another talk shop rehashing matters with which we are all too familiar. The best way to advertise would be to send to the different dioceses a copy of the program to let them see that it is a high-powered conference well worth their while.

Father George noted that few dioceses were represented and that the diocesan clergy were conspicuous by their absence! What a waste! What an unspeakable tragedy! I am sure if the program had been circulated beforehand, that would have made a considerable difference. I for one would certainly have been there, and I would have encouraged some of my colleagues to accompany me. My only hope is that the talks were all recorded so that I can listen to them and bring myself up to date.

> *Father Leonard Alfonso*
> *Barbados, West Indies*

One and a half million people and over fifty Catholic organizations joined Pro-Life Philippines in a mammoth protest/prayer/vigil rally that started at 5 p.m. February 13, ending at 10 today, February 14, 1993.

Prolife speakers, all laymen and women, took turns explaining to the people the horror of abortion; the contraceptive mentality; the myth of overpopulation; the real meaning of love, sex, and marriage; the value of children; and, repeatedly, the protest against the condom campaign of the government.

Families, many with infants, came with their picnic baskets and mats and camped all night long, listening on their transistor radios to the aired speeches where the sound system could not reach them. The thousands of lighted candles glimmered like stars of hope in a country torn by natural disasters, economic crisis, and moral degradation because of Western-influenced media and population-control programs.

Guest speakers included prolife senators and the mayor and vice mayor of Manila. The films "Silent Scream" and "Eclipse of Reason" were shown on five huge outdoor screens.

At 5 a.m., Cardinal Sin celebrated Mass and dwelt once more on the theme of the rally: "Save the Child, Save the Family."

Sister Mary Pilar Verzosa, RGS
Pro-Life Philippines
Manila, Philippines

This is to acknowledge receipt of the package containing the pamphlets, reprints, and summaries. They are very helpful in our apostolate, which is to fight the enemies of the papal encyclical *Humanae Vitae*. I have already read most of them and find them very informative. In other words, they are good materials in combatting the propaganda of the murderers of the unborn.

The Most Rev. Salvador L. Lazo
Bishop of San Fernando of La Union
Philippines

The Lord continues to open doors. I have received good feedback from people who have heard me preach prolife in the Baguio Cathedral on Sundays. Thanks for the materials you gave me. The people here are desperate to listen to solid teaching. It is unfortunate that we often give vague homilies.

Father Mark Achilles Villanueva
Baguio City, Philippines

"A teacher's influence never ends" (Fr. Marx in Singapore)

Defending the children of the poor with Mother Teresa (Calcutta, 1989)

Costa Rica and Colombia

No. 86   Christmas 1991

A ugust 13-19 found me in beautiful, resource-rich, mountainous, volcanic, and earthquake-prone Costa Rica. HLI and our branch, the Asociación para la Defensa de la Vida (ADEVI), cosponsored a three-day Seminar on Morality and Sex Education in San José, the capital. With me on the faculty were HLI's incomparable Barbara McGuigan from California and Ruth Stearns of Catholics United for Life.

Costa Rica is the charming, democratic paradise of Central America. On his third journey to the New World in 1502, Christopher Columbus gave it its name (Rich Coast), assuming the land was filled with precious metals. Her real treasures include aquamarine waters, glistening beaches, sprawling inland valleys that give way to vast green savannas, mountain slopes canopied with majestic trees, balmy breezes caressing stunning plateaus, and, down below, dense jungle stretching out under a blanket of mist.

NEVER-ENDING SPRING

The country's botanical and biological resources are second only to Cuba's. Merck, the world's largest pharmaceutical company, is spending millions to screen plants, microbes, and insects from the lush tropical forests for possible use in drugs. Costa Rica has 12,000 square kilometers of protected lands.

Colorful, vibrant flowers flourish everywhere, and thousands of varieties of orchids dazzle the senses. Scientists are still discovering exotic flora and fauna. Costa Rica's soil is home to twice as many species of trees as are found in the continental USA.

At the heart of Costa Rica a jagged, mountainous spine runs through the country, tilting the landscape steeply on the Pacific side; the sloping terrain, etched with fast-flowing rivers, gives Costa Rica an abundance of electrical power, which neighboring countries buy.

The country enjoys a perfect tropical climate, a kind of never-ending spring. Three outstanding wilderness areas (12 percent of the national territory) contain exquisite national parks and shelter almost all of the 12,000 varieties of plants, 237 species of mammals, 848 kinds of birds, and 361 different reptiles and amphibians that are native to the country. Fascinating, too, are the 120 volcanoes (some are active), caves, and hot springs.

This diminutive country (smaller than West Virginia) lies just ten degrees north of the Equator. At the narrowest point (east to west), just 75 miles separate the Atlantic Ocean from the mighty Pacific; the widest span is only 180 miles. From north to south, Costa Rica stretches 275 miles.

At 12,606 feet, Mount Chirripo is the highest mountain in Costa Rica. Twelve miles from San José the famous *Ojo de Agua* (Eye of Water), a natural fountain, spouts 6,300 gallons of water per minute from an undergound river.

Costa Rica's first export is coffee; she's second only to Ecuador in exporting bananas and second only to Hawaii in the production of macadamia nuts. From her flat northern plains, the country also exports a great deal of frozen beef, mainly to Europe.

The commitment to peace and democratic freedoms has earned Costa Rica its reputation as "the Switzerland of the Americas."

A NATION WITH NO ARMY

Invading Spaniards massacred the fiercely resisting Guaymi Indians. So few survived that Costa Rica today is unique among Latin American countries in that almost all her people are of European descent, mostly Spanish. With 2.7 million *ticos* (the local name for the inhabitants), Costa Rica is one of the oldest democracies in the Americas. After a civil war in 1948-49, the nation abolished its army. The commitment to maintain peace and democratic freedoms has earned Costa Rica its reputation as "the Switzerland of the Americas"; in fact, the varied terrain and the beautiful, sloping green mountains with their grazing animals do remind you of Switzerland.

As early as 1848, the country established a free but compulsory educational system. Next to Chile, she has the highest literacy rate in Latin America (93 percent-plus), an extremely low infant-mortality rate, and an average life expectancy of more than seventy years. With a large middle class, Costa Rica is the most stable country politically in Latin America and the best off economically, even if she does bear a fearsome $4 billion foreign debt.

Kindly, peace-loving Costa Ricans took in 400,000 refugees from Panama and Nicaragua during the '70s and '80s. The government estimates 40,000 illegal Nicaraguan immigrants are living in the country. Former Contra guerrillas rob, rape, and rustle. Planned Parenthood (PP) tells Costa Ricans they have too many people, but fully one-third of the land isn't being used; the year-'round growing season could support many more people.

Costa Rica's telephone system is one of the best in Latin America. There are six Spanish-speaking TV stations, including one operated twenty-four hours a day by evangelical sects; one English-language cable channel from the USA is now available in most of the central valley. There are more than 100 radio stations and three daily newspapers.

In 1969, the International Planned Parenthood Federation (IPPF) established an affiliate deceptively called the "Asociación Demográfica" (AD), under the leadership of a "Catholic" doctor, Victor Morgan. The eloquent, very wealthy Morgan can be found lecturing for IPPF all over the world. (Oddly enough, his daughter appeared as a sincere volunteer at a meeting promoting chastity.) The man is subtle and dangerous.

As in other countries, AD-PP networks with various groups, including the "gay" movement, which surfaced last year; AD-PP hides behind many fronts. Because it has faced little opposition, it has become very bold, even suggesting a pornographic sex-"education" program for the schools. Strangely, Archbishop Román Arrieta Villalobos, a pleasant and gracious man, approved of it. However, the intervention of the papal nuncio and a group of alert Catholic laymen stopped its development. A committee of the latter was to study the issue and propose a good program. According to the latest reports, though, it was unable to prevent reintroduction of the AD-PP plan.

The condom is advertised freely as the great preventer of VD and AIDS. An AD-PP-affiliated company calling itself "Pro Familia" (!) sponsors highway billboards showing a father with one child above the caption "Have only as many children as you can make happy." The same company sells baby foods and baby clothes but apparently believes it can make more money on birth-prevention paraphernalia.

A university law professor told me a doctor had offered him 10,000 free condoms if he'd give them out to students at a campus fiesta. Who paid for them? You did, most likely, through grants from the U.S. Agency for International Development (USAID) and tax-supported IPPF.

KNOW YOUR ENEMY

As usual, PP has directed its tentacles toward the media and government, particularly health and education departments. I pleaded with all my audiences to understand who their enemy is, told them about IPPF's tactics all over the world, and begged them to picket the home of Dr. Morgan (Costa Rica's Public Enemy No. 1) and the AD-PP headquarters—Satan's nerve center in this beautiful land.

The most common means of birth control are the abortifacient Pill, the condom, and the abortifacient IUD (Copper-T), in that order. There's no organized natural family planning (NFP) program; a U.S. couple, the Timothy Robinsons, made a good start, but the bishops refused to support them financially, and so they left to work with the great Father Aloysius Schwartz in Mexico. (By the way, please pray for him: he's gravely ill.)

Besides the Archdiocese of San José, the country supports five dioceses. I spoke to all the priests of the archdiocese (80-90 men), with the archbishop and his auxiliary present. They listened attentively as I described the anti-life situation around the world, the activities of IPPF, and the remedies: promoting chastity and preparing people for truly Christian marriage (including NFP). We armed them all with prolife literature (provided by your generosity) and promised every pastor anything he needed. Because many Costa Ricans speak English, we sent a mountain of English-language material in advance and lugged in as much as we could, with our office in Miami supplying the Spanish-language literature and audiovisuals.

Costa Rica's one major seminary has 190 theologians; there are six minor seminaries, some of which teach philosophy also. The number of vocations compares very favorably with other countries in Latin America. In this small country there are 500 priests and some 1,300 nuns, all in habit. Good Catholic parents told us how, in the late '60s, Franciscan nuns and priests from the USA set up two high schools, St. Francis for boys and St. Clare for girls. They introduced a strange, heterodox liberalism, but the local sisters refused to imitate the fashionably dressed *gringo* nuns.

Our seminar was a huge success, drawing 420 paid participants from all over the country. Besides Barbara, Ruth, and yours truly, local doctors and university professors gave talks. Theirs was a high-quality performance, and audience response was magnificent.

Chastity, *I was told again and again,* means celibacy—*as if there were no chastity in married life!*

WE WARN THE FIRST LADY

One highlight of our trip was an evening when I spoke to sixty university students housed by Opus Dei priests. Another was a half-hour chat with President Rafael Angel Calderón's gracious wife, Gloria. We left key prolife/pro-family literature with her; she is wined and dined by IPPF, whose false statistics she cited. I showed her the pornographic sex ed that IPPF taught to the children of her nation.

Costa Ricans, like all Latin Americans, find it difficult to understand chastity. They often trace the problem to the freewheeling Spanish invaders who abused many local women. *Chastity,* knowledgeable locals told me again and again, means *celibacy*—as if there were no chastity in married life! We emphasized again and again that if there's no chastity *before* marriage, there'll be none *after*. People were shocked by our abortion films, pictures, and posters, all of which they will use well against their mortal enemy.

Barbara spoke to 5,000 Catholic high-school girls, who gave her a standing ovation. She also did several radio interviews. I appeared on TV once and did three programs for the national Catholic radio. Most gratifying was the large number of nuns attending. Fewer than ten priests came; low priestly turnouts are typical worldwide.

We couldn't have come at a more opportune time: the battle over sex-"education" is raging. I'm afraid the bishops don't understand the dangers of sex-ed in the schools, where contracepting/sterilized teachers are often in charge and the immoral ideas of AD-PP have already been implemented. There are some Catholic grade schools and high schools, but most Costa Rican children go to public schools. By law, two hours of religion must be taught; an Institute of Religion trains the teachers.

I saw AD-PP's proposed books on sex-"education." Their content is subtly satanic. Because AD-PP faces little resistance, it's much bolder and takes advantage of the local situation, brazenly spreading its lies. At least one high school gives condoms to the students. Thanks to AD-PP, condoms are sold at subsidized prices in grocery and liquor stores, gas stations—everywhere. Radical feminists are coming on strong and meet little resistance. ADEVI-HLI has shown "The Silent Scream" some 250 times, though.

KILLERS FLOUT THE LAW

I never did have my planned meeting with an active Protestant prolife organization that has enthused over contraception as a remedy for abortion. The push is on to legalize abortion in cases of rape and incest; the current law allows abortion only to save the mother's life. No one will estimate the number of abortions, but there are many, 99 percent of them being performed in doctors' offices, pro-life doctors assured me. One ex-abortionist admitted to us that he had been making $5,000 a week inducing abortions as a sideline. Any doctor can receive, free of charge, the latest suction equipment to perform early abortions. Most likely, the baby-killing tools come from North Carolina's International Projects Assistance Service, but who pays for them?

Many of the killer-doctors were trained in the USA to sterilize adults and kill babies. They came home to practice on Costa Ricans, and when they became expert their country became a training center for Latin America, financed by U.S. money. Today the birthrate has fallen to 3.1 children per family. Although Costa Rica has the fewest slum-dwellers of any country in Latin America and the best division of wealth, almost one-third of the families are headed by only one parent.

Our efforts brought us invitations from a diocese in Panama and from nuns in Nicaragua to repeat the seminar; we continue to be overwhelmed with requests for help from all over the world. By the way, because we publish in three languages—English, French, and Spanish—HLI is being quoted and reprinted worldwide. You make all of this possible.

P.P. AND REDS V. COLOMBIA

In October 1990, HLI sponsored a weekend prolife seminar in Colombia's largest city, Bogotá. In *Special Report No. 76* I gave you a picture of this resource-rich but very undeveloped and violent country of thirty million people, and of her Church. This September I spent eight days in Colombia for another HLI seminar in Medellín, the country's second-largest city and the world's drug capital.

The only Latin American country to honor Columbus by name is plagued with poverty, high unemployment, hundreds of thousands of street children (many the offspring of prostitutes), violence of every kind (including frequent kidnappings), a shortage of clergy and religious, and many other problems.

A recent report of the World Bank maintains that thirteen million people out of thirty million live in utter poverty, deprived of education, health care, housing, and public services. The country needs a large army to control the many leftist guerrilla groups that inflict enormous damage on the country's productivity and order. The army dispatched 60,000 troops across the country to make possible a recent national election. You see soldiers and police everywhere. For $10 you can have someone murdered (it costs much more to have a policeman "hit"). Colombians joke that there are two ways to lose your money: getting robbed on the street or taking a taxi.

While I was there, rebels dynamited the oil pipelines, spilling 19,000 barrels of raw petroleum. Such attacks have spewed thirty-five million gallons of crude into rivers and jungles, three times the amount spilled in the *Exxon Valdez* disaster in Alaska.

Every week since 1986, the National Liberation Army has bombed the Catatombo River, one of scores of riverways, marshes, lakes, and forests polluted by Red attacks on the country's main oil pipeline, the 500-mile-long Cano-Limón. Millions of impoverished peasants are caught in a bloody, 35-year-old war pitting government soldiers against the guerrillas.

In Medellín alone, fifty people are killed every night. From 6:30 p.m. on Friday to 7:30 a.m. on Saturday when I was there, 100 were killed. A priest took me to a morgue, where I saw twenty-seven victims, post-autopsy. One had died of natural causes, four in car accidents; a man had brought in a dead, three-month-old baby girl; six had been killed with knives and sixteen with guns. Most of the victims were innocent. When I asked the pastor of a parish of 45,000 how he handles all the funerals, he replied, "Well, people are often not buried; they just disappear."

God blessed Colombia with enormous water resources, no change of seasons (and therefore 365 days of crop production), varied terrain, and coastlines on both the Atlantic and Pacific Oceans. Virtually everything grows in this beautiful country, which is as big as Texas and New

Mexico combined. Coffee is the chief export, followed with bananas, other fruits, and flowers, of which Colombia is one of the world's chief exporters.

Medellín is known as the "City of Eternal Spring"—and also as the drug capital of the world.

A CITY IN THE SKY

Because of her flowers and pleasant weather, beautiful Medellín is known as the "City of Eternal Spring." She's also known as the drug capital of the world, a reputation this city of three million people high in the Andes is trying to change. The province of Antioquia, where Medellín is located, is the richest and also the most religious, producing the most priestly and religious vocations. However, the archdiocese has only 450 secular priests and 250 religious priests. The cathedral is the seventh largest in the world, containing 1.2 million large bricks. Many seminaries grace the area, including that of a Colombian foreign-mission society that has 150 seminarians, as well as 2,000 priests working in ten countries.

PP, known as "Pro Familia," has been more successful in Colombia, perhaps, than in any other Latin American country. Its antibaby programs have so greatly reduced the birthrate and the population that in 1989 the U.N. Fund for Population Activities (UNFPA) gave it a special award. The bishops protested, but to no avail. The many abortions and sterilizations are performed not in hospitals and so-called clinics but in numerous "houses" owned by PP.

Seven years ago, through the national Health and Education Departments, Pro Familia (typically) invaded the schools with its horribly graphic sex-ed. Its workers freely give students abortifacient Pills, often with little instruction; condoms are so easy to get that they're not given out in the schools. They're promoted there, however, and also on TV, with the slogan "If you love your girl, use a condom." The many slum dwellers are showered with free

Pills and condoms. The poor can buy a cycle of Pills from many sources at the subsidized price of ten cents.

Obviously, the aim is to get young people to start fornicating; the more fornication, the greater the damage to family life and the lower the birthrate. As a result, Latin America today is in a strange situation: there are many teens but comparatively few small children. In the future there'll be many old people and not enough workers to support them—thanks to "Planned Hell."

Poor couples still have an average of four children, but middle- and upper-class couples have barely two. The most common means of birth control for the latter groups are sterilization, the Pill, the IUD, and the condom, in that order. Estimates of illegal abortions run between 400,000 and 500,000. Last July the nation adopted a new constitution that condemned divorce and proclaimed the unborn child protected, but later slipped in the comment that a woman has the right to control her own body. This insertion opens the way to legal abortion in the future.

PROBLEMS IN THE CHURCH

Hours of conversation with ten wonderfully Catholic women who teach NFP and do other archdiocesan family/welfare work truly proved to be a revelation. Colombian NFP began fifteen years ago and is quite sophisticated, but only about 5,000 couples practice it in the archdiocese. The women said priests often claim that NFP "doesn't work," but it is the clergy who haven't worked to learn it. Priests rarely preach on contraception, sterilization, or abortion; some dismiss baby-killing as inevitable or even necessary.

According to a grim joke, "the only virgin in Latin America is the Blessed Virgin."

The women confirmed what I've often sensed when in Latin America: the clergy and religious aren't trained to handle the gigantic onslaught of sexual sins encouraged by the ubiquitous PP and fueled by millions of dollars from wealthy countries (especially the USA and England).

My contacts decried the immorality of Catholic teachers. They said upper-class Catholic mothers often provide their teen daughters with Pills. They insisted that some girls as young as nine have intercourse, and the grim joke was that "the only virgin in Latin America is the Blessed Virgin." They told me that rampant promiscuity and VD are rather recent phenomena, arriving with Pro Familia, condoms, and the Pill.

Being on the front lines, these women knew the problems: too few priests and religious; the evil media, which extol and advertise sterilization, condoms, and the Pill; and advertisements featuring naked women. Again and again, they emphasized how vicious the moral environment is, how hard it is for young people to be virtuous, how little the truth is known and taught and learned, and what masterful and satanic deceptions abound. Meanwhile, cable TV is slithering through the country, bringing pornography into home and school.

PROLIFERS BATTLE BACK

Marriage-preparation courses are poor, but caretaker Auxiliary Bishop Carlos Prada San Miguel assured me the Archdiocese of Medellín is trying to build a total marriage-prep course, no small task in a country and city where immorality is king. The archdiocese has little money or equipment for this gigantic task; it has virtually no prolife literature, films, audiotapes, or videocassettes. Meanwhile, the sects are making serious inroads, as they are in all of Latin America—in fact, throughout the developing world.

The archbishop's seat is now vacant. Last January the pope appointed the energetic, 48-year-old Cardinal Alfonso Lopez Trujillo president of the Pontifical Council for the Family in Rome. Once president of the Colombian bishops' conference, Cardinal Lopez Trujillo was an articulate foe of liberation theology. In eleven years he reportedly built 120 parishes.

The rector of Medellín's major seminary, which is educating 140 major seminarians, told me liberation theology is only a theme in a strictly orthodox theological course. But I found not a bit of prolife literature in the library; I assured them that Magaly Llaguno of our Miami office would ship them all they need (provided by you).

By shipping the best prolife materials to the seminaries of the developing world, where there are so many vocations, we're defending God's babies and families at the very nerve center, because future priests desperately need to know how to promote family life, to prepare young people for holy marriages, to foster chastity, and to resist the incredible onslaught of antibaby forces such as PP and its many international cohorts, which include the entire U.N. and, not least, contraception-pushing UNICEF.

Attending the seminar in Medellín were 200 leaders, including a dozen priests and forty religious. We had to turn away more than twenty people for lack of space. Listeners were shocked by my description of the worldwide antilife/antifamily mess. I left them a clear picture of what they needed to do to save their country, which is still the healthiest one spiritually in Latin America, considering the many vocations and seminaries, among other things. Next year we'll hold a similar seminar in Cali. Please pray for Colombia!

Letters

With the support of HLI we successfully finished our youth program last Saturday. We gathered together 600 teen-agers from all over the country. Although most of them came from low-income families, they had the opportunity to take along with them pamphlets about chastity, the dangers of contraception, the effects of abortion, sad pictures of aborted babies, and pamphlets on population control and the dangers of Planned Parenthood.

The press didn't pay attention to this important event, but the radio stations gave it a big promotion.

HLI is an inspiring organization that shows us how to do our prolife work. It's very important to realize that thanks to Father Paul Marx and Magaly Llaguno we have a lot of rising prolife groups all over Latin America. We hope to keep promoting the respect and sanctity of human life.

Thanks for your help in saving Hispanic babies.

Eduardo Loria
Costa Rica

Congratulations, Father Paul, on your being named "Catholic of the Year," 1991, along with ex-hostage Terry Anderson.

All of my associates at Catholic Aid Association join me in extending to you our sincerest congratulations, esteem, admiration, and sincere thanks for all your efforts in behalf of Life. There is no one known to us who has expended more energy with such effectiveness for the cause as you have, Father Paul. You are a "saint"!

I take great pride in the fact that I was a student of yours in school and that I have been able to nurture a relationship through the years. I have been a much better person as a result of your influence on my life, and I thank you sincerely.

> *F.L. Spanier*
> *The Catholic Aid Association*
> *St. Paul, Minnesota*

On July 18, I celebrate my one-hundredth birthday. Sending Father Paul Marx this check is my only celebration!

> *Helma Krauch*
> *Tucson, Arizona*

As I recall, it was in the mid-sixties that my brother, James, and I had the opportunity to meet you here in the Coon Rapids area. We listened to you closely and have carried the message faithfully since: "The progression all begins with *contraception*, to sterilization, to abortion, and finally to euthanasia."

I hope the bishops will see their error and begin their duty to educate the faithful as to the true teachings of the Roman Catholic Church! A few good priests are doing just that.

Thank you! You have done more than any other single human being in the whole world to instruct and educate everyone!

> *Joseph D. Moriarty, MD*
> *Coon Rapids, Minnesota*

(Written to the Liturgical Press, Collegeville, Minnesota):

There came to my attention recently the most excellent little book by the Rev. Paul Marx: *Death without Dignity: Killing for Mercy*. Although Father Marx's book is now eighteen years old, it still is one of the most cogent, powerful revelations of the pagan philosophy underlying the abortion/euthanasia movement. The good father may well be seen as a prophet in the light of recent developments.

How may I obtain more copies of this book? I am a member of a committee in our denomination that will produce a positive statement on the "right-to-die" movement. I need at least four copies of the book. If you have published others in this field, I should appreciate learning how I may obtain them. Your help is much appreciated.

Pastor Peter B. Grassmann
Emmanuel Reformed Church
Sutton, Nebraska

Planes, trains and automobiles—
Fr. Marx's mobile offices

Fr. Werenfried van Straaten
receives HLI's International
Human Life Award
(Houston, 1993)

Conferring with a Colombian bishop about the global struggle

Vatican Summit and "Gay" Convention

No.87 January-February 1992

The Pontifical Council for the Family invited HLI to attend a summit meeting of the world's prolife leaders in Rome, 14-16 November 1991. Attending were 160 people from thirty-seven countries, plus ten bishops, three cardinals, and (typically) only two nuns.

Accompanying me were Father Albert Salmon, substituting for Father Matthew Habiger, and Magaly Llaguno, who runs HLI's Miami office and coordinates our comprehensive program in Latin America. The three of us gave a twenty-minute report on HLI's international work. Magaly's husband, Julio, also came and did yeoman work in leading discussion groups.

Incidentally, Magaly and Julio had just returned from very successful HLI seminars in Mérida, Mexico, and one in Tegucigalpa, Honduras. Thousands attended, to the consternation of the population-controllers and family-destroyers. I wish I had space to tell you about these most successful gatherings.

It's impossible to sum up the numerous reports at the Vatican summit. Many speakers mentioned how essential the help of HLI was; throughout the meeting, there was no doubt about which organization was most active around the world saving babies, teaching chastity, preparing people for marriage, and building up family life. It was most edifying and gratifying to hear, and I thank you for the prayers and gifts that made it possible.

One theme ran through virtually all of the talks: bishops, priests, and religious don't realize how devastating the antilife colossus is and do far too little to oppose the death-peddlers and Planned Parenthood (PP). No hierarchies received more vigorous (but charitable) criticism than those of Italy, South Africa, and Ireland.

Latin American leaders reported that too many priests

and religious think it's up to the couple to decide the means of child spacing. Some priests even condone abortion. Most do not know what needs to be done, and those who do know lack the means.

ABORTIONS OUT OF CONTROL

The worldwide total number of abortions, including not only surgical killings but also abortifacients such as the Pill, the IUD, Norplant, Depo-Provera, RU-486, and the morning-after Pill, is truly mind-boggling. Bogomir Kuhar, founding president of Pharmacists for Life, estimated that in the USA alone there are 9.85 million to 12.30 million abortions of all kinds annually.

Austria's Opus Dei Bishop Klaus Küng told us there are more abortions in his country than births, divorces are increasing constantly, more and more couples are living together without getting married (we used to call it "shacking up"), and the birthrate is far below the replacement level. Meanwhile foreigners, including the proliferating Moslems, are moving into the vacuum (a Europe-wide, indeed, a Western-worldwide phenomenon).

The report from Dr. Claude Newbury, the head of HLI-South Africa, was truly frightening. When TV came to South Africa, he said, it brought in the worst ideas of the West; they have destroyed the moral structures that the Christians, particularly the Calvinists, had built up over hundreds of years.

Nelson Mandela has made it clear that he'll impose abortion-on-demand and punish any prolifer who resists.

Dr. Newbury accused the West of hypocrisy for imposing economic sanctions on South Africa because of apartheid while pouring in millions of dollars for depopulation. These millions, managed mostly by PP, are destroying black families above all, with abortifacients such as Depo-Provera, the Pill, the IUD, and Norplant. Now the antilifers are pushing for wider legalization of abortion and pornographic, antiparent sex "education."

South Africa's abortion law gives babies some protection (thanks to HLI) but will be repealed when Nelson Mandela and his Communist Party colleagues take over. Mandela has already made it clear that he'll impose abortion-on-demand and punish any prolifer who resists. What's more, contraceptives, abortifacients, and sterilization will be made available to all at taxpayers' expense. In 1990 this hero of the liberals said in Angola, "There's one thing where [Cuba] stands head and shoulders above the rest—that is in its love for human rights and liberty."

Working with a weakened government that's too distracted to control them, wealthy PP and its cohorts conduct the worst sex "education" in youth "clinics" that PP set up all over the country, even in the vast rural areas. Resource-rich South Africa numbers only thirty million people in an area the size of Germany, Belgium, Holland, France, and Italy combined. There are twenty-two million blacks, five million whites, two million people of mixed ancestry, and one million Asians. Despite the low population density and the natural wealth, the country is the target of massive overpopulation propaganda. The blacks' birthrate is 4.9, the "Coloureds'" is 2.9, the Asians' is 2.3, and in last place are the wealthy whites with 1.7. These whites are dying out fast.

A great scandal is the *New Nation,* a left-wing newspaper controlled by South Africa's Catholic bishops and financed 100 percent by German Catholic money. It prints articles promoting contraception and abortion, and showing genitalia in obscene detail. After running this offensive series of articles purporting to give the Church's official teaching, the paper condoned contraceptives as "the lesser of two evils," in total contradiction to *Humanae Vitae.*

Dr. Newbury and his wife Glenys give some 300 prolife talks every year!

H.L.I.-NIGERIA REACHING MULTITUDES

Another interesting report from Africa was that of Dr. Lawrence Adekoya, the head of HLI's Human Life Protection League (HLPL) in Nigeria. Dr. Adekoya has been working miracles in that country, thanks HLI supporters who helped buy him a four-wheel-drive vehicle for Nigeria's bad roads and helped him publish 100,000 copies of our *Love and Let Live* pamphlet.

Dr. Adekoya reported that last August 2 Nigeria's health minister announced as a trial balloon that the military government may legalize abortion. The Catholic hierarchy immediately responded sharply, as did all forty of our HLPL chapters.

Obviously, the regime wants to impose abortion by decree before it turns over the reins of government to civilians late this year. Because of Catholic and Moslem opposition, a democratic government would never be able to legalize abortion. That opposition is stiffened by the many prolife films, videos, and projectors we've sent, not to mention the tons of literature we've put into this most important and populous African country (115 million).

Dr. Adekoya reported that in less than two years he'd given talks to some 300,000 people, distributing HLI materials everywhere through HLPL. Some of his audiences had more than 5,000 people—one had 8,000! I know of no other country in the world where prolifers can draw that many people and show them films, give them literature, teach them the evils of contraception/sterilization/abortion, and explain to them the merits of chastity/fidelity, proper marriage preparation, and natural family planning (NFP).

Dr. Adekoya recently showed abortion films to ninety Anglican pastors. They were so stunned they vowed they'd go home to fight this "huge animal." Your prayers and generosity make all of these victories possible. From her many vocations, Nigeria will reward you with missionaries to the West; ten are in the USA already.

On the plane to Rome I had a long chat with Randy Terry, evangelical leader of Operation Rescue. We discussed everything from the Bible to birth control. Randy is totally opposed to contraception and even to NFP, which he really doesn't understand. He sees no moral or metaphysical difference between the two. But he's open-minded, and I hope I enlightened him a little. He gave a moving six-minute inspirational talk at the end of the three-day summit meeting.

Randy will soon begin presenting an hour-long national radio talk show, five days a week, to stir up opposition to abortion and related evils. A very prophetic man, this good Protestant; the world will hear much more from him. He believes most bishops, priests, and ministers are sleeping, where abortion is concerned; hence, the success of the baby-killers—especially PP, which runs ninety-six U.S. abortion mills that kill 120,000 babies yearly.

It was obvious from all the reports that, wherever abortion has been legalized in the Western world, prodeath forces are systematically promoting euthanasia with much the same tactics and deception. Even the European Economic Community (EEC) will discuss "mercy" killing next year at Strasbourg. By the way, last year the Italian prolife movement sent 500 teenagers to a session of the European Parliament to give witness to life. Italy hopes to send 1,000 this year.

Pope John Paul II: "No person is born by accident; each person...is called, from the moment of conception, to eternal communion with God."

PROLIFE POPE ENCOURAGES ACTIVISTS, KNOCKS CONTRACEPTION

Pope John Paul II spent an hour with us; he met and posed for photos with every participant, greeting each one personally. In a fifteen-minute address he reminded us that "no person is born by accident; each person is the result of an act of God's creative love and is called, from the moment of conception, to eternal communion with God." Citing St. Paul, he urged us never to despair, reminding us that we're living in a "culture of death." This culture must be fought with the "Gospel of Life," both preached and lived.

"You have a self-sacrificing, giving strength which comes from spiritual values," the pontiff observed. "You have the agility of the person who acts without ideological

conditioning or the weight of bureaucracy." (We took this
to mean we don't let bishops hamper us.) The pope mentioned society's lack of awareness that "the moral disorder
of contraception" was part of the death mentality, indeed,
the *source* of abortion! He went on to reaffirm Vatican
opposition to abortion, sodomy, and the ordination of
women.

Cardinal Alfonso Lopez Trujillo, the new president of
the Council for the Family, asked us to generate wide support for the pope's imminent encyclical on life. Each "language group" was asked to make three suggestions in a
final statement for episcopal and papal guidance. Dr. Jack
Willke and his colleagues wanted no mention of contraception. They also opposed the suggestion that sex education
be left to the parents.

It was fascinating to watch the international politick-
ing. But even Our Lord, after instructing His apostles for
years, had to rebuke them several times for debating who
among them would be the greatest in Heaven! If there's
one thing that does not change in this world, it is human
nature, "prone to evil from the beginning," as the Bible
says—a doctrine little or never taught, and even ridiculed
by heretics such as Father Matthew Fox, OP, who,
strangely, is still allowed to propagate the many horrendous errors of his "creation spirituality."

The trip to Rome confirmed my longstanding impression that Vatican officials aren't always fully informed on
vital issues. For example, as far as I can learn, Cardinal
Joseph Ratzinger was the first high-ranking Vatican official to mention that the Pill is an abortifacient (in his
keynote address to the cardinals' April 4-5 meeting); I've
known and proclaimed this fact for twenty-five years.
Ironically, "most women don't know it," the cardinal went
on to say. But no wonder, when most bishops and Catholic
doctors don't tell them! (In his most recent encyclical,
Centesimus Annus, the pope mentions chemical birth prevention.)

The forthcoming encyclical on life will definitely condemn contraception. But will the U.S. bishops and their
theologians do so? They seem most reluctant, even though
by now it's glaringly evident that contraception is a huge

source of abortions, as prominent abortionists such as Dr. Malcolm Potts, Dr. Judith Bury, Dr. Irvin Cushner, and PP's late president Dr. Alan Guttmacher have admitted.

Recently a prominent U.S. cardinal was asked to condemn contraception and sterilization along with abortion. "Oh, no," he replied. "We bishops must remain united on abortion." In the cardinals' five-minute talks at their April meeting in Rome, not one mentioned that contraception leads to abortion. Chicago's Cardinal Joseph Bernardin presented his sick (or do I mean slick?) seamless-garment (wet-blanket?) theory.

A notable exception is Bishop Glennon Flavin of Lincoln, Nebraska, who last fall addressed an eloquent pastoral on the evil of contraception to his faithful and to doctors (send me a stamped, self-addressed envelope if you would like a copy). For years Bishop Flavin has promoted NFP and other good programs; that is one reason his diocese enjoys so many vocations. Spiritually, Lincoln seems to be the healthiest diocese in the USA.

FATHER MARX AMONG THE "GAYS"

My seminary and sociological training taught me always to be sure to know who are the real enemies of God and humanity. That's why, years ago, I used to attend PP meetings incognito. That's how I caught doctors, hospital administrators, PP personnel, judges, lawyers, politicians, and even clergy at a secret meeting in Los Angeles in January, 1971, plotting to bring down every abortion law in the USA, by any means necessary. My best-selling book *The Death Peddlers* reported that meeting to the world, to the anger and consternation of the "respectable" participants. As Pope Leo XIII wrote in 1890, "We must look at the world as it really exists, and then look elsewhere for the solace of its troubles."

That is why I spent an afternoon and evening at the biennial convention of Dignity, August 31-September 1 in Washington, D.C., where that group maintains its headquarters. Dignity/USA is an organization of Catholic homosexuals who reject the Church's teaching. Its new president, Kevin Calegari of San Francisco, told the convention that

Dignity will promote "new models of the Church and assault Catholicism" nationwide. Desperate for allies, he said Dignity would work not only with homosexual and lesbian groups but with pro-aborts and divorced Catholics as well.

The convention, held at the Hyatt Regency Hotel on Capitol Hill, drew about 600 members from across the USA. Only about twenty lesbians came; when I asked why there were so few, they told me that lesbians were even angrier at the Church and that Dignity wasn't radical enough! Only 15 percent of Catholic lesbians belong to Dignity. The more radical ones have formed their own organization, the National Conference of Catholic Lesbians.

Other topics discussed were Eastern spirituality, dissent in the Church, women's ordination, ACT-UP's storm-trooper tactics, the militant Queer Nation, "safe sex," handling the bishops, "Gospel values," the alleged hypocrisy of the Church, spirituality for homosexuals, lay-led liturgies, and legal/economic issues for those engaged in "domestic partnerships." These homosexuals purport to belong to "the Church that transcends the institutional Church."

I also noticed these talks listed: "A Lad's Guide to Lust and Love (Men Dating Men in the '90s)," "Wet, Wild and Well: Lesbian Sex in the '90s," "Sex, Safe and Hot: Eroticizing Safer Sex for Women," "In God's Image: Women Liberating the Church," and "A Legal Primer for Unmarried Couples." All of this discussion reminded me of St. Paul: "They exchanged the truth of God for a lie....therefore, God handed them over to degrading passions. Their females exchanged natural relations for unnatural, the males likewise gave up natural relations with females and burned with lust for one another" (Rom. 1:24-31).

A surprising number of priests and ex-priests attended, plus men claiming to be priests, a few rebel nuns, and dissenters of every kind. Kissing and caressing went on during an "exodus liturgy" marked by a sermon given by an ex-priest, songs by songwriter and ex-Jesuit Dan Schutte (in person), candles, and ritual embracing. (Every Sunday night 400 "gays" fill St. Rita's Episcopal church in Washington for a "gay Mass.")

The sodomites know their friends—and their enemies. They hate no one more than Cardinal Ratzinger, unless it's Cardinal John O'Connor of New York. Cardinal James Hickey of Washington, which claims the largest Dignity chapter, was called "a damn liar." These malicious, lying "gays" are out "to expose the bishops": "We must get those daddies to come out," they declared—"coming out" meaning to publicly admit one's homosexuality.

Because AIDS has killed many Dignity members, the group isn't growing much.

There are eighty Dignity chapters in the USA. Individual homosexuals told me privately that AIDS has killed many Dignity members, and so the group isn't growing much. The "gays" cringe reflexively at the very mention of Courage, a group of Catholic homosexuals who try to live chastely. The militant "gays" intend to expose a certain archbishop in the Midwest in case he gets or already has AIDS, develop "nontraditional" religious communities without celibacy, go after allegedly racist Catholics, and so on.

Like PP, the homosexuals are masters at networking. They, the feminists, the environmentalists, the New Agers, and the pro-aborts work together. They abhor prolife rescuers. People who object to sodomy are labeled not just "homophobic" but "breeders." So it's the "gays" versus the "breeders"—the elite versus the slaves or drones! The hatred and vengefulness they displayed were frightening indeed. After examining the pornographic literature on four exhibit tables, I rushed home and took a shower. Dignity will celebrate its twenty-fifth anniversary in New Orleans in 1993.

BISHOP QUINN'S "GAY" MASSES

Catholic sodomites seem most at home in the dioceses of Chicago, Milwaukee, Sacramento, Louisville, and Baltimore. In Sacramento they have the falsely compassionate, praise-addicted Bishop Francis Quinn. Bishop

Quinn turned over his cathedral to pro-abort Governor-elect Pete Wilson and his PP-type second wife Gail for an inaugural bash (see *Special Report No. 78*).

The bishop coddles the "gays" and provides a Sunday Mass for them—which he himself sometimes offers—at St. Francis Church. During the exchange of peace at one of these Masses, a homosexual handed the bishop a teddy bear to caress. Teddy bears are a symbol of the homosexuals, and pederasts use them as bait to seduce children into perverse acts.

On November 22, a TV reporter from Channel 31 stood in front of Sacramento's Cathedral of the Blessed Sacrament and proclaimed, "The Church is not as archaic as many people think. It does want to help in the prevention of AIDS, even if it means using a condom. There are guidelines." Bishop Quinn then appeared, stating, "If they genuinely used a condom for health purposes, that, in the eyes of the Church, would not be wrong. It's the contraceptive that's the wrong part."

The bishop muddled the Church's teaching on sexual morality again in an article entitled "Church Stance on AIDS, Condom Controversy" in his diocesan paper, *The Catholic Herald*. On December 13, he rented his cathedral for a concert by San Francisco's "Chanticleer," a men's chorus that's well connected within homosexual/lesbian circles. Bishop Quinn personally and actively lobbied for California's recent "gay rights" bill, which even the homosexual-courting Governor Wilson vetoed; it would have persecuted people, including Catholics, who refused to hire or rent to sodomites. But more on this, Chanticleer, and the bishop in my next report.

> **It is not sinful to have the homosexual inclination; *it is the homosexual acts that are intrinsically unnatural and therefore immoral.***

The pope has said many times that the faithful have a right not to be confused. So let's be clear: it is not sinful to have the homosexual *inclination*; it is the homosexual *acts* that are intrinsically unnatural and therefore immoral, and, of course, enormously harmful to society. Let me refute the possible accusation of "homophobia" (a ridiculous word!) by assuring you that I could see myself working as chaplain in an AIDS hospital.

The famed French geneticist Dr. Jerome Lejeune has observed that if people want to make of AIDS disappear, they should quit sodomizing. Likewise, the bishops of Zimbabwe said bluntly in a national pastoral that if people want to be rid of the "slim disease" (as it's known in Africa), they should stop sinning sexually.

American Catholics—and millions of other Americans—wait in vain for the bishops to speak out as frankly against the politically protected plague that kills 150 Americans every day. What a blessing it would have been if the bishops had emerged from their recent national meeting with a ringing document on chastity, written by the best theologians and psychologists.

It could have pointed out the theological and human wisdom of observing chastity before marriage and fidelity within marriage; showed how the family is possible and healthy only if the unruly sexual appetite is curtailed by sacrificial love; explained true human love and the error and folly of giving condoms to teens by citing the abundant factual evidence; and recommended a modern, up-to-date Catholic marriage-preparation course with built-in, mandatory NFP training. Instead, in this age of condomania, the "authentic teachers" discussed which holy days of obligation to abolish, the environment, and the plight of the Indians.

Last year's medical bill for AIDS in the USA was $5.6 billion; by 1994 it will be $10.4 billion. During my recent checkup at the Mayo Clinic, medical authorities predicted that AIDS will overwhelm the health-care system. Today, teenagers are the most venereally diseased segment of our (literally) sex-sick society. Every fourteen months the number of teens with AIDS increases by 100 percent. The "safe sex" propaganda, the horrible sex-ed programs, and the insane high-school condom giveaways will only add fuel to the fires of lust.

In my next report I'll tell you where I stand on the Catholic sex-"education" controversy. Meanwhile, read our critiques of *The New Creation Series,* Coleen Mast's *Sex Respect* program, Franciscan Communications' *In God's Image, Family Life* (Benziger), Molly Kelly's *Let's Talk to Teens about Chastity,* and her "Teens and Chastity" video.

Letters

I wish to acknowledge with immense gratitude receipt of the projector which you so kindly sent to me. I shall always remain grateful for any other materials you can send to us for our apostolate in the Human Life Protection League.

I wish you and all your dedicated co-workers God's blessings in abundance. Let us pray for each other.

> *The Most Rev. Stephen N. Ezeanya*
> *Archbishop of Onitsha*
> *Nigeria*

Things are oppressively tough around here, and our country is in a rather messy situation economically, politically, and socially. Of course our antilife adversaries are exploiting the situation maximally. More grants, loans, and Greek gifts are being offered virtually every month. These apparent palliatives have not made much impact on the populace in spite of our government's efforts to tackle our massive socio-economic problems. The pervasive mood is one of low morale.

I am quite convinced that today's carrots will turn out to be tomorrow's sticks and that that deadly tomorrow which is really not a distant one has already begun. In our beginning is our end (with due deference to T. S. Eliot). We are already witnessing the veritable signals of tomorrow's decay—AIDS, abortion galore, surreptitious sterilization of villagers, massive distribution of condoms to young people, etc.

Unless our people are awakened to the truth, there may not be any tomorrow. If we are like the legendary ostrich, we will probably bury our heads in the sand, making believe not only that we do not know what is going on but that others do not see us either. That will be a double coincidence of tragedy.

Be assured, however, that HLPL will not give up the

good fight. We need the prayers and assistance of the few sane voices of the Friends of Life remaining in the wilderness of the Western world. We shall overcome.

Lawrence A. Adekoya, KCSS
Human Life Protection League
Ijebu Ode, Nigeria

I am writing to acknowledge receipt of the VHS tape "The Silent Scream." It caused a stir in our studios the very day I had the materials dubbed onto the u-matic tapes we use.

Arrangements are now being made to air the program to our over three million viewers.

Matthew Otalike
Nigerian Television Authority
Nigeria

I have just read your leaflet *Behind the Mask of UNICEF*. I found it very revealing. This has prompted me to write you to request some of your past publications, and future ones meanwhile, pending when our league can officially subscribe to these publications.

Our new prolife group is involved in the task of promoting and preserving the inherent dignity in human life.

The situation in Nigeria as regards population issues makes mass enlightenment with such publications as yours a necessity. Under much pressure from international organizations (World Bank, USAID, Planned Parenthood, etc.), the Nigerian government has collaborated in spreading the false alarm that our numbers and population growth are the root cause of our economic problems. It is also being used as a tool for encouraging the abortion and contraceptive culture. The illiteracy rate and lack of adequate and authentic information sources are playing into their hands.

Njoku Chiedum N
University of Ibadan
Oyo State, Nigeria

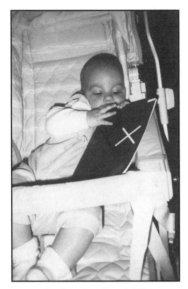

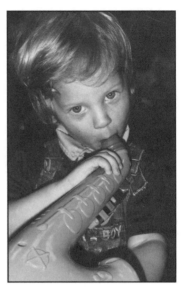

"Maybe there's a **Special Report** *in here…"*

"We prolifers have to blow our own horns"

Bishop Austin Vaughan teaches at HLI weekend conference in St. Louis

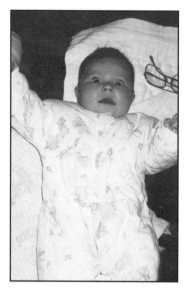

"The voters elected Clinton?!"   *Baptizing a new prolifer (Belgium)*

Prolife seminarians—who'll be the next Fr. Marx or Fr. Matthew?

Putting Sex Education on the Couch

No. 88   March 1992

In my last *Special Report* to you, I disclosed that Bishop Francis Quinn of Sacramento, California, rents the Cathedral of the Blessed Sacrament to various groups hostile to Christ's Church. These include the proabortion participants in Governor-elect Pete Wilson's inaugural bash and San Francisco's Chanticleer, an a cappella male chorus that's well connected in the homosexual and lesbian populations.

Chanticleer concerts are promoted in various "gay" publications, including Sacramento's *Mom...Guess What!* The group got $40,000 of your tax money from the National Endowment for the Arts, which funds blasphemous and pornographic "art" such as the notorious "P---Christ." Another $40,000 came from Hewlett-Packard, the computer giant well-known for its financial contributions to baby-killing Planned Parenthood (PP).

CATHOLICS KICKED OUT, PAGANS WELCOMED

I've carefully studied the latest documents from the Holy See and, in particular, Cardinal Paul Augustine Mayer's "Concerts in Church" of 5 November 1987. In no way do these documents allow Bishop Quinn's renting of his cathedral to these secular groups; nor do they justify excluding the faithful who want to come in to pray or to visit the Blessed Sacrament during the events; a Catholic man who wished to do so during the Chanticleer concert of December 13 was ordered out of the cathedral. The police physically ejected another Catholic man who wished to pray. (Too bad these two forgot to turn over the tables in the cathedral where money-changers were selling audiocassettes, videos, and literature.) To accommodate one of these secular groups on another occasion, a scheduled Sunday Mass was canceled.

The concert audience consisted mainly of trendily

dressed individuals and couples, including many males, and people who apparently had never graced the cathedral before. Some couples embraced. A woman with a container of some liquid refreshment poured drinks into red plastic cups.

Before and after the performance, and during the intermission, people talked, laughed, called out to one another, and strolled about freely. They wandered into the sanctuary and into the alcove where the tabernacle containing the Blessed Sacrament stands on a side altar; the flickering sanctuary lamp indicated that Our Lord had not been removed.

According to the printed program, both secular and religious music filled the cathedral, including songs such as "A Christmas Song" ("Chestnuts Roasting on an Open Fire") and "Winter Wonderland."

At the end of the performance the chorus received a standing ovation amid shouts of "Bravo!" One of those applauding was Father Bill Holland, the assistant pastor, who was vested in a casual, patterned sweater.

Sacramento's secular newspapers reviewed the event in their "Amusements" and "Music Review" sections, just as they'd review any performance of a major act. Both mentioned the cathedral as the site of the concert. One newspaper referred to the "capacity crowd" and the "entry [of the group] into the sanctuary," the procession of the singers to the "front altar," and so on.

Bishop Quinn provides all of his diocesan employees an insurance policy that includes abortion, contraceptives, sterilization, and more.

DIOCESAN WORKERS GET ABORTION COVERAGE

Bishop Quinn has done other strange things, such as buying for all of his diocesan employees an insurance policy that includes abortion. For this policy he pays almost $50,000 a month to Kaiser-Permanente, whose hospitals are notorious abortion centers. This insurance plan gives teachers and other diocesan employees access to abortions, contraceptives/abortifacients, prenatal testing directed toward abortion, genetic counseling directed toward aborting "defective" children, sterilization, and "safe sex" programs. These "services" are also available to the minor children of diocesan employees without parental knowledge or permission.

Also operating in the diocese is Sister Sheila Walsh, SSS, She organized Jericho, a lobbying project that networks with wild liberal groups such as NOW, the California Council of Churches, and PP.

Perhaps it's not surprising that Bishop Quinn has supported California's homosexual agenda. This agenda includes a "gay rights" bill, the final version of which was too much even for pro-"gay" Governor Wilson, who vetoed it. "I think bigotry and political ambition were the forces at work here," pronounced Marist Father Rodney DeMartini, director of AIDS education for San Francisco's Archbishop John Quinn. People should be "outraged," he said, and should complain to their elected officials. The California Catholic Conference has also backed the "gay" agenda. It took no stand on the bill, which was designed to persecute people, including Catholics, who refuse to hire or rent to sodomites.

Father William Wood, SJ, who for some five years was director of the conference, openly supported "gay" pseudo-rights and other questionable legislation. He was weak on abortion and pornography. He even hired Kathy Lynch, a pro-abort, as the conference's lobbyist in Sacramento. Father Wood recently became president of the National Catholic Rural Life Conference, headquartered in Des Moines, a city apparently too much of a backwater for his taste: he still lives in California.

SEX ED *V.* MORALITY ED

Many ask where Father Paul Marx stands on sex education in Catholic schools. First of all, some clarifications:

"sex-ed" is education in the male and female reproductive systems. Children need some prudent instruction in the biology and physiology of human reproduction, but it must take place in the context of the study of the entire body. The reproductive system should receive no more emphasis than the respiratory, nervous, or digestive systems. The student doesn't need reproductive information constantly repeated throughout twelve years of schooling.

In the appropriate context, learning doesn't personalize sexual acts for the student; the child must take biology classes more seriously because he knows the grading is important. That's not true in "sex-ed" classes, where teachers often grade students on their attitudes rather than their biological knowledge. But parents must be very watchful, because any opening of the delicate subject of sex can be the crack in the door through which sex educators slip in. No matter how good the textbook, "the teacher is the curriculum."

Never forget that sexuality is a complex, body-soul, multifaceted and profound reality—a mystery—the understanding of which reaches into theology, philosophy, biology, physiology, sociology, psychology, genetics, and more. The fact that we're male or female marks each person's total function and, indeed, every cell of our bodies. Sexuality, personality, and spirituality are coterminous.

That is why teaching only the physical side, as so often happens today, deals with only one facet, a sliver of the total reality and mystery that is human, holistic sexuality. To focus solely on physical sex distorts the truth.

Every pope who has dealt with this matter has warned that we must handle this area of human life and education with supreme delicacy and care. Pope John Paul II told the U.S. hierarchy in 1979:

> Sex education, which is the basic right and duty of parents, must also be carried out under their attentive guidance, whether at home or in educational centers chosen and controlled by them. In this regard, the Church reaffirms the law of subsidiarity, which the school is bound to observe when it cooperates in sex education, by entering

into the same spirit that animates the parents.

Today, educators often shut out the parents, ridicule their advice and protests, and totally ignore the central role of the principle of subsidiarity.

The tragic results of today's constant, obsessive barrage of sex-ed, engineered by PP and its offspring, the Sex Information and Education Council of the United States (SIECUS), are obvious for all to see. (For documented facts on the dismal failure of PP's and SIECUS's sex-ed programs, funded by millions of your tax dollars, order *Public School Sex Education: A Report*, by the American Family Association, from HLI for $2 postpaid.)

The U.S. Senate Report, *Code Blue*, notes the bitter fruit borne since the sex revolution and modern sex-ed began in the '60s: a 600 percent rise in teen pregnancies; a 300 percent rise in teen suicides; a 232 percent increase in teen homicides; and 400,000 abortions exterminating the babies of teenage girls yearly.

Then there are the phenomenal increases in divorces, illegitimacy, single-parent families, AIDS, teen VD, and infertility, and the drop in the U.S. birthrate. According to the latest information from the federal Centers for Disease Control, 72 percent of high-school seniors have fornicated and 43 million Americans have acquired incurable sex diseases. We're rotting from within.

There's no such thing as morally neutral or "value-free" sex education.

PUBLIC SCHOOLS, CATHOLIC SCHOOLS, AND HOME SCHOOLS

There's no such thing as morally neutral or "value-free" sex education, despite what PP and Catholic quislings assert. Sexual behavior is inseparable from our spiritual lives and religious values. That is why public schools cannot, even under the best of circumstances, spiritually form and inform young people, because Supreme Court rulings forbid public schools to teach about religion, morality, God, and the afterlife.

What about "Catholic" schools, CCD programs, and sex/chastity/abstinence sessions? First, you should know that only about 5 percent of Catholic teachers of childbearing age in Catholic schools accept *Humanae Vitae* and/or practice natural family planning (NFP). Thus, most of them are involved in contraceptives/abortifacients/sterilization and, in some instances, even surgical abortion. How can they teach, generate, or inspire chastity when they live unchastely themselves? And how could it be otherwise, when Catholic priests rarely discuss abortion from the pulpit and virtually never preach on contraception or sterilization, and when the majority of Catholic theologians reject *Humanae Vitae*?

Using the words "chastity" and "abstinence" doesn't guarantee that a program will coincide with parents' expectations or even with Catholic moral teaching. Many "chastity" programs present the same "choice" thinking and much the same graphic information as PP programs do, dressed up with some "God talk." Their creators don't seem to realize that even PP's *methodology* is objectionable from the standpoint of Catholic theology.

HLI now publishes valuable critiques of all major Catholic-school sex-education courses and chastity/abstinence programs. We didn't decide to produce these booklets without a great deal of thought, research, and consultation. I knew they'd be controversial. But after studying the programs and seeing that their content often was inconsistent with Catholic teaching, I decided it was important to inform parents, bishops, religious, priests, and others.

What's more, as Cardinal John O'Connor has remarked, we've raised a generation of illiterate Catholics, and they're falling away from the Church in droves. The insightful Father John Hardon, SJ, maintains that 70 percent of "Catholic" schools are no longer Catholic—hence, the healthy trend toward Catholic home schooling.

REMEMBER "OCCASIONS OF SIN"?

A common error is to think that mere knowledge and information are enough. But even the best sexual information won't make anyone chaste; the powerful sex appetite must be reined in by spiritual formation and religious practice. Pope Pius XI put it in a nutshell when he said that "the reason young people get into trouble sexually is not ignorance, but weakness of will and poverty of spiritual life." (Think of the flimsy CCD programs to which parents bring their children on Sunday—after which they drive home instead of staying for Mass.)

Drawing upon Pope Pius XI's masterful encyclical *The Christian Education of Youth* (30 December 1929), the Vatican's Holy Office gave us all the following directive in 1931:

> The first care must be the full, strong, and uninterrupted religious instruction of the youth of both sexes; they are to be taught above all to be instant in prayer, regular in the sacrament of penance and in receiving the Blessed Eucharist, to have filial devotion to the Blessed Virgin, the Mother of holy purity, and to place themselves entirely under her protection; they must carefully avoid dangerous reading, immodest shows, bad company, and all occasions of sin.

Not one sex-ed or chastity program now in existence comes close to observing this directive.

We must return to teaching the whole faith: the Ten Commandments (including the sixth and ninth, presented in nongraphic terms), the cardinal virtues (one of which, temperance, governs chastity), the theological and moral virtues, the unadulterated Gospel message, the reality of original and actual sin, the need to go to confession and receive Communion frequently, the lives of the saints, and so on. If we did, the foundation of chastity would be assured, as it formerly was. We must constantly emphasize the mastery of the soul over the body.

To all of those priests, religious, and teachers who are

so ready to talk to youngsters about physical sex and to inflict on them the horrendous literature and videos that they themselves often haven't scrutinized, I say: Examine your own lives, values, and practices. Priests must begin to instruct parents from the pulpit and at every other opportunity, helping those parents who don't know their faith to learn and practice it. This instruction will rearm the primary educators of the family, wherein the foundations of children's personalities are laid down and in terms of which they learn everything else.

HOW TO TEACH CHASTITY TO YOUNG PEOPLE

Of course, sincere, well-prepared Catholic teachers, priests, and religious who know their faith and have the gift of cultivating it can help parents to bring back good religion textbooks to Catholic schools, books that teach the whole of morality without equivocation. This teaching will help young people acquire more and more spiritual wisdom and the discernment and strength to avoid as many occasions of sin as possible, by practicing what the saints treasured, "custody of the eyes."

Our young people desperately need this solid spiritual formation, rooted in the sacraments, daily prayer, and exposure to authentic Catholic principles. Sadly, the vast majority of Catholic boys and girls today never learn these principles, because countless priests, religious, and lay teachers have caught the Modernist virus or have fallen for the propaganda of the "sex jockeys" (sex educators) from PP and SIECUS.

The best sex education or formation anyone can have is to live in a home with loving parents.

So often we hear, "But parents don't teach their kids." I resent that charge with all that's in me: the best sex education or formation anyone can have is to live in a home with loving parents. Mom and dad don't have to say much explicitly about sex, as the past proves; their example says everything. Chastity is more "caught" than taught.

Some people argue that if the school doesn't teach "the facts of life," kids will learn them "on the streets." But information that a boy gets from his friends is more like a secret and doesn't pretend to be authoritative; thus, it doesn't destroy the mystery of sex for him. Nor does it deprive sexuality of its spiritual and moral character or desensitize him through classroom instruction given by an authority figure.

If we've learned one thing from our research into the major "Catholic" sex-education programs (with their heretical literature and often pornographic audiovisual aids), it's that sex-ed programs are woefully inadequate, very dangerous, and therefore best eliminated. Giving one or even several hours on sex-and-chastity to religiously ignorant students may or may not do much harm, but no one should believe it imparts the information and formation needed for truly chaste Christian living in a sex-soaked culture.

Some scientists dispute the existence of a latency period, but any perceptive person with any experience has seen it verified again and again in the innocence of young children—say, before ten or eleven years of age. It's precisely this innocence of little children that's so touching. What a tragedy it is when grown-up "sexperts" barge into these "years of innocence" (as Pope John Paul II calls them in *Familiaris Consortio*) with endless physical details, in mixed classes. All authentic experience proves that. No wonder our youth are so unhappy, confused, diseased, sexually immoral, and suicide-prone! The incredible AIDS/sex programs, with their condomania, will only make a bad situation far worse. PP is using the AIDS crisis and its high school sex "clinics" to inject even more explicit sex programs into the schools.

How much better to let formed and informed parents teach their own children in this crucial area! We should never trust public-school teachers. We can no longer trust even "Catholic" teachers with chastity education, because so many have been duped by Modernist theologians, secular humanists, and proponents of values clarification.

My advice is to preoccupy yourself with learning your faith and living it in today's culture of death, as the pope calls it. You'll bring common sense into this delicate area where, as I mentioned earlier, parents are so often trampled, ridiculed, and ignored. Speaking of parents' "most solemn obligation" to educate their offspring in sexual matters, Vatican II says, "Their role as educators is so decisive that scarcely anything can compensate for their failure in it" (*Gravissimum educationis*).

PITFALLS OF CHASTITY EDUCATION

Discussing physical sex before a mixed class of boys and girls is already an occasion of sin for them, in many instances. The very intimacy of sex demands that every reference to it be made with the greatest reverence and sensitivity. Publicity is the enemy of this intimacy; such violations are so serious that giving sex instruction to a mixed class of students of various emotional ages is harmful even if the teachers are sincere and cautious.

When we consider the reality that most public-school students will get their sex-ed from teachers taught with PP methods, and when we consider the proabortion, antiparent agenda of the National Education Association (NEA), we have no choice but to eliminate sex-ed from our public schools. Likewise, because of the shortage of orthodox teachers in Catholic schools and the desensitizing effect of twelve years of sex-ed, when few Catholic school children even know their faith, we must also consider Catholic sex-ed a disaster, overall. "The teacher is the curriculum." Sex-ed has failed in every country, including Sweden, the pioneer.

We recommend to every parent the wise Father Vern Sattler's new book, *Challenging Children to Chastity: A Parental Guide*, which you can order from HLI for $8 postpaid. Another "must read" new book is psychiatrist Dr. Melvin Anchell's *What's Wrong with Sex Education?* now available from HLI for $9 postpaid. For a grim picture of diseased teens, read Dr. Stephen J. Genuis's *Risky Sex:*

The Onslaught of Sexually Transmitted Diseases, yours for $9 postpaid. Every parent, priest, bishop, and teacher should read these books.

I also hope you'll order all of our critiques of the major "Catholic" sexuality programs: *The New Creation Series*, Coleen Mast's *Sex Respect, In God's Image*, and Molly Kelly's book and video, *Let's Talk to Teens about Chastity* (all four critiques for only $12 postpaid). What you read will shock you, to say the least.

The very term "chastity education" is a kind of misnomer. The practice of chastity entails a whole constellation of virtues. We need to instill in our young people much more than just part of the virtue of temperance. One-issue moral-education programs have been notorious failures. Drug education among young people has led in general to more drug use, antismoking programs have led to more smoking, antisuicide training has increased the number of deaths, and "death education" classes have only produced a morbid preoccupation with that subject.

Preoccupation with physical/ biological sex in public and parochial schools has been a colossal failure.

Preoccupation with physical/biological sex in public and parochial schools has been a colossal failure, resulting in more VD, unwed pregnancies, abortions, single-parent families, sexual sins of all kinds, and so on. Emphasizing physical/biological sex only confirms in the minds of young people that physical intimacy is the be-all and end-all of life and that pleasure is the sole, or at least the main, purpose of sex. The popes and the magisterium have always had it right: teach the total faith, make sure children understand basic morality, and you'll gain the most.

So, finally, am I opposed to education in Christian sexuality, understood as moral-spiritual training and formation for living a life of unselfish love in which the sexual impulse is contained and controlled? Of course not. Can it be provided in public schools? No!

Am I opposed to such education in so-called Catholic schools? It depends: Are the parents involved? Do they know what's being taught? Have they examined the audio-visual aids and literature? Are the teaching materials derived from Scripture, papal encyclicals, and official Church teachings, or from PP, pop psychology, and the opinions of well-meaning but inadequately educated lay people? Do the teachers practice chastity themselves by living up to and proclaiming the ideals of *Humanae Vitae*? Are they known for their exemplary Christian lives, especially in this area? Do they have special training? Is this education presented in mixed classes? Does it take up more than its share of the curriculum? Is it integrated into comprehensive religious instruction? (I could ask a few more questions.) If in doubt, don't let your precious children be sex-educated.

Far better for formed and informed parents to take charge, with—where necessary—the help of truly Catholic teachers under close parental control. Otherwise, stay away from it! Learn your faith and live it intensely in a home-protected environment. Today, the truly Christian family and home are our only havens.

Planning strategy with Bishop Venmani Selvanather and the great
Fr. Anthony Antonisamy (India)

Letters

A concerned Catholic parent brought me your "question-naire," and both he and I cannot believe you honestly believe in what you are doing.

It seems that your great fear about educating our youth *responsibly* is rooted in your own inability to come to terms with your own sexuality. People who have accepted themselves as sexual beings (and this includes those of us who have chosen celibacy) are unafraid of human sexuality and unafraid of educating young people in the beauty, goodness, and mystery of human sexuality expressed in the marriage relationship, as the Church teaches.

Wake up, brother priest! Kids will learn about sexual-ity one way or another—and there is nothing you or I or Catholic parents can do to control all the opportunities they have to learn about sex. Few parents are as responsi-ble as you or I would like them to be. Teaching human sex-uality in Catholic schools is one of the best ways to offset parental irresponsibility. Better for kids to get wholesome, Catholic teaching from their parents (if possible) or in our parochial schools than from the many non-Christian sources that are now available to them. Think about it and you'll agree.

Get your head out of the sand and look about you! The world is changing faster than you imagine—and the Church, to be effective, must constantly update itself in its mission of Christian education. You cannot impede the work of the Holy Spirit begun at Vatican II!

I am both saddened and amused by the pathetic lamen-tations of those of you who are so deperate in refusing to accept a changing Church in a changing world. I am sad-dened because you on the Far Right are a burden, a scandal, and a source of total confusion to our American Catholics who, by and large, rejoice in the spirit of *aggiornamento* begun by John XXIII and continuing in the Church—all implications of which you simply refuse to accept. You are pitiable hangers-on of a Church mentality that is obsolete and that cannot and will not be resuscitated.

I am amused because you use the word "Modernist" to denounce every churchperson and every postconciliar idea that you—with your hardened hearts and closed minds—cannot accept. Why, most Catholics today don't even know what "Modernism" is—nor do they care! Thus, all the effort you and your fellow conservatives (whose numbers are, naturally, shrinking with the passage of time away from the Church of Pius XII) put into putting down the elusive so-called Modernist thinking in the Church is a very ludicrous waste of your time, and God's!

Conservative Catholicism has no future, because it is rooted only in a nostalgic past which most Catholics today want to—and will eventually!—forget. The Spirit of Jesus is moving the rest of us forward, and you who refuse to go along will drown in your Twin Circles of fear and ignorance. As Fray Junipero Serra said in his motto: "Always look forward and never turn back!"

I pray that God who "makes all things new" *renew* your time-warped mind and spirit.

I am a postconciliar Chicago pastor.

> *(No signature)*
> *(No name)*
> *(No address)*

In your newsletter you gave some examples of horror stories from your large file of graphic sex-education classes in Catholic schools. The horror stories are exactly what you would expect. They are consistent with the training that has been given in Catholic seminaries for some time.

I am afraid that we need a lot more than a survey and putting Mrs. Engel's book into the hands of bishops, priests, and teachers. Frankly, I think that what we need is good bishops and good priests. This is not to say that I think that all bishops and priests are not good. Some are worthy of their calling. Far too many are not. With the right kind of priests, Mrs. Engel's book would be surperfluous.

I thank God that my children are grown, but I fear for my grandchildren in more than sex education. The Catholic Church is not there for them as it was there for their grandmother and me.

Thomas J. Padden, PhD
Commander USN (Ret)
Casselberry, Florida

There was much satisfaction for me in learning of your survey regarding sex education in the Catholic schools. Bravo!

My husband and I are the parents of a fourteen-year-old girl who spent seven years in a Catholic school and has just completed the seventh grade in public school.

I, too, have been frustrated by the sex-education program of my local Catholic school. I first learned there was reason for concern when attending the presentation to parents for the fifth- and sixth-grade sex-ed program. A video was shown which left me scarlet-faced. When the lights came on, I noticed several other red faces. I was particularly concerned that all material was presented to coed classes. When I asked the teacher in charge how they planned to preserve a girl's modesty under these circumstances, she said merely that boys also have modesty! It became clear to me that the eighth-graders were taught birth control by the priest. I later heard that his theory was that at thirteen the students are having sex and need to be prepared.

My daughter Sara's sex education began when she was four. Following the theory that one answers a child's questions, I found myself telling her, answer by answer, the entire facts of life one evening. From that night on, the subject has been open for discusion in our home whenever events suggest it.

When Sara was in fifth grade, I chose to take her out of the sex-ed class. The material was being presented by a nurse from the local country-health organization; no Catholic moral teaching was presented in conjunction with

this curriculum. I took material to the principal that
indicated that teaching abstinence was the most successful
approach to reducing teen pregnancies and promiscuity,
but my efforts to have it taught fell on deaf ears.

This year Sara is in public school. Her faith has
increased enormously. She has been taught abstinence in
the school sex-ed course. I have had no concern about R-
rated movies, since she has seen very few movies at school
(unlike the Catholic school). In general, those students she
has chosen for friends are more faith-oriented than
students in her former school had been.

> *Charlene Tomenchko*
> *Monroe Falls, Ohio*

Thank you so very much for all the reading material you
sent me. I especially enjoyed reading *Is Humanae Vitae
Outdated?* When I had my change of heart, I had very few
facts to support what I was doing except blind faith, but
now I do, thanks to you and others.

I spent almost six years at Emory doing obstetrics only
and in fact did two years of additional training in high-risk
obstetrics. Dr. David Grimes was there when I was—he
was head of abortion surveillance at the CDC (Centers for
Disease Control) and popularized the notion that it was
safer to have an abortion than to have a child. I shudder
when I think of those days.

The problem of teenage sexual activity has accelerated
the past five years. Over the past eighteen years in this
field I have seen such an increase in the number of girls
sexually active, at earlier ages. We, as a society, are
definitely on a downward spiral.

One of the last departmental conferences before I left
Emory in 1984 was the annual report on the Teen Services
program. If they had listened to what they were saying,
they would have realized that their services resulted in an
increase in the numbers of abortions and deliveries. What
have we done? However, all ob-gyns in this country have
been brainwashed into thinking that single motherhood,
abortion, contraception, and sterliziation are society's

norm. We have a lot of backtracking to do.

> *Kathleen M. Raviele, MD*
> *Tucker, Georgia*

Thanks for allowing many concerned Catholics to help you voice our firm opposition to the Planned Parenthood type of scandals being perpetrated in some "Catholic" schools.

> *Fernando E. Pasquelle*
> *Daly City, California*

I want to thank you for all that you and the whole HLI team have been doing to defeat the evil agenda of Planned Parenthood and the abortionists, and to save human babies all over the world.

PP and the abortionists have had their evil way so often. If we can stop them in their satanic plans in Ireland that will be a great witness to the world. With the liberal theologians eating away at the true faith in the seminaries there and through the media—both secular and religious— we can win only through God's mercy and blessing.

> *Father James E. Haran*
> *Chattaraugus, New York*

May God bless you for the great and important work you are doing to save the lives of unborn children. You are a prophet in our times.

I have just read your special issue, No. 88. It is excellent. Your writing is powerful. Please put me on your mailing list.

> *The Most Rev. William J. McNaughton, MM*
> *Bishop of Inchon*
> *South Korea*

Malaysian Madonna and Child

With Ireland's Norma Crosbie and Mairéad Waldron (1992)

IPPF didn't get this one! (Nigeria)

*"Grownups have made
a real mess…"*

"The future of humanity passes by way of the family"
(Familiaris Consortio)

*Children are numerous and welcome at Sunday Mass
at world headquarters*

Children are the only future any nation has (Nigeria)

Our Asian-Pacific Conference

No. 89   April 1992

I **n 1974 I traveled** to Manila, where Sister Pilar
Verzosa and I launched Pro-Life Philippines. During
four subsequent mission journeys, I managed to give
talks on all eleven major islands. My latest trip, in
February, was perhaps the best.

The Philippines' 7,107 islands comprise 116,000 square
miles, an area larger than Ireland and England together,
and slightly larger than Nevada. The country is home to
sixty-two million people, and seven million live abroad.
Between two and three million are in the USA, including
23,000 doctors and 50,000 nurses. More than a million
Filipinos live in Arab countries, and the rest are scattered.

THE IRELAND OF ASIA

Indeed, the chief export of the Philippines is people. Just
as the Irish once did, the Filipinos are now spreading
Christianity to many parts of the world, including Japan,
which recently agreed to let in 200,000 Filipino workers.
The Filipinos are 83 percent Catholic. About 5 percent are
Moslem, and 2 or 3 percent belong to a powerful, unified,
schismatic "Catholic" group known as Iglesia ni Kristo
(Ferdinand Marcos was a member). The remaining 10
percent are Protestant. The Catholic bishops fear an influx
of sects over the next five to ten years.

Because of HLI's four speaking tours and the thousands of dollars' worth of prolife/profamily materials we've
pumped into this island nation since 1974, her prolife
movement has truly flourished. From January 31 to
February 2, HLI sponsored and mostly paid for a historic
Asian-Pacific Pro-Life Conference in Manila, attended by
1,700 souls, including 600 nurses, 120 nuns, some 30
priests, and delegates from all seventy-two provinces. The
gathering was a huge success, thanks in large part to your
prayers and offerings. People came from nine other

countries—Japan, South Korea, Taiwan, Thailand, Indonesia, Malaysia, India, Pakistan, and Australia. All took home an abundance of prolife/profamily videos, films, and literature that we'd shipped over in advance and carried in with us.

Just as the Irish once did, the Filipinos are now spreading Christianity to many parts of the world.

The international faculty that we assembled took HLI's total approach. The speakers covered everything from contraception to euthanasia, including sex education, chastity promotion, "overpopulation," the formation of conscience, radical feminism, postabortion syndrome, the attacks upon *Humanae Vitae*, marriage preparation, natural family planning (NFP), and related subjects. We audio- and videotaped all of the sessions for use in educating thousands throughout Asia.

A significant fruit of the conference was the founding of the Asian Council for Life and Family, with headquarters in Manila. Its chairwoman will be the incomparable Sister Pilar, a tiny, wise, courageous, and totally orthodox Good Shepherd nun who enjoys the total confidence of both bishops and lay leaders. It's incredible what she's accomplished, under HLI's guidance.

The Asian Council will be the hub of prolife/profamily promotion throughout Asia. It was founded at the personal request of Manila's powerful Cardinal Jaime Sin, whom the people jokingly call "His Political Eminence." The Filipino bishops were meeting during our conference, and so the cardinal couldn't attend. But two bishops of the Family Commission, Juan de Dios Pueblos and Jesus Varela, took an active part, joking that "we can abandon the bishops, but not the prolifers and family promoters." CNN filmed the entire opening Mass, by the way. They'd asked HLI to help them work up a telecast on how religion, especially the Catholic Church, affects abortion laws worldwide.

The Philippines have a long and interesting history, which I've related in past *Reports*. The Filipinos describe their national history as 400 years in a convent (with the Spaniards), fifty years in Hollywood (with the Americans), and three years in hell (with the Japanese, in WWII). Today the developed nations, the international contraceptive imperialists, and the multinational corporations brutally exploit this richly endowed island nation of poor, gentle, and humble people.

The Philippine archipelago stretches 1,150 miles north to south and 690 miles east to west. The Filipinos inhabit 115 islands, and 4,000 islands are still unnamed. The country could be prosperous if developed properly and not exploited. She's well within the tropics, though, and suffers from typhoons, floods, volcanic eruptions, and earthquakes.

Paying the foreign debt gobbles up 40 percent of the national budget. More than 20 percent of the people are unemployed, and the situation is fast getting worse. The inexperienced, wealthy President Cory Aquino has failed. On May 11, thirty million voters will choose a replacement. But better days are hard to foresee. The country has no democratic tradition and is burdened with corruption of all kinds, everywhere. The international population-controllers have bought off many legislators. The threat from the Communist "New People's Army" is allegedly receding, but the Philippines maintain 158 private armies, and only eighteen have been disarmed.

MARCOS AND P.P. *V.* BABIES

The population growth rate is still 2.3 percent, but births per family have fallen from five in 1980 to three today, thanks to President Marcos's vicious depopulation plan, which began in the 1970s under U.S. pressure. Running it were the World Bank, the U.S. Agency for International Development (USAID), the International Planned Parenthood Federation (IPPF), and other antilife organizations. Filipinos tell you that Marcos, who ruled the country from 1965 until his ouster by "people power" and prayer in 1986, reduced the birthrate by one-third and that people today are much poorer anyway. Depopulation has been a disaster, as has the vicious sex education introduced in the 1970s. Schoolbooks are loaded with procontraception, too-many-people propaganda. Sixty percent of the population are 17-24 years old. The depopulators have sterilized 40-50 percent of all married couples in Manila. A woman who agrees to be "ligated" receives a 500-peso ($20) reward from the Depopulation Commission. Doctors like to do caesarean sections because it's easy to sterilize the mother at the same time. The abortifacient Pill and IUD are used widely. For years Upjohn of Kalamazoo, Michigan, illegally injected the abortifacient Depo-Provera (so dangerous that it's banned in the USA) into Philippine women; many thought they were getting vitamin injections. The depopulators are implanting the abortifacient, matchstick-like Norplant into Filipinas again, in the name of health and family welfare!

The Planned Parenthood (PP) depopulation network and propaganda ensnared the bishops at first, but they quickly broke free when they saw they'd been deceived. Today the Church promotes NFP widely, with some success. Various forms of subtle coercion accompany depopulation programs fueled by millions of U.S. dollars. PP, known as the Philippine Family Planning Association, has done seminars on sex-ed for priests, religious, and teachers. The depopulation movement has brainwashed most of the teachers in the many Catholic schools on contraception and "overpopulation."

The USA's most antifamily university, Johns Hopkins, creates pop music and other entertainment with depopulation themes. This entertainment instills antilife/antifamily ideas around the world, above all in the Catholic Philippines. A Filipino recruited by USAID told me that battery-powered abortion suction machines "clean out the women" in the remote hills and mountains. It's incredible how widely the tentacles of the diabolical antilife movement have reached, and how deeply they've penetrated. Meanwhile, only two or three of the Philippines' twenty medical schools offer a course in medical ethics.

HOW FARES THE CHURCH?

When Pope John Paul II visited the islands, he proclaimed the Filipinos the hope of Asia and begged them, as the only Catholic nation in Asia, to evangelize that continent as much as possible. Despite the Philippines' acute shortage of priests and nuns, you find Filipino missionaries in a number of countries. There are 20,000 laymen for every priest. Parishes of 50,000 and 80,000 people aren't unknown. Imagine baptizing 250 babies on Christmas Day, and then more than 300 on the favorite Filipino feast day, Santo Niño (Holy Child) in January! Priestly and religious vocations are decidedly on the upswing, though.

Seminarians are victimized by rebel theologians, the worst being the Jesuits and the Divine Word Fathers.

Priests and nuns sometimes seem poorly educated. In one seminary, the rector asks students to date girls "to become strong"! Seminarians are victimized by rebel theologians, the worst being the Jesuits and the Divine Word Fathers, both of whom reject *Humanae Vitae* brazenly. The Salesians and forty Opus Dei priests are clearly the most orthodox and are doing great work. One Salesian priest told me that doctrinal conditions in the schools are so bad, the birth-control virus so pervasive, and many teachers so misled by foreign contraceptive propaganda that one pretty much has to start with the parents and kindergarten to "set things aright" for the future. Incidentally, some 50,000 homeless children roam the streets of Metro Manila. Philippine women, too, are very much neglected. Their proper education and development would help reduce poverty and many other problems.

The influential Benedictines of San Beda Abbey run a complex of schools in Manila, including one of the country's best law schools. Ever since 1974, I've tried but failed to interest them significantly in the prolife movement. A similar situation exists among the Benedictines in the USA. I'll have more to say on this sad story in the future.

My colleague, Father Matthew Habiger, OSB, preceded me to the Philippines for a ten-day prolife speaking tour. He was astonished by the large audiences and the enthusiastic response he got from high schoolers, university students, seminarians, religious, and priests. "The little Filipina nuns surely know how to work you," he reminisced wearily but happily. I recall the sisters' calling me "the tireless priest" during earlier stays, then working me to the bone.

Here's a brief rundown on what Father Habiger and I learned at the conference:

TAIWAN

There are only 350,000 Catholics among twenty million people. The island is very prosperous, with an economic growth rate of 6.7 percent and a great deal of international money-lending. Consumer confidence is the highest in the world—Taiwan's currency has grown in value more than any other, e.g., 4.8 percent against the U.S. dollar.

There's virtually no prolife movement beyond what HLI has instigated recently; I was there in 1974, but the work I started petered out. The government legalized abortion eight years ago, and abortionists kill many, many babies. After embracing PP's suicidal prodeath policies, the government has finally become alarmed at the nation's nonreproductive birthrate and "youth deficit." Abandoning its "stop at two" policy, it now declares that it's quite all right to have more than two children. Sterilization is common. Priests preach rarely on contraception, and not very often on abortion; after making a strong protest when the government first weakened the abortion law, both bishops and priests seem to have gotten used to baby-killing. We need to reawaken Taiwan's NFP movement, too. Affluence is Taiwan's curse.

BANGLADESH

Only 1 percent of this Moslem country's 120 million people are Catholic. Although it's illegal, abortion is common; abortionists kill an estimated one million babies annually. "Menstrual regulation" (MR), a form of early abortion, is a massive problem; because doctors are in very short supply, the many foreign-trained paramedical personnel perform the MR procedures. The foreign depopulation *apparat* is swarming all over this, the poorest country in Asia. The depopulators use every known antibaby weapon, including the abortifacient Norplant (see Report No. 84), encouraging enormous abuses and suffering. Bangladesh is one more Moslem country that has found it impossible to resist the international antilife monster. But the delegation at our conference is raring to go, with the materials we gave them.

SOUTH KOREA

The chipper Sister Dominica, Korea's prolife leader, said there are 1.5 million abortions annually among 42 million people—4,500 per day! Korean prolifers began their efforts last year, with a national meeting of 700 people in Seoul. HLI has poured in literature, the best of which has been translated into Korean. A delegation of fourteen people begged us to repeat the Manila gathering in Seoul.

Prosperous South Korea is a nation of contrasts. Next to Ireland, Korea gave Pope John Paul II the largest Mass congregation ever, 600,000 souls out of fewer than two million Catholics. There are four major seminaries and many vocations, not to mention one of the highest convert rates in the world. This booming nation is 6 percent Catholic, with its own Catholic medical school. The first Christians to arrive in Korea, the proabortion Presbyterians, are the largest Christian group. The government strongly urges people to have only two children. HLI must come to the aid of the Koreans. The hierarchy is ready to move. HLI's friend, Bishop Thomas Stewart of Chun Cheon, has promoted NFP for years, more than any other bishop in the world.

INDIA

I've reported extensively on this nation of 750 million people in past *Reports*, such as *No. 53*. Thanks to widespread commercial amniocentesis programs and sex-selection abortions, the sex ratio is now 900 girls to 1,000 boys; there's much infanticide of females, too. Incest and prostitution are rife, as is AIDS. India's fifteen million Catholics suffer from rampant liturgical abuses.

India has the second-largest contingent of Jesuits in the world; they haven't always been a blessing, often having loused up theology, as Richard McCormick, SJ, did in the USA. (Did you see his shameful performance on TV recently in "Sex and Catholics"?) Sexual scandals among the clergy are increasing. HLI has decided to hold its next Asian prolife/profamily conference in 1994, the Year of the Family, in centrally located Bangalore. This city has the only Catholic medical school in India and the country's best prolife group, under the leadership of the great Drs. Alfred and Marie Mascarenhas.

MALAYSIA

The Moslems are persecuting the Catholic minority more and more in this country. Only a few remain of some fifty Catholic schools founded by Christian Brothers from Ireland. Abortion is illegal but by no means unknown. Moslem authorities dream of tripling the fast-growing population—of Moslems, that is. Our best efforts haven't resulted in a concerted prolife movement. The Malaysian delegation promised us renewed efforts and dedication. Bishop Anthony Selvanayagam of Penang is very eager to move.

Thailand is burdened with the most AIDS cases in Asia, thanks to Planned Parenthood's contraception campaign.

THAILAND

This country is burdened with the most AIDS cases in Asia, thanks to PP's contraception campaign over the last two decades. A government minister estimates that by the year 2000, two to four million Thais will be infected. Tourism is this Buddhist country's main source of foreign exchange. The many "kamikaze sex tours" cause enormous harm. Illegal child and adult prostitution flourishes in

Bangkok's 600 brothels, with more than 500,000 prostitutes in a nation of fifty-seven million souls. Beautiful Thai girls work in houses of ill repute in other countries, e.g., in Europe. Thailand's prolife movement is spotty, but religious vocations are many, surprisingly.

INDONESIA

This oil-rich nation of 180 million people is the world's largest Moslem country. Three percent of her people are Catholics, and 90 percent of them live on the island of Flores. Five of Indonesia's thirty cabinet ministers are Catholic.

For some time we've been helping Sister Robertilde Vander Meer, a Dutch Holy Ghost sister who's a prolife missionary in the interior. There she teaches NFP to rural people and saves baby after baby from abortion. At the conference, we loaded her down with literature, films, and a projector. She must've been quite a sight, with the projector hanging on the side of the horse she needs to get back to her people. Sister is a *mulier fortis*, if ever I met one! She showed us sad photos of babies who had survived botched abortions. Indonesia's 216 Holy Ghost sisters staff many high schools and kindergartens, eight hospitals, and an even greater number of free-standing outpatient health centers, mostly on Flores.

The uneducated rural folks observe the myth that you can't cut the umbilical cord unless the placenta comes out with the baby. So, when a mother recently died after giving birth, they put both mother and child in a coffin; when the baby cried, they opened the coffin and rescued the baby! We have a photo! You may meet some Indonesian abortion survivors at our world conference in Ottawa.

Indonesia is under strong international pressure from the antilife imperialists to strip her preborn children of legal protection. The Moslem minister of health spoke out against it recently, however. Sister Robertilde begged me to airmail the maximum possible number of pictures and posters of aborted babies, prolife videos, and our twelve-week fetal models to her and to Sister/Dr. Mary Veronica Woonga, who's with the government. For years Sister

Mary Veronica has been teaching NFP successfully. Now she's desperately going around the country giving talks to prevent legalized baby-killing and to show the people the reality of abortion. When I got home, we air-shipped $2,000 worth of fetal models, videos, films, posters, and pictures to each nun. We're also in touch with several other Dutch and American missionaries. Pray for them and their people!

HORRORS IN HAWAII

In *Report No. 78* I described the sad situation created by the strange bishop of Honolulu, Joseph Ferrario. Since then, Bishop Ferrario has taken his diocese from sad to worse. For example, when the state legislature established a legal holiday to honor Martin Luther King, Jr., it did so by abolishing Good Friday as a legal holiday. Bishop Ferrario did nothing to prevent the abolition.

This anti-Marian bishop has forbidden his people to recite the rosary at funeral homes, preferring liturgical/psalm prayers. In the Hawaiian tradition, priests had offered funeral Masses for the deceased at chapels attached to funeral homes. Bishop Ferrario forbade this practice, and so now many Catholics are buried without any Mass because of the extra cost of transporting the coffin to the church, and for other reasons. According to the diocesan paper, only 125,000 Catholics attend Mass regularly, down from 250,000 when Bishop Ferrario took over in 1982. Liturgical abuses abound. The bishop has also forbidden priests to hear people's confessions during Holy Week. And he made himself the laughingstock of the U.S. hierarchy by excommunicating five lay people, some of them excellent Catholics.

In 1991 Bishop Ferrario of Honolulu
personally lobbied for the "gay rights"
bill that later passed.

In 1991, Hawaii's legislature considered an oppressive "gay rights" bill (H.B. 1346), one of the worst in the country. Most of those testifying opposed the bill, but Bishop

Ferrario favored it. He lobbied for it personally by writing to every legislator and sending two priests to lobby. (Never mind that this procedure was in total disobedience to Rome, which forbids bishops to give any encouragement to the homosexual movement.) The bill passed.

Five years before, the Knights of Columbus had opposed a similar bill in Hawaii. In 1991, every K of C council but one proved spineless and endorsed it by default. If today's Knaves of Columbus had lived in the sixteenth century, they might well have followed the bishops loyal to Henry VIII out of the Church—"our bishops, right or wrong!"

During the 1989 meeting of the National Council of Catholic Bishops in Baltimore, a certain David Figueroa embarrassed the hierarchy by accusing Bishop Ferrario of having abused him homosexually for years. Figueroa also filed charges against the bishop. Judge Harold Fong threw these out of a federal court in Honolulu last year, ruling that the statute of limitations on the allegations had expired. Fong happens to be Bishop Ferrario's golfing partner. Appeals are pending. Geraldo Rivera's nationally syndicated "Now It Can Be Told" TV show did a program on priestly sex abusers that included allegations against the Honolulu bishop, who also made *Time*'s religious section over the matter.

The 1992 public-policy statement of the Diocese of Honolulu supports "the durable power of attorney for medical decision-making" and "education for responsible sexuality, including full information on HIV-positive infection and prevention." The sex ed in Hawaii's Catholic schools is atrocious.

Good Catholic lay people prevented Bishop Ferrario from selling beautiful, historic St. Augustine's Church on Waikiki Beach for $50 million to a Japanese hotelier. As a replacement, the bishop had proposed a meeting-hall church built on top of a five-story parking lot, with three elevators! Bishop Ferrario, by the way, likes to call himself a "CEO."

On my way to the Philippines, I stopped in Honolulu to renew prolife contacts. I took time to join prolifers picketing PP. Later, a pastor invited me to preach; Bishop Ferrario forbade it, thus becoming the first bishop in eighty-four countries to do that to me, over forty-five years! I could say much more, but prudence dictates silence. Pray for Bishop Ferrario and his people.

FATHER HABIGER REPORTS FROM PUERTO RICO

In February 1991 I spent eight days with Father Marx, taking the prolife/profamily message to the PP-ravaged people of this island (see *Report No. 79*). These efforts came to fruition over the weekend of February 14-16 this year, at the Casa Manresa retreat center near the city of Aibonito in the diocese of Caguas. HLI Puerto Rico's first Congress on Love, Life, and the Family drew 350 leaders, including representatives from Mexico, Costa Rica, Guatemala, the Virgin Islands, Colombia, and all parts of Puerto Rico.

Cardinal Luis Aponte Martinez, the archbishop of San Juan, Bishop Sean O'Malley of the Virgin Islands, Bishop Blasco F. Collaco, and the apostolic delegate of Puerto Rico joined in the formal opening of the congress at the territorial state department in Old San Juan. Carmencita Acevedo, the First Lady of San Juan, greeted the participants. Bishop Enrique de Rivera of Caguas attended the congress and took part in a TV interview.

The fruits of this congress were many, bringing hundreds of prolife/profamily leaders together and giving them an opportunity to be briefed on the life issues by an international faculty. HLI-Gaithersburg and our Miami office distributed large amounts of Spanish-language literature, videotapes, and models of preborn babies. We sent packets of prolife/profamily material to all eight seminaries. A special daylong conference attracted 100 young people on Saturday.

Major Caribbean prolife leaders met on Saturday evening. Local leaders strategized for two hours on Sunday afternoon. Two days before the congress, visiting faculty spoke at universities and to the media, and taped programs for local TV stations. Priests, sisters, and seminarians heard the prolife message at the congress. People from all walks of life are now ready to take the next steps in advancing the prolife/profamily movement in Puerto Rico. And Puerto Ricans need it: they endure the highest HIV-AIDS rate in the Western world, an estimated 40 percent of the women have been sterilized, and their legislature is trying to put the "right" to abortion into the law in case the Supreme Court overturns *Roe*.

Alejandro Sanchez, a third-year major seminarian at Mount St. Mary's in Emmitsburg, Maryland, accompanied me everywhere. Alejandro edits our Spanish-language Seminarians for Life International newsletter and no doubt will assume more leadership in the prolife movement in Puerto Rico in the years to come. The effects of our Congress will ripple throughout all of Central and South America. We thank the good Lord for His many blessings upon this gathering, and His mother for her maternal care. You, too, deserve much credit for helping make all of this possible. Please pray with us that the people of Puerto Rico, 75 percent Catholic, may continue to grow in their love of families, babies, and good marriages.

Letters

I am a teacher in Stella Maris secondary school. I've been involved with youth for a few years. I've realized the need for youngsters to know the truth about God's plan concerning love and life.

Just the other day I had a discussion with youth about sex, marriage, abortion, and pregnancy crises. Once again I couldn't help feeling astonished at how little they know about these matters. I could see a hunger in them for the truth. It's obvious that they have been exposed to arguments that are proabortion.

Here in Malaysia, the local newspapers each day carry stories of babies found in garbage bins.

We need youth with Christian values to reach out to their peer groups, and I want to help them. Any assistance from you, Father, would be greatly appreciated.

Charmine A. Wong
Sabah, Malaysia

Thank you so very much for sending me the two video tapes, *Candlelight Conflict* and *The Most Important Work on Earth*, to help me in my prolife campaign. I am sorry that India is following the other countries and has legalized child-murder, but I will not give up the fight.

I congratulate you and your supporters in your vigorous campaign to save human beings. May God bless you and your work.

The Most Rev. Alan de Lastic
Archbishop of Delhi
India

We are disappointed and saddened by the results of the U.S. presidential election. We will continue praying that unborn babies in the States will be protected and that the new president will not be able to institute laws that will be even more detrimental to the American people and the unborn babies.

Please support us strongly in your prayers and rush us whatever materials could be of use to alert our religious and educational authorities to the announced plans of the Family Planning Association of India to invade our schools, both Catholic and secular.

Kevin L. Fernandes
Abundant Life Education Research Trust
Bombay, India

I am angry and concerned about the recent presidential election. I am numb and broke from the fight. I ran for our state legislature and missed by nine votes. I campaigned hard on the prolife issue and should have won in our conservative district. I campaigned exhaustively against Bill Clinton based on his proabortion stand alone.

Yes, I told them it would be a sin for Catholics to vote for Clinton. I was branded as hateful and narrow-minded even by people in my own church. Funny, but I cannot ever remember hating anyone, and I have never really been that outspoken before. I just did what God called me to do at the time.

But I felt so alone that I even began to feel that it was I who was wrong, and started to doubt my faith. I have gone through many long, sad nights since the election. Thanks for your letter; it was so uplifting!

So many Christians lack the sense of urgency about the prolife issues that it sometimes looks hopeless. I see the same problem throughout our country. They are voting from their pocketbooks and not their hearts. However, you are a tremendous source of courage. If you can continue, so will I.

Robert Brechtel
Casper, Wyoming

*HLI-Canada staffers—Leoni Cere, Jill Watts, Erik Vink, Filip Vink,
Theresa Bell*

Undercover at the Dutch Euthanasia Conference

Ireland in Turmoil

No. 90   May 1992

I n **1969 the Irish** Family Planning Association, one of 117 national affiliates of the International Planned Parenthood Federation (headquartered in London), moved across the Irish Sea to set up shop in Ireland.

In 1972 I journeyed to the Land of Saints and Scholars. My purpose was to warn the Irish bishops, through Dublin's Archbishop Joseph Ryan, that IPPF (International Planned Parenthood) always starts by promoting contraception but always ends by pushing legalized abortion-on-demand, using every possible means, including testing the law, breaking it, and so on. I assured Archbishop Ryan that I'd seen IPPF's tactics in forty-eight countries and offered him documentation. He refused it, saying, "Ireland is Catholic, and there is no danger of abortion; contraception, perhaps."

Archbishop Ryan, in 1972: "Ireland is Catholic, and there is no danger of abortion."

I was stunned. I told him that I'd heard such comments before in other countries, eventually to see IPPF's affiliates ruin the young people with sex education, the family with contraception/sterilization, and society with legalized baby-killing. The archbishop was most pleasant and kind. After half an hour, he gently ushered me to the door. I distinctly remember thinking, "You will see the day." He did.

I immediately gave a series of slide-talks across Ireland, spreading prolife literature and films in all parts of the country. Some people reacted unfavorably, not sensing the danger, but many were alerted and interested. The anti-Catholic, pro-abortion press crucified me.

HOW CONTRACEPTION LED TO ABORTION

In the 1970s, the antilifers tested Ireland's birth-control law with the McGee case, a fabrication involving a married woman who had several children. A doctor declared that her life was in danger if she became pregnant again; therefore, the State should let her have the Pill, which had to be released by Customs. A court ruled in her favor. By such methods did legalized contraception enter Ireland. (Since then, Mrs. McGee has had more children.)

At first, the sale of contraceptives and abortifacients was limited to medical and pharmaceutical outlets, and then only to married people. But eventually all regulations broke down. Today, contraceptives and abortifacients are available to virtually all comers. Reportedly, some nightclubs have installed condom machines. Since 1969, Ireland's birthrate has fallen to slightly above the replacement level because of widespread use of condoms and the Pill, and increasing sterilization.

Ireland's constitution was modeled on the USA's. Under Irish law, abortion was clearly forbidden. But alert Irish lay people were concerned that legalized abortion might follow legalized contraception. And because in 1973 the U.S. Supreme Court had imposed virtual abortion-on-demand 'til the day of birth, the Irish prolifers and the bishops eventually foresaw that the only way to keep legalized baby-killing out of Ireland would be to add an amendment to their constitution.

In 1983, 67 percent of the voters approved the eighth amendment to the Constitution. The amendment declared, "The State acknowledges the right to life of the unborn and, with due regard to the equal right to life of the mother, guarantees in its laws to respect, and as far as is practicable, by its laws to defend and vindicate that right."

Irish prolifers thought they'd excluded legalized abortion from their country forever, because they'd rightly trusted neither the courts nor the Dail (parliament). For nine years the amendment, as interpreted by the Supreme Court in various cases, served the Irish well. For example, in one case, the Court decreed that it was illegal for abortion "counseling" and "information" centers to steer Irish women to abortionists in England.

ANOTHER PHONY CASE?

But the Irish underestimated the satanic forces promoting anarcho-sex and the killing of the resulting babies. In February of this year, the pro-aborts came up with a highly emotional "hard case" that's suspiciously similar to the McGee case: a fourteen-year-old pregnant girl, allegedly raped, who supposedly threatened suicide. No professional has evaluated the girl except a psychologist who admitted he'd never counseled a girl of her age. He pronounced her suicidal. The alleged rapist, the father of a friend of the girl, denies the accusation and volunteered every proof through genetic and other specimens. The police have made no arrest.

Strangely, the parents took the girl to England to have her baby aborted, but before the killing took place they came home and called the Dublin police to ask whether they should preserve a specimen of the aborted baby as possible evidence against the alleged rapist. Why didn't the parents just quietly go through with the English abortion, as happens in 4,000 other cases annually?

The police took the case to Attorney General Harry Whelehan. The High Court ruled that the girl couldn't leave the country for nine months. The shrieks of rage from the Irish media reached levels not measurable by decibels, putting pressure on the government and the Supreme Court, and riling up the people emotionally even more. Orchestrated worldwide publicity added more pressure.

Ireland's vitriolic anti-Catholic media attacked prolifers and the bishops relentlessly for having secured passage of the 1983 amendment. With help from students in British-controlled Northern Ireland, Irish university students held marches demanding the poor baby's death. Other students held counter-demonstrations in defense of life (the media hid *their* demonstrations from you). The demonstrations are still taking place.

The world's liberal Catholic press, e.g., the leftist

London *Tablet* (29 February 92 and 14 March 92) joined in. Invoking "pluralism" and ignoring the experience of other countries, the *Tablet* naively pontificated, "It will not open the floodgates to abortion on demand...." Worldwide proabortion propaganda portrayed the Irish as narrow-minded, medieval, and, by implication, stupid, not allowing abortion even in "hard cases."

On Ash Wednesday, by a four-to-one vote, the Supreme Court interpreted the constitution to allow abortion, ruling that when "it is established as a matter of probability that there is a real and substantial risk to the life as distinct from health of the mother [e.g., by a threat of suicide] which can only be avoided by the termination of her pregnancy, ...such termination is permissible, having regard to the true interpretation" of the eighth amendment!

By this edict, the Court deprived Ireland's preborn children of all legal rights. They now have even fewer rights than animals, which are entitled to a humane death. The proof required is minimal: any pregnant mother can threaten suicide, and as soon as a shyster psychologist "verifies" the threat she can legally abort her child *in Ireland*. The Court imposed no time or age limit; in this respect, Ireland now has the most permissive abortion law in the world!

The judges made no distinction between direct abortion and indirect "abortion," e.g., the unintended death of a baby during the removal of a cancerous uterus. They ignored the baby's right to life, which the amendment guarantees. They also ignored the normal medical procedure of treating potential suicides until the danger is passed. The judges were more concerned with the possible, easily avoidable death of the mother than with the certain death of her preborn baby. Inconsistently, the Court, by a narrow three-to-two majority, retained the power to prohibit travel abroad for abortions. But neither the backers of the amendment nor anyone else in 1983 ever envisioned or desired a ban on travel.

What's more, the Court completely overlooked evidence that many more girls commit suicide *after* abortion than *during* pregnancy; scientific studies prove that pregnant women rarely commit suicide.

ABORTION BY JUDICIAL TYRANNY

The Supreme Court's verdict was shallow, inept and lacking common sense. The justices undemocratically—indeed, tyrannically—reinterpreted the amendment to legalize abortion, the exact opposite of the clearly expressed will of the people. They twisted the wording of the amendment to mean what they chose, rather than what the people intended it to mean. Like the U.S. Supreme Court, the Irish Court invented a new "right" in the Irish law, a "right" open to flagrant abuse. The Court used an amendment meant to bar legalized abortion forever to give Ireland the world's most wide-open law.

Like the U.S. Supreme Court, the Irish Court invented a new "right," open to flagrant abuse.

The Court's shameful decision triggered a constitutional crisis. From the logical, factual, and legal points of view, the decision is perhaps worse than *Roe v. Wade*. The Irish decision created a huge judicial and legal mess, with many unanswered questions. The Court said nothing about the rights of the father. It sought no qualified, independent medical evidence to confirm the opinion of a questionable clinical psychologist regarding the mother's purported suicidal tendencies.

The lone dissenting justice, Anthony Hedeman, had it right: "There cannot be freedom to extinguish life side-by-side with a guarantee of protection of that life, because the termination of pregnancy means the destruction of an unborn life. The State must, in principle, act in accordance with the mother's duty to carry out the pregnancy and, in principle, must also outlaw the termination of pregnancy."

Last December the Irish government added a protocol to the Maastricht Treaty on European Union. The protocol guaranteed the Irish that the EEC would never tamper with their abortion law. Until recently, the government still hadn't decided what to do about the Supreme Court decision, except to propose (with British support) an amendment to the protocol saying, "This protocol shall not limit freedom to travel between member states or to obtain, in Ireland, information relating to services lawfully available in member states." But Ireland's European Community (EC) partners said no, for fear other countries would want to make changes, thus scuttling the whole treaty.

On April 8, Prime Minister Albert Reynolds decided to stage a June referendum on the treaty and his amendment, with a November referendum on abortion. Family Solidarity, a prolife group, declared that no one who believed in legal protection for preborn babies could in conscience vote for the Treaty now. Prolife leader Dr. Mary Lucey was blunt: "Unborn Irish babies are being sold for a mess of potage, for money." Ireland is a major recipient of EC funds.

BISHOPS STAND FIRM FOR BABIES AND MOTHERS

On March 13, the Irish bishops (with no dissenters) made an excellent statement on the situation. They said they shared the "widespread dismay" over the Supreme Court's decision as well as the anguish of women before and after abortion. "The lives of both the child and the mother are sacred," they explained. Abortion "is the direct taking of innocent life and no motive can justify it, no court judgment, no active legislation can make it morally right." The Irish people had understood that the constitution protected the life of the preborn child. The new situation created by the Court "poses an inescapable challenge for the whole of our society," the bishops insisted, "and this challenge must be faced without delay." They will tolerate no exceptions.

The bishops wisely observed that "wherever abortion is legally permitted, there is continual agitation to alter the legislation." They then proved they know what most U.S. bishops (especially the hierarchy of Louisiana, who abandoned babies conceived by rape) and the National Right to Life Committee don't seem to know: "Experience has shown that laws permitting abortion even in restricted circumstances rapidly lead to abortion on demand."

If it takes another national referendum to restore

protection for each and every preborn baby in Ireland, so be it, said the bishops' spokesman, Bishop Joseph Duffy. As an indication of how strongly these wise shepherds feel, their statement is the first of its kind since the 1970s that doesn't explicitly acknowledge the "right" of legislators to make laws in accordance with their "consciences." Meanwhile, through an organization called CURA, the bishops will continue to offer women all possible help.

Revising Irish laws to satisfy the domestic and European requirements needed to pass the Maastricht Treaty in June is next to impossible. The government cannot repair by law the huge gap that the Court tore in the constitution. The only way to restore the situation to what everyone thought it was after the eighth amendment (and to reassert the people's rights under article six to decide these matters) is to add to the amendment clear-cut wording banning all direct abortions and providing for necessary medical treatments in cases such as tubal pregnancies and cancerous uteri.

It seems the massive, worldwide propaganda influenced the justices. They proved their ignorance of the world's experience with abortion legalization; some even used abortion-propaganda language. The majority justices blame the government for not writing guidelines based on the eighth amendment. But why do they need guidelines when the intent of the amendment and the nation was clearly to outlaw abortion forever? Prolifers say that the situation now is one of media-incited mob law.

***But since when is it a "moral crusade"
to defend the right to life?***

Prolifers rightly don't trust the legislators. Prime Minister Reynolds sounded an ominous note:

> In a modern democratic state the government cannot function as a paternal authority seeking to control the decisions of its citizens relative to personal

morality. Similarly, we cannot live in isolation of our neighbors in Europe or forbid our people to travel to countries where they organize things differently. It is not the function of government to conduct moral crusades.

But since when is it a "moral crusade" to defend the right to life—the fundamental human right upon which all other rights are based? This isn't a matter of "personal morality." It concerns the most essential element of true democracy and the entire familial/social order. From bitter experience worldwide, Reynolds should know the consequences of making exceptions and the chaos that follows legalized abortion.

Of course, he and the Dail are much concerned about Ireland's June 18 vote on the Maastricht Treaty. The Irish people could reject the treaty in retaliation. If they do, the EC will have to start all over on a new treaty, and Ireland will lose millions of dollars she needs badly.

To summarize, the Irish Supreme Court imposed potential abortion-on-demand upon Ireland. Any pregnant woman can threaten suicide, find a conniving psychologist to verify her threat, and then legally proceed with the abortion. We see once again how diabolically clever the enemy is. Meanwhile, British abortionists are poised to move into this Catholic land to kill Irish babies for money. Father Patrick Hannon, a retired professor from the national seminary at Maynooth, believes the situation in Ireland is the worst it's been since St. Patrick came.

H.L.I. AIDS IRISH PROLIFERS

I rushed over to Ireland for a week to learn all I could and to find out how HLI could help. I spoke to six audiences, did two one-hour radio talk shows, gave three news interviews and set up a weekend seminar on prolife issues that will take place in Cork next October 30-November 1.

While in Ireland, I desperately called home for prolife videos and postcards and posters of aborted babies, to bring the reality of abortion to the Irish as soon as possible. Thanks to our friends' generosity, we've air-freighted much material to Ireland. "The Silent Scream" is an ideal film for the Irish now; we've already sent over at least fifty videocassettes of it.

I agreed with Irish prolife leaders that the film should be shown to every citizen twelve years old and up. I urged them to show it to parliament, as we did in South Africa with great results. After 1983, the Irish relaxed somewhat, assuming that they'd driven the abortion snake from their land forever. Instead, they should have organized a national prolife/profamily education program covering contraception, sterilization, abortion, euthanasia, and related subjects. The bishops should have promoted chastity and created a modern, orthodox catechetical program and an intensive, orthodox marriage-preparation course with built-in natural family planning (NFP).

The Irish bishops must take their share of the blame: they've done almost nothing to promote NFP. They seemed unconcerned about contraception. During my many trips to Ireland, I've always heard bitter complaints about episcopal indifference to NFP. This time, one NFP teacher-couple told me they had instructed only one couple last year; another teacher-couple told me they had helped five, but four of them were taking the course in order to *achieve* pregnancy.

Today one has to be blind and obtuse not to see the connection between contraception and abortion, but I've yet to hear of an Irish priest or bishop who has made this connection publicly. Nor have I heard of one who condemned contraception as the root cause of so many evils today, destroying youth, family, Church, and nation. One astute Catholic layman in Dublin told me that he'd buy me ten Guinnesses if I could find ten priests who have preached consistently against contraception and sterilization. Alas, Father Enda McDonagh (Ireland's Father Charles Curran) still teaches at Maynooth. A professor of moral theology there recently published a book that totally distorts the Church's teachings on abortion and related subjects.

And consider the National Catholic Marriage Advisory Council, which gets money from both Church and State and has the approval of all the bishops. Every married couple must take the council's episcopally approved, unbelievable marriage-preparation course, which describes and proposes all kinds of contraceptives and abortifacients nondirectively. Everything is left up to the conscience of the couple, meaning, in practical terms, "Do as you wish."

All of the ills afflicting the Catholic Church in the USA are now afflicting the Irish Church as well, although their damage is not so far advanced. I'm talking about New Age practices, feminism, Modernism, sex education, and so on. Particularly disturbing is the "life skills" program, launched in the schools about five years ago. This is a combination of values clarification, nondirective counseling, self-esteem/self-actualization, "choice" theory, sex-ed, comparative religion, New Age, and feminism. Irish teachers, and most Irish nuns and priests, need to meditate on Pope John Paul II's admonition at the International Congress on Moral Theology (10 April 86): "Love for whoever errs must never bring about any compromise with error."

Ireland is no longer a source of foreign missionaries. Most nuns have rejected the habit, and many more are tinged with the New Age virus. The witchcraft-promoting Father Matthew Fox, OP, and the angry feminist theologian Rosemary Ruether have been to Ireland, as have other rebels. Every week some Irish religious community is selling off buildings and property for lack of vocations.

Still, 85 percent of all Irish Catholics attend Mass every Sunday, perhaps the highest percentage in the Western world. Daily Masses are well attended. The Legion of Mary is active and healthy. Medjugorje prayer groups flourish everywhere. One thousand young Dubliners gathered in front of the Dail on short notice to plead for total protection of preborn babies. The eighty university students I talked to during my last evening in Ireland were uniquely inspiring.

Ireland is boiling, and the people are angry. And now we know that not even constitutions can protect the hapless preborn child in this New Age of pervasive paganism.

WORLD BANK PUTS BOUNTY ON CHILDREN'S HEADS

Live children are a liability, not an asset, in the eyes of the World Bank, which has entered into a Machiavellian partnership with the worldwide abortion industry.

The World Bank has entered into a Machiavellian partnership with the worldwide abortion industry.

The World Bank and its antilife, antifamily sister organizations have joined in the so-called Safe Motherhood Initiative to put a bounty on the lives of preborn children. The bank, headquartered in Washington, D.C., is misusing its enormous, global economic and political clout to ordain and bankroll a misanthropic effort to "assist humanity" by destroying preborn human beings. It's introducing unsafe, intrusive, culturally repugnant and often abortifacient methods of birth control, and mutilating healthy people through wholesale neutering programs.

Through such initiatives, women in the Third World are being used in medical experiments. Their children are the target of a massive, well-financed eugenics campaign aimed at the poorest and most defenseless members of the human family.

Operating under the deceptive slogan of "Safe Motherhood," a gaggle of international depopulation policy-makers gathered in Washington (March 9-11) to launch their latest offensive against the children and families of developing nations. World Bank President Lewis T. Preston has promised to pump $2.5 billion into abortion, contraception, sterilization, and other "women's health" programs by 1995—double the amount the bank has been spending.

Preston made the pledge when he addressed the opening session of the three-day conference, attended by 120 delegates from twenty developing countries. Organizers gave lip service to the general health needs of women in "Third World" nations, but the heart of the program is depopulation. Meanwhile, women's real health needs are being underfunded.

The meeting was sinister and hypocritical. Sponsors of the Safe Motherhood Initiative are the UN's World Health Organization (WHO), the UN Fund for Population Activities (UNFPA), the UN Development Program, UNICEF, the World Bank, the Population Council, and the ubiquitous IPPF.

Here you have the world's worst enemies of preborn children, women, and the family gathered to discuss "safe motherhood." IPPF is the world's largest purveyor of abortion-on-demand. IPPF's model of "safe motherhood" is a sterilized woman with a dead baby, preferably a baby killed at one of IPPF's numerous and lucrative abortion mills. And one has only to examine the ideology of IPPF's founder, white supremacist Margaret Sanger, to discover its racial/eugenics agenda.

Last January 31, in a blatant and crude act of imperialism, the World Bank ordered every Latin American government to legalize abortion and make baby-killing the center of maternal and infant "health" programs. Mexican officials quickly gave a favorable response.

That edict came at another misnamed conference—one held in Guatemala and called the "Central American Conference for Maternity Without Risk"—where World Bank official Anne G. Tinker demanded that governments provide "safe abortion" in all maternal and infant health programs. Politicians must make the necessary legislative changes immediately, she told the gathering. Currently, abortion is illegal in every Latin American country except Uruguay, Barbados, and Communist Cuba. The reason Ms. Tinker supplied for this planned holocaust is that it will allegedly reduce hospital costs. The Safe Motherhood Initiative is genocide by economic blackmail.

Meanwhile, the socialist government of the Province of British Columbia is now *forcing* public hospitals to kill unborn babies and giving grants to private abortion businesses. Who said Nazism is dead?

Letters

Just recently I was beaten, jailed twice—once for ten hours and the other time for six days—threatened by death, and accused by the corrupt policemen and justices of "potential murder" of an abortionist!

And this in a country where abortion is forbidden by law! You just can't imagine the degree of corruption of this country!

I also was dismissed from my job in a government bank that defends the abortionist instead of obeying Brazilian laws!

This is the land of the absurd, where everything is head over heels, where the Good is the Evil and the Evil is the Good.

In North America, you go to jail with your friends, but I go to jail alone. I don't think you can know the terrible sensation of abandonment I have felt. But let's keep up the fight!

Tarcisio de Barros
Joinville, Brazil

I am sending the enclosed contribution *not* because your organization is staunchly prolife. While this part of your work is admirable and important, there are many other organizations that are just as deserving of my support due to their efforts in this area. However, yours is perhaps the only organization, Catholic or otherwise, that has had the courage and insight to recognize the connection between the proliferation and widespread acceptance of contraceptives and the tragedy of abortion.

Our society's efforts to take into our own hands matters better left to the will of God began with the vigorous promotion of birth control and found their logical conclusion in *Roe v. Wade.* Your recent article decrying the continuing and now almost universal acceptance of birth control was not only timely and courageous—it was Godly and correct. As usual, men are reaping the woe they sow for themselves when they seek to elevate themselves above their rightful stations with respect to our Sovereign Lord. Alas, as the men of Babel found, such efforts are rarely costless.

The voices in opposition to such thinking are fewer and fewer, even in the Church. I watch sadly as each of the powerful and courageous stands taken by the Catholic Church is trampled in the rush to "modernism" and "sensitivity." While I am not at all in agreement with every tenet of Catholicism, I find that only Catholics can point to any consistency in their prolife stances, if they hold to the strictures against contraception.

You probably get protests from those who see no connections between the two issues—please ignore them. I often wonder if our failures with respect to this subject have hindered Christians in the battle against the holocaust of abortion. In what is above all a spiritual battle, are we ignoring the will of our Commander?

John F. Dowd
Cambridge, Massachusetts

During our Strategy Weekend in Nova Scotia,
Fr. Matthew made time to hit the airwaves

"Planned Parenthood called me their Number One Enemy!"

With Austria's great
Martin Humer at a monument to
victory over the Turks at Vienna
three centuries ago

Defending Ireland's anti-abortion
constitutional amendment

Irish leaders map out their strategy (1992)

HLI's candlelight procession for Life in Ottawa (1992)

Canadian proaborts called them "violent"

"Let your light shine before men" (Ottawa)

**With the great Drs. Carlos Perez Avendaño and Jerome Lejeune
at HLI-Miami**

Nigeria and Sparkill

No. 91 June 1992

Our world conference in Ottawa was a huge success. Some participants said it was our best conference yet; if so, our enemies helped to make it so! Some eighteen antilife/antifamily, feminist, homosexual, socialist, and other groups called on Ottawans to "stop the assault on choice" by HLI. Flyers throughout the city raved that

> Human Life International is coming to Ottawa. They are anti-woman, anti-gay, anti-choice, opposed to abortion, birth control, gay rights, even sex education. These religious zealots are sponsoring an international anti-choice conference....Your freedom is under attack! Their 1,500 delegates will be organizing how to take away a woman's right to control her own body and her own life....Bring banners and signs, bring your friends, lovers and children and march.... Shock the right!

DEMONSTRATIONS *V. DEMON-STRATIONS*

Our wise vice president, Bob Lalonde, went to court seeking an injunction to prevent their *demon*-strations. That stunned the opposition and brought us endless news interviews and publicity—more than we've had in all of our preceding conferences combined! We lost the court battle, but we also won it, because the judge agreed with us that violence was possible and that it was the duty of the police to protect our people.

So, while 300 pro-aborts (and even satanists) screamed outside, we celebrated a beautiful opening-night Mass at St. Patrick's church. Afterward, 1,200 of HLI's global family proceeded with candles for 1.4 miles to Parliament Hill, enjoying the kind of police protection usually reserved for heads of state. Howling pro-aborts, bused in from other cities, followed us as we prayed the rosary and sang Marian hymns. None of us will ever forget it!

On Friday afternoon we formed a huge, blocks-long life chain in front of Parliament. Again, the pro-aborts, homosexuals, and witches screeched their obscenities and slogans: "Hey, hey, ho, ho, HLI has got to go"; "HLI, your name's a lie, you don't care if women die"; "Not the Church, not the State, women must decide their fate"; "Keep your rosaries off our ovaries" (one priest wondered out loud whether these angry, screaming "females" even *had* ovaries); "Choice NOW, now and forever"; "Bring on the lions"; "Death to the Christians," etc. Some of their epithets were so foul I wouldn't dare to quote them here, but I was reminded that the new pagans are like the old.

Because *HLI Reports* has told our readers about the great talks our speakers gave, and many other fascinating details, I'll end my Conference commentary here.

PROLIFE MISSIONARIES AID NIGERIA

Father Matthew Habiger's report: Between February 26 and March 4 (Ash Wednesday), I was in Nigeria for a conference sponsored by HLI and HLPL (the Human Life Protection League, founded by the Nigerian bishops). I brought with me two movie projectors, a slide projector, many prolife videos, and much literature, all of which are now saving babies throughout Nigeria, thanks to our benefactors' generosity.

Dr. Peggy Norris, a tireless researcher/writer/speaker and officer of England's Doctors Who Respect Human Life, met me at London's Gatwick Airport. Together we made our first visit to an African country. Nigeria is twice the size of California. According to a recent census, this largest black country in the world has fewer than 90 million people—not the 120 million projected by the contraceptive imperialists, who have scattered contraceptives and abortifacients across the country and now are pushing legalized abortion. Nigeria has roughly equal numbers of Moslems and Christians, plus millions of animists.

The Catholic faith is strong here: the churches are full and priests are overworked just providing the sacraments.

Every one of the thirty-nine dioceses supports at least one minor seminary. There are eight major seminaries, three having 500 seminarians each; vocations are many. The culture abounds with Christian symbols; e.g., large trucks are covered with folk art using religious motifs and Scripture verses. Babies appear everywhere, too: the average Nigerian family has five or six children. The bishops are thoroughly Catholic in their teaching and leadership.

> *The Nigerian bishops are thoroughly Catholic in their teaching and leadership.*

Nigeria, which is just north of the equator, is very hot. The largest city, Lagos on the southwestern coast, endures high humidity, but farther inland the air is drier. There are just two seasons, rainy and dry. This was the dry season. I understand why the people begin their day at 5 a.m.: they must lie low during the afternoon heat. If I lived in Africa, I'd want the same rich, dark pigmentation of the locals for protection against the fiery sun.

Traveling in Nigeria requires immunization from malaria. The disease is hatched in swamps and carried by mosquitoes. The remedy is quinine, which comes from the abundant cinchona bark. I mistakenly took too much and had an adverse reaction. Fortunately, with so many doctors at our meeting, and with the prayers of all the participants, I made a rapid recovery.

We drove six hours to Okpuno, Awka, in south central Nigeria, to attend the conference at the pastoral center of the Diocese of Awka. It was an ideal setting with its beautiful chapel, conference building, cafeteria staffed by ten religious sisters, and apartments for all participants. Awka's Bishop Albert Obiefuna, a moral theologian, gave an excellent paper, "Conscience and Personal Responsibility."

Dr. Adekoya, who is HLI's employee, fits the hardworking HLI mold well. Each day began with Mass at 6:30, breakfast at 7:30, and the first talk at 8:00. There were usually nine sessions each day, with a break for lunch and rest. Lawrence had invited leaders from each of the forty HLPL chapters he's founded, and so many of Nigeria's pro-life leaders were together for these five days. Among them were three great bishops, several priests, twelve doctors (three of whom were religious sisters), two dozen nuns (including two mother superiors), university professors, a journalist, and several tribal chiefs.

Topics ranged from abortion around the world, *Humanae Vitae*, *Familiaris Consortio*, conscience, and chastity to more specific areas such as euthanasia, teaching fertility awareness in the schools, making use of the media, Nigeria's depopulation policy, and the harmful effects of contraception, sterilization, and abortion.

BISHOPS DEFEND THEIR FLOCKS

Father Matthew's report continues: Bishop J.E. Ukpo of the Ogoja Diocese, who is chairman of the bishops' Marriage and Family Commission (and who spoke at Ottawa), welcomed everyone and explained the bishops' plan in view of the population scare. The bishops condemn contraception and encourage natural family planning (NFP). Sr./Dr. Leonie McSweeney, MMM, gave several talks on NFP. Sponsored by the bishops, she has taught the Billings NFP method for years all over Nigeria. She's a prolific writer, too.

The Right Rev. John Onaiyekan, coadjutor bishop of Abuja, Nigeria's new capital, enlightened us with his paper, "Christian-Moslem Collaboration in Pro-Life Activism." Participants at HLI's world conference in Santa Clara heard this great bishop and theologian speak on a similar topic. Space doesn't permit me to describe the other outstanding talks.

Bishop Ukpo's conclusion to his welcoming address sums up the conference well:

> The Bishops of Nigeria are firmly behind HLPL. They commend HLI's efforts to protect life. All Christians and Moslems must do all they can, to join hands with you to counteract the antilife

campaign and also step up their prolife activities. The contraceptive/abortifacient culture of the West and of the so-called developed world is being pushed down our throats.

They have transferred their regrets of depopulated cities and the lack of youth to man the factories, etc., to this country under the guise of concern for the Nigerian standard of living, fear of overpopulation and the AIDS epidemic. Let me reiterate *Humanae Vitae* [section] 23: "Do not allow the morals of your people to be undermined. Do not tolerate any legislation to introduce into the family practices which are opposed to the natural and divine law....There are other ways by which a government can and should solve the demographic problem, that is, by enacting laws which will assist families and by educating the people wisely so that the moral law and freedom of the citizen are both safeguarded."

He continued:

If those who are directly affected, husbands and wives, do not resist the commercialization and veterinary mentality introduced by the antilifers to birth regulation, then Nigeria, like European countries, will soon be importing humans to produce babies. Nigerians must resist being used as guinea pigs, or a junkyard, or dumping grounds for abortifacients in the name of "International Aid."

The bishop concluded, "Make the best use of this opportunity in order to be well-equipped to do battle not only with the evil one but with anti-human life propagandists."

Many good results came from these five days. Nigerian prolife leaders were brought up to date on all the major life issues. They received accurate information on the depopulation and "family planning" strategies of the Planned Parenthood Federation of Nigeria, the tax-funded Johns

Hopkins University, the World Bank, the International Monetary Fund, and USAID.

These agencies, funded lavishly with U.S. taxes, want to destroy Nigeria's culture in terms of family life, contraception, sterilization, abortion, and numbers of children. They're willing to use *any* means to accomplish their goals. One of the most effective ways to combat them is to expose their plans, goals, and sources of funding. Once local leaders learn what the population doomsters are planning, they can react accordingly. These Nigerian prolife leaders *know* what's happening in their country.

With $10,000 that our friends helped to provide, Dr. Adekoya can now hire a staff of five people for one full year! He used to work as the registrar at a university and only part time for HLPL. Now he'll work full time for HLPL to organize a major prolife/profamily effort in Nigeria, aided by the Toyota four-wheel-drive vehicle HLI helped buy for him. We can expect great results from his energy and his management skills. We can also expect a ripple effect upon the surrounding countries of this great, more-or-less empty continent. (End of Father Matthew's report)

What would St. Dominic have done about the "homophobia" conference at Sparkill, New York?

SCANDALS AMONG THE DOMINICANS

What do you suppose St. Dominic would have done about the goings-on at the Dominican Convent in Sparkill, New York?

Almost 100 homosexual priests and religious attended a special one-day conference at the convent on April 9 to discuss "the homophobia [that] the lesbian and gay religious experience in the Church." As if that weren't bad enough, just before last November's elections, eight nuns from the convent signed a newspaper advertisement endorsing a proabortion county legislator.

The full-page ad in the 4 November 1991 issue of the local *Our Town* proclaimed, "We proudly endorse the re-election of Ed Clark to the County Legislature." Among the signers of the ad were Sr. Ursula Joyce; Sr. Adele Myers, OP; Sr. Noreen Nolan, OP; Sr. Una McCormack, OP; Sr. Lesley H. Block, OP; Sr. Marcella Marie Tucker, OP; Sr. Mary E. Dunning, OP; and Sr. Anne Foley. The "Sr." was attached firmly to each name, as was the "OP" to six of them. ("OP" stands for "Order of Preachers," the official name of the Dominicans.)

As *The Catholic Register* pointed out in a story about the ad, Sister Una McCormack is executive director of the Catholic Home Bureau of the Archdiocese of New York. (We also note that she appeared on the program at the Respect Life Institute meeting of 18 May 1991, along with Cardinal John O'Connor and Helen Alvare, director of planning and information for the Secretariat for Pro-Life Activities of the U.S. bishops.) Sister Noreen Nolan is principal at St. Elizabeth's Elementary School in New York City. Sister Ursula Joyce runs a senior citizens' apartment complex that the Dominicans operate in Rockland County.

Contacted by *The Register*, none of these three nuns said they knew of Clark's proabortion stand. "But none would say they would have refused to sign the ad," the story said.

Clark, who won re-election in November, earlier voted for a resolution calling on Congress and President Bush to overturn the administration's regulations cutting off Title X funds for abortion-selling "clinics." A week before the elections, Clark told a radio audience, "I am a pro-choice candidate. I was a pro-choice person when I ran for the legislature. I have always had those feelings....I am not about to put those young people in a position where they will be forced to go to a back-alley abortion mill that could threaten their health or even their life."

A PLANNED BARRENHOOD "CATHOLIC"

Clark received a $225 donation from the Rockland chapter of the National Organization for Women (NOW) in November. In September, he attended a Planned Parenthood (PP) dinner in a nearby city. In 1990 he voted against a resolution endorsing parental consent legislation. Oh, yes, a priest at St. Margaret's Church in Pearl River described him as an "active" parishioner.

Sister Ursula Joyce told *The Register* that Clark's proabortion stand "...is not an issue in a local election. It is not of significance." Someone should have told this news to NOW and PP—not to mention Clark! Where has Sister Ursula been?

On 28 October 1987, a group calling itself the "Rockland Coalition for Free Choice" ran an ad entitled "1987 Pro-Choice Voting Guide" in *The Rockland Journal News*. The ad endorsed Clark and other candidates who voted to give $13,000 of the taxpayers' money to PP. "The above Pro-Choice candidates answered positively to questions concerning Safe and Legal Abortion, Medicaid Funding for Eligible Women's Abortions, Equal Access to Abortions for Minors, Allotment of County Funds to PP, and Support for Increased Sex Education to Prevent AIDS," trumpets the ad.

Meanwhile, thanks to the political influence of Clark and his accomplices in office, prolife rescuers in Rockland County are being crucified. Monsignor John M. Harrington, vicar of Rockland County and pastor of Immaculate Conception Church in Stony Point, accused the town judge and district attorney of "brutal, cruel, oppressive, and unjust treatment" of rescuers who tried to save babies and mothers at an abortion chamber there last October 19. "They've become political prisoners because the Democratic Party—which is the party in power in Rockland County—is going to show that no more Operation Rescues will take place," the priest told *Catholic New York*. "Many of the politicians are so-called 'good Catholics' who run on pro-choice platforms."

And these politicos are getting help from some of the Sparkill Dominican nuns. Meanwhile, the *loyal* nuns there who know what's going on are shocked and have been in anguish for a long time. They're also grieved that they're being unjustly branded with guilt by association. They've asked for an apostolic visitation several times, but, as so often happens these days, they've gone unheard by Church authorities.

MEET THE NEW ALBIGENSIANS

The "homophobia" conference at Sparkill—sponsored by
New Ways Ministry (co-founded by Sister Jeannine
Gramick, SSND, and Father Robert Nugent, SDS)—
provided a Catholic forum for homosexuals and lesbians to
further vent their spleen against the Church, i.e., against
God, because He clearly forbade sodomy and the other
vices that homosexuals engage in.

Perhaps the millions of people who engage in *heterosex-
ual* fornication will get their act together someday and form
a movement denouncing "forniphobia." Or maybe those who
bed their neighbors' spouses will get an "adulterophobia"
crusade going against the Church. After all, she does "dis-
criminate" against both fornicators and adulterers, as well
as homosexuals and other classes of sinners. Don't the "fornicators' community" and the "adulterers' community"
deserve their own "ministries," Masses, and "rights"?

But the "gays" want special privileges, and they por-
tray themselves as yet another poor minority being
oppressed by the powerful, narrow-minded, and bigoted
Church. A cadre of nuns at Sparkill wants to help them
spread their poison. *The Rockland Journal News* carried a
long story about the "gay" meeting, with a photo of a lesbian Sister of St. Joseph and a homosexual Capuchin
priest. They weren't very gay about the way they think the
hierarchy is treating them.

The Capuchin, Father Richard Cardarelli, is forbidden
to function as a priest in the Archdiocese of New York.
Another participant, New Ways Father Nugent, is forbidden to exercise his ministry in the Archdiocese of
Washington, D.C.

St. Dominic fought the Albigensian heresy back in the
13th century. If he were to visit Sparkill and other convents today, he'd immediately discern many of the same
antilife, anti-Church, anti-Christ spirits at work. Among a
host of other errors, the Albigensians taught that hetero-
sexual acts were among the greatest of evils because they
tended to beget life, thus adding to the number of souls
that were incarnate and therefore subject to the possible
fates of Hell or Purgatory.

In other words, the Albigensians were antilife—even though they didn't believe in self-defense or in any war (or in eating meat, for that matter). These muddled heretics considered suicide laudatory. They denied the divinity of Christ and elevated Satan to the level of a god, crediting him with the creation of all matter. Today's New Age/Modernist movements embrace most of these dangerous ideas in one form or another.

Such heresy was clearly intolerable at the time of St. Dominic, and it's intolerable now. The faithful are being scandalized and souls are being lost as people such as this handful of Dominicans and their "gay" guests spread their errors and flaunt their rebellion, not unlike the bizarre "Dominican" theologian Father Matthew Fox.

Some people close to the situation at Sparkill are pressing for the Vatican to come in and straighten out the mess.

WHEN WILL THE CHURCH ACT?

"There were also false prophets among the people, just as there will be false teachers....Many will follow their licentious ways, and because of them the way of truth will be reviled," complained the first pope (2 Peter 2:1,2). Time hasn't changed much.

Some people close to the situation at Sparkill are pressing for the Vatican to come in and straighten out the mess if officials in the Archdiocese of New York refuse to do so. Clearly, the Church must take forceful action, immediately.

Currently, Rockland County is buzzing with the news that the Sparkill convent "leaders" plan to build a five-story complex for the "frail elderly." A feasibility study is underway. Convent grounds belonging to the motherhouse, the patrimony of the order, would be the site of this commercial nursing home, which would *not* be for frail elderly *religious*. The contemplative atmosphere would suffer greatly, and likewise the convent. Critics will be told, no doubt, that they lack compassion for the elderly. Never underestimate the subtlety of those who want to destroy the Church. They'll do it nick by nick, brick by brick, or whole walls at a time if they can.

We don't mean to criticize all Dominicans; many are loyal. Some of them work with HLI. The Nashville Dominicans, with their well-deserved throng of novices, are flourishing. And one can only admire the great work of the Dominican sisters at Hawthorne, New York. Please pray for the sons and daughters of St. Dominic!

AN APOLOGY TO BISHOP FERRARIO

In *Special Report No. 89* I erred: Hawaii's state legislature did not abolish Good Friday as a legal holiday. Instead, it abolished Discoverer's Day to make room for a Martin Luther King holiday. We'd accused Honolulu's Bishop Joseph Ferrario of doing nothing to save Good Friday. We sincerely apologize to him.

But we've also just learned that Bishop Ferrario has abolished all holy days of obligation—except the Feast of the Immaculate Conception, December 8, and Christmas. The U.S. bishops recently decided to retain all six holy days of obligation. But Bishop Ferrario learned that the Bishops' Conference of the South Pacific had asked for and received permission for each diocese to decide which holy days to retain, as long as they included a Marian feast and Christmas. So the bishop asked the Holy See to let his diocese have the same freedom granted to those bishops, basically because of Hawaii's proximity to their dioceses, and because people came to Hawaii from the South Pacific.

He was bound and determined to eliminate holy days of obligation. Now he uses the term "holy days of celebration" (not obligation) for All Saints Day, the Feast of the Assumption of Mary, and the Feast of Mary, the Mother of God. He moved the Solemnity of the Feast of Ascension Thursday to the Seventh Sunday of Easter.

In his *Hawaii Catholic Herald*, Bishop Ferrario asserts, "There were no holy days of obligation in the Christian community described in the New Testament." Please pray for Bishop Ferrario and his flock.

Letters

Congratulations for your numerous successes in Ottawa—
especially your *major* media coup.

Your wonderful unselfish team did a great job! Our
entire family *loved* HLI's conference.

John Finn
Redondo Beach, California

Cameroon is in a precarious position because of the
activities of the International Planned Parenthood
Federation. This evil, sneaky organization has developed a
legal body in my country to carry out all the satanic
activities you know about.

You have mentioned several times in your publications
that the hope of the Church and the world is in Africa. I
am afraid that if you do not double your efforts in
supporting in every way possible the prolife groups in
Africa, your dream will not come true. The antilife groups
have targeted Africa as the testing ground for all their
goals and objectives. Anything in the way of
contraceptives, sterilization, etc., that is banned in the
West is flourishing in the markets and hospitals of Africa.
Africa has become the dumping ground for all antilife
activities.

My prayers are that organizations like the Couple to
Couple League and Human Life International should put
aside special funds to rescue Africa from the staggering
position into which Planned Parenthood has taken her. In
a typical African rural market in my diocese, pills and
condoms are displayed openly for sale by people who do not
even know how these things work.

I am happy to inform you that all the nice books and
pamphlets you sent did arrive safely. You can send more. I
have distributed them to priests, women's and men's
groups in Kumbo Diocese, youth groups, Bible groups,
major seminary of our province, bishop, seminarians, and

some influential people.

Ephraim Lukong
Family Life Office
Kumbo, Cameroon

"It's great to be alive!" Dr. Joe Stanton and euthanasia survivor Nathan Post—prolife heroes

Saved by HLI's abortion photo: Anthony Joseph Speers and his mother, Shelah

Hungary and Czechoslovakia

No. 92 July 1992

I n early June I spent nine traumatic days in
Hungary, helping that country's prolifers to build resistance to abortion.

Among the last barbarians to migrate to the West from
the steppes east of the Urals in the 9th century were the
Magyars, a unique race distinct from the Slavs with a
unique language similar to Finnish. After ravaging
Western Europe, the fierce Magyars finally settled down in
the basin of the Carpathian Mountains in the 10th century.

In the 11th century, their first king, St. Stephen,
whose crown and right arm are still preserved, converted
to the Catholic faith and brought his people to
Christianity. Beginning in 1526, the Ottoman Turks occupied Hungary for 150 years. After World War I, Hungary
separated from the Austrian-Hungarian Empire. In 1940,
the country joined the Axis powers. After World War II
came the Communists. In forty years, those fanatical athe-
ists destroyed the Church, morality, the family, and the
economy.

THE DEVASTATED VINEYARD

At the end of World War II, there were sixty-three religious orders with 636 monasteries and 11,538 religious. By
means of Ordinance No. 34 in 1950, the Communists dis-
solved 94 percent of the orders; they closed 90 percent of
the monasteries and confiscated their assets. They allowed
only four teaching orders to remain, totaling some 250
members: three orders of men (the Benedictines, the
Franciscans, and the Piarist Fathers) and one of women
(the Sisters of Our Lady). The Reds reduced the number of
major seminaries from thirteen to six and allowed only
eight other Catholic schools to function; they kept all of
these under careful surveillance.

Hungary once had twenty-six denominations; 60 percent

were Catholic, 23 percent Calvinist, and 3 percent Lutheran. Meanwhile, the sincere and wealthy fundamentalist sects have moved in recently, mostly from the USA; they're making many converts. In World War II, many thousands of Jews perished. Hungary still has the largest Jewish community in Eastern Europe, 80,000 strong.

The number of Catholic schools today has grown to twenty, and in ten years the Church supposedly will get back most of her now-dilapidated buildings, but without her supportive property, such as land. Last year the primate's Archdiocese of Esztergom regained its seminary, but in such bad condition that the archdiocese bought a hotel for its thirty-five major seminarians. There are eight major seminaries.

Hungary has eleven dioceses and a fifteen-parish abbey *nullius* (a kind of mini-diocese) centered around the famous, ancient Benedictine monastery of Pannonhalma, founded in 996 amd well-endowed by King St. Stephen. Pannonhalma and its famous 300,000-book library sit atop a 900-foot-high promontory. Even the barbaric Nazis and Communists respected this venerable institution, a seat of learning and scholarship through the centuries.

There were five Benedictine abbeys before the takeover by the Reds, who confiscated all of them and banished the monks.

Hungary was once Benedictine country. There were five Benedictine abbeys before the takeover by the Reds, who confiscated all of them and banished the monks. Before the Red era, the Benedictines ran nine gymnasia (high-class university-preparatory high schools); today only two are operating. In fact, the Church once ran more than half of the schools.

Hungary today has 2,300 priests. Their average age is seventy, yet some country pastors care for four or five parishes. There are forty priestless parishes. The Red barbarians destroyed the nuns' convents. No one knows how many sisters are still alive; it may be 1,000 or so. Many are very old.

Today, thanks to forty years without religious instruction, only about 10 percent of the Catholics attend Mass regularly. Basic religious and catechetical materials are sparse; week-long "catechism camps" try to interest young people in the faith. The gracious, well-informed, prolife archabbot/bishop of Pannonhalma, Asztrik Varszegi, told me, "Seven million Hungarians remember when grandmother was Catholic and practiced her faith; a portion of these go to Mass two or three times during the year, say, at Christmas and Easter."

The Communists let the bishops publish only 60,000 books yearly. *Humanae Vitae* appeared only in 1986, eighteen years after its issuance. Some encyclicals—but not all—have been published, but many other basic papal documents, such as *Familiaris Consortio*, have not. Again and again, people told me that outsiders cannot imagine what it's like, what the teenagers and young adults are like, after forty years of no religious instruction and atheistic persecution.

It's hard to assess the bishops' performance. But trustworthy Catholic intellectuals and professionals accuse some of them of collaborating with the Reds. (In the 1964 Partial Accord with the Holy See, the government acquired a strong say in the choice of bishops.) Hungarian Catholics have little respect for Cardinal Agostino Casaroli's *Ostpolitik*; some still resent the enforced resignation of Cardinal Jozsef Mindszenty in 1971. (By the way, I prayed for all of our friends at his tomb, which is bedecked with flowers and memorabilia, in the cathedral at Esztergom. When his body was returned from Austria last year, Church officials found it to be incorrupt.)

In 1956 the bishops issued a pastoral against abortion, allegedly written by laymen. The next time they spoke out was shortly before the pope visited Hungary last year, perhaps at his request. Under the Reds, any priest who criticized abortion was expelled or neutralized. Meanwhile, natural family planning (NFP) is only beginning.

COMMUNIST CHAMELEONS

Hungary is one of the most densely populated countries in Europe. Her 35,919 square miles (the size of Indiana) are home to 10.35 million people. Some 1.6 million Hungarians live in the province of Transylvania, stolen by Stalin and added to Romania after World War II. A million more are scattered across the Western world, with some 500,000 in the USA. Cleveland was once the second-largest Hungarian city in the world.

Inflation (26.2 percent) and unemployment (400,000) create problems, as do thousands of refugees from Russia, Croatia, Romania, etc. Many Hungarians work at two or three jobs to make ends meet. The minimum wage is less than $200 a month; tenured university professors, after ten years, receive $300 per month. At least 20 percent of all Hungarians live below the poverty line. And the economic situation is worsening.

In 1956 the Freedom Fighters, believing the West would aid them, revolted against the Communists and freed their land—for a week. Soviet Premier Khrushchev ordered a brutal invasion, killing thousands and destroying much of beautiful Budapest. Some 250,000 Hungarians fled their country as the Reds regained power.

Today, the many new cars that clog the streets are evidence of the highest standard of living behind the crumpled curtain, but the socioeconomic problems are great. No longer a part of the Soviet system, the economy must be rebuilt. But the Communist chameleons—now called the "free" Socialists—have connived to protect their homes and their positions in large companies and in the media; they still dominate the country.

The ultra-liberals and the radical socialists have formed a party; a coalition with two other parties, including the small Christian Democrats, runs the country. There are six major parties. The media are viciously anti-Catholic. They make fun of the Church, whose many seemingly weak bishops appear to be groping their way as the Church struggles to come out of hibernation.

MORE COFFINS THAN CRADLES

In the 1950s, the Red health minister, contrary to the clear prohibition of abortion in the constitution, allowed abortion-on-demand. He argued that abortion was cheaper than raising children, that women had a right to abort, and that it would serve the equality of women. Hungary became a disastrous "abortion paradise." A recent book asserts that "abortion cleans out women."

Since the 1950s, Hungarian gynecologists have legally killed five million babies in this nation of 10.35 million; for twelve years there've been more abortions than births, more coffins than cradles. In the 1970s, the number of baby-killings surpassed 200,000 per year; even the Communists were alarmed by the consequences, which they never allowed the popular press to publicize. They tightened up the abortion law somewhat, eventually reducing the number of killings to about 100,000 per year. Even so, baby-killing was allowed for ten "indications"! (Today, about 65 percent of the abortions are performed on married women.)

Only gynecologists may murder preborn babies. They were required to kill during the first trimester for virtually any reason, and up to the twentieth week for "medical" reasons. I wonder how Catholic "doctors" could take part in such killings and still practice their faith, at least minimally.

Hungarian doctors who refused to kill babies lost their positions or licenses or suffered other severe penalties; the best students never entered the OB/GYN field. Last year 94,000 babies were killed and 125,679 born. The national head count has plummeted by 40,000 since 1989, according to the Hungarian Center for Statistics. The present population of 10.35 million equals the 1970 level. Last year there were 71 abortions for every 100 live births (it's 30 per 100 in the USA).

And so Hungary, aged and shrunken, languishes in the long shadow cast by the declining West. The population soon will fall beneath ten million, fewer people than live in metropolitan New York. More than 20 percent of the nation are over sixty years of age. Pensioners constitute 24 percent of all Hungarians, a growing burden for the ever-shrinking working population. Hungary is heading for national socioeconomic suicide.

Hungary's annual death rate of 14.1 per 1,000 people is the highest in Europe and one of the highest in the world (the USA's rate is about 9 per 1,000). The average life expectancy is very low: 65.1 years for males and 73.7 for females. Compare this with the wine-loving French, who live to 72.9 and 81.3 years, respectively.

Hungary is a national laboratory that gives the lie to the pro-aborts and population controllers who tell us legalized abortion is safe.

Hungary is a national laboratory that gives the lie to the pro-aborts and population controllers who tell us legalized abortion is safe (or even healthful, as the Reds once maintained). Several hundred thousand Hungarian women have become sterile. The number of premature births is the highest in Europe, thanks to "the procedure." And a huge incidence of Post-Abortion Syndrome (PAS) is latent; it's now being addressed, because of HLI.

You cannot separate baby-killing from Hungary's other peculiar social problems, such as an astronomical 65.9 suicides per 100,000 men and 25.7 per 100,000 women in 1991—the highest rate in the world (the USA ranks fifteenth). So far this year, 4,133 Magyars have taken their own lives! Hungary has 500,000 known alcoholics; a massive drug problem is just around the corner. Masonry, pornography, prostitution, dirty video stores, topless bars—the worst of the West has moved in, reminding us of Pope John Paul II's warning to Eastern Europe not to replace atheistic Communism with atheistic consumerism.

Hungary's greatest killers, after abortion, are lung cancer (from smoking) and heart disease (from stress). Doctors report 2,000 cases of AIDS, but many more people have the virus. Divorces are common. Besides surgical abortion, the most common means of birth control are the abortifacient Pill and IUD. IUDs have caused much infection, sterility, and pain, not to mention ectopic pregnancies.

When you add unenlightened health habits, ineffective health-care policies, polluted urban environments, and other environmental factors, plus "immeasurables" such as apathy and hopelessness, you begin to understand why, for many Hungarians, life tends to be "nasty, brutish, and short."

PROLIFERS BATTLE BACK

On the positive side, Hungary has many good people who are working to restore the vineyard. I addressed the Society of Christian Intellectuals (mostly Catholic) in Budapest. I also spoke to the annual meeting of the 12,000-member Association of Large Families (you must have at least three children to belong). I discussed abortion briefly on national radio and TV, too. The assembled Catholic hierarchy listened patiently to my twenty-minute discourse (in German) on abortion. I spent an evening with the Association of Christian Physicians and an afternoon with the 1,100-strong Society for the Protection of Unborn Children. God also arranged a two-hour meeting with eleven prolife members of Parliament.

I had a most interesting discussion with the minister of public welfare, Dr. Laszlo Surjan, a fine Catholic who has six children. He's the only member of the minority Christian Democratic Party in the cabinet. Because abortion is still in the Criminal Code, the reconstituted Constitutional Court declared the present abortion "law" invalid last December and told the Parliament to pass a new one.

The impetus for this declaration came from doctors and lawyers from the Pacem in Utero (Peace in the Womb) Society, founded in 1989, and the Society of Pro-Life Obstetricians (HLI has been working with both). Dr. Surjan is to come up with a proposed bill by the end of the year.

He described to me, with anguish, the impossible current abortion situation: he hoped the law would protect all Hungarians, born and unborn. But because women are so prone to abort—talking about it as casually as going shopping—he said they should consult a committee before having an abortion. And maybe only two abortionists would be tolerated in a given hospital, instead of ten. (The Reds long ago took over all Catholic hospitals. The bishops want to start one now but have no money.)

The minister also said that the bishops influenced perhaps only 20 percent of the people but that polls showed 70 percent favored women's "freedom of choice" to kill. Hungary's budding feminists, goaded by U.S. Peace Corps members, scream for legalization of all abortions. What are prolifers to do when the atheistic Socialists have a majority in Parliament!

As I left Hungary, the International Planned Parenthood Federation (IPPF) moved in. A family-planning center (FPC) will start up in Budapest later this year. It's being organized by the Society for the Protection (!) of the Family and Women (a front for IPPF), supposedly to reduce the number of abortions and to make available "positive" family-planning methods on a wide scale.

They announced these plans at a June 10 news conference held by the CILAG pharmaceutical company. This Swiss firm, which makes abortifacients mostly, will give extensive help to the new center. (Of course, spreading Pills and IUDs throughout Hungary will only lead to more fornication, adultery, and abortions, as worldwide experience proves.)

The FPC will promote a program covering all areas of "family planning," according to Gyorgy Garamvolgyi of the society. The FPC won't push for compulsory sex "education" and "family planning" in the schools or in premarital counseling—at least in the beginning. But the center's volunteers—doctors, nurses, social workers—will provide sex "education" in the "traditional" manner in the schools. So far there's none.

Budapest's city government is also supporting the center. Once a suitable building is available, the work can begin: IPPF will provide large-scale assistance (*Magyar Nemzet*, 11 June 1992).

Please pray for Hungary!

CZECHOSLOVAKIA'S MARTYRED CHURCH

Father Matthew Habiger's report: In late May, I represented you, HLI, and the World Council for Life and Family in Bratislava during the Second World Pro-Life Conference for Eastern Europe.

Czechoslovakia's sixteen million people live in three republics: (1) Bohemia in the west (capital: Prague), (2) Moravia in the center, and (3) Slovakia in the east (capital: Bratislava). The country is surrounded by Poland, Ukraine, Hungary, Austria, and Germany; her borders have shifted back and forth for centuries.

The land is dotted with churches, monasteries, and convents, some of them 1,000 years old. Slovakia boasts graceful "wooden churches" constructed entirely of wood. Our Masses during the congress took place at the beautiful, neo-Romanesque Church of the Assumption of Our Lady (1899).

When the Communist Party seized power by a *coup d'état* in February 1948, the Reds shut down more than thirty Catholic newspapers and every Catholic publishing house. All of the Catholic primary and high schools had already come under state control.

During the nights of April 13-14, 1950, the Bolsheviks disbanded all male religious communities and confiscated all of their centuries-old cultural treasures and libraries. All female religious communities were banned soon after. Without any trials, the Reds imprisoned the Franciscans, the Jesuits, the Salesians, and others in "concentration communities," forcing them to fell trees in the forests for ten years. People with a couple of university degrees had to look after pigs.

In May 1950, the Communists closed every diocesan seminary and outlawed the Greek Catholic Church in Slovakia. They detained both the resident bishop and the suffragan bishop. All seminarians were forced into military service.

Anyone who travels regularly to the Eastern countries knows that Communism left its mark even on people in the Church. The Reds wiped out almost all initiative, creativity, and sense of responsibility. The Marxist system not only destroyed the structures of the Church; when it deprived people of their faith, it took away their hope.

The Reds wiped out almost all initiative, creativity, and sense of responsibility.

THE UNDERGROUND PRIESTS EMERGE

Father Matthew's report continues: Rome has asked men who served as clandestine priests to present themselves to their local bishops. Those who are unmarried are invited to apply for ordination, following tests of their doctrinal and liturgical knowledge, and perhaps some further training.

Underground priests who married must give up performing priestly functions but may serve as deacons, assist other priests, or teach. They may also apply for ordination in the Greek Catholic (Uniate) Church, which is strongest in eastern Slovakia and allows priests to marry.

The Vatican thanked the secret priests for their sacrifices but said a "double priesthood" could no longer exist. The 300 underground priests back up about 3,000 official priests. Estimates suggest that two-thirds of the sixteen million people are Catholic.

Rome sees the underground as a courageous counterbalance to the Communist state, which allowed only a trickle of entrants to the country's two Roman Catholic seminaries and sometimes jailed priests who said Mass in private homes. But by the early 1980s, as the regime gradually allowed more religious activity, the Vatican grew uncomfortable with the underground's growing independence and began to criticize it publicly.

PROLIFERS, BISHOPS FIGHT WITHOUT WEAPONS

Father Matthew's report continues: Dr. Zdenek Hejl related that in 1968 the Reds tried to remove all legal protection for preborn babies. The Church's struggle to resist this policy succeeded in part. The abortion rate dropped from 66 abortions per 100 births in 1968 to 40 per 100 in 1974; births rose from 214,000 to 296,000 in that period.

Later, especially in the 1986 abortion law, the Communists removed the last bits of legal protection for preborn children. Abortionists now kill some 185,000 babies every year, resulting in a rate of 95.8 abortions per 100 births.

Prolifers are delivering petitions to the new government asking amnesty for all preborn babies. Professor Klener, the new minister of health and a Catholic, has already (on February 22) criticized the 1986 law in the Czech National Council. And twenty new bishops have been consecrated over the past few months; prolifers gave a translation of Father Marx's "What Bishops Could Do about Abortion" to each new shepherd.

On 22 March 1992 a pastoral letter from the bishops on abortion was read at every Mass. But a lack of funds cripples the efforts of prolifers. HLI will send prolife literature, which must be translated. Even paper is a scarce commodity and must be paid for by outside sources. One urgent need is to print 100,000 copies of our "Love and Let Live" brochure in both Czech and Slovak for immediate distribution. HLI-Czechoslovakia also plans to show "The Silent Scream" on national television.

H.L.I. HELPS FORM 4,000 LEADERS

Father Matthew's report continues: Four thousand souls gathered for the Bratislava conference. By all standards it was a thundering success.

It was organized by Donum Vitae (Gift of Life) of Slovakia and presided over by Dr. Miroslav Mikolásik. The honorary presidents were Cardinal Alfonso Lopez Trujillo, president of the Pontifical Council for the Family, and A. Rakús, minister of health for the Slovak Republic.

Twelve prolife organizations and international bodies took part, including HLI-USA and the World Council. Eastern Europe is a melting pot of many languages, something difficult for a Yankee to get used to! Translations were provided in English, Spanish, German, French,

Slovak, Czech, and Italian.

The local organizers included many M.D.s and medical students. They understand the serious need to bring moral principles to bear upon all the life issues facing the East after the collapse of Communism. Despite the lack of financial resources, Bratislava was chosen because of the strong Catholic presence there.

Fifty major seminarians were volunteer helpers, along with many teenage girls dressed in their traditional costumes. These seminarians learned much about the life issues they'll face as priests. We're sending them copies of the *Seminarians for Life International Newsletter.*

This congress was crucial because abortion, a curse from the former regime, won't go away without an all-out effort. Catholics, especially, realize that. Eastern European leaders know that unless they defeat abortion, sterilization, and contraception *now*, those evils will become permanent fixtures in the rebuilding of their cultures. Catholic Poland is a good example of a country learning to extricate itself from the clutches of a death culture of abortion, euthanasia, and sterilization.

Through the grace of God, we made many contacts and met folks who wanted to see a representative of HLI. We displayed HLI literature (which vanished in minutes!) and met with forty prolife workers from all over Czechoslovakia.

Speakers included French geneticist Dr. Jerome Lejeune, Rev. Dr. Michel Schooyans of Belgium, Dr. Bernard Nathanson, Rev. Dr. John Berry of England, and Dr. Janet Smith of the USA. I spoke on "Preparing for the 25th Anniversary of *Humanae Vitae.*"

Czechoslovakia's political tensions recently forced out President Vaclav Havel, the former playwright/poet/political prisoner who became a symbol of the democratic movements straining to reshape Eastern Europe. Thank God, there are parallel efforts by Catholic lay people to retrieve respect for the sacredness of all human life. Through HLI, our benefactors are playing an important part in this work.

At HLI's second Abortion Holocaust Survivors meeting (Houston, 1993)

Sarah Smith, abortion survivor (r.), and her mother, Betty (Houston)

Sr. Pilar Verzosa, RGS, a Filipina prolife powerhouse

Don't tell them that preborn babies aren't human beings!
(Abortion survivors in Ottawa)

*Of such is the Kingdom of
Heaven: abortion survivor
Lauren Pulliam*

*Abortion survivor Gianna Jessen
and survivor's daughter
Michelle Miller*

***Meet the press! HLI's first Abortion Holocaust Survivors meeting
(Ottawa, 1992)***

Bishop, priests and Queen: Opening Mass,
Ottawa World Conference (1992)

Abortion survivors' meeting: Eduardo Loriá (interpreter), Hilda Espitia,
Diana DePaul (mother), Gianna Jessen

Holland, Belgium, and UNICEF

No. 93 August 1992

HLI vice president Bob Lalonde and I spent a fruitful week recently in Holland, Belgium, Germany, and Ireland exploring ways to expand HLI's total-approach, prolife/profamily apostolate.

With our friends' support, we founded HLI-Holland, with an office in Eindhoven; from there we'll work in the Netherlands, neighboring Belgium, and eventually all of Western Europe. We also founded HLI-Belgium.

Both countries desperately need our total approach: the truth about everything from contraception/sterilization, education in Christian sexuality, natural family planning (NFP), and marriage preparation to abortion and euthanasia. Next March 11-14 (1993) we'll sponsor a badly needed European prolife leadership conference in Eindhoven. We continue to be overwhelmed with appeals for help from all over the world, and with opportunities to advance the cause of Life. Our friends' support and prayers are making a difference!

HOLLAND: EMPTY CHURCHES, EMPTY WOMBS

Until the 1960s, Holland was 40 percent Catholic; it sent out more foreign missionaries than Ireland and boasted five daily Catholic newspapers and a flourishing Catholic radio/TV network. Today, this nation of fifteen million is rotting from within, as are other European countries, only more so. Only 3-5 percent of the people are practicing Catholics.

In 1985, when Pope John Paul II visited the Netherlands, a movement called the "8th May Celebration" coalesced into an opposition group to the Holy See. They reject the pope's authority, *Humanae Vitae,* and other Church teachings; they plead for priestesses and a married clergy; they embrace contraception and sterilization and wink at abortion.

Active religious orders are collapsing or have collapsed. No fewer than 4,000 retired nuns, who faithfully bore the heat of day, suffer to see their younger sisters getting their hair done weekly or wearing modern dress. There are few religious vocations. One community of nuns has had only one vocation in Holland in twenty years, although it has many in Africa and Indonesia. Sadly, radical feminism and Modernism have taken over. The bishops surrendered their authority long ago; today they're not taken seriously and are opposed, derided, and divided.

Last year a homosexual/pedophilia scandal among faculty and students at the seminary at Rolduc in the Diocese of Roermond shook unshockable Holland. This seminary used to teach some 100 major seminarians but today teaches only thirty. Holland's other seminary, in the Diocese of 'S-Hertogenbosch, has thirty-five students, and three houses of study attached to universities have about thirty seminarians each. Vocations are few, but increasing.

The Dutch claim their share of drug worshipers, VD, and AIDS. A recent study found at least 15 percent of the young people "utterly confused" about life goals. The huge Dutch drug company, Organon, is leading the drive for raw sex "education" in the schools; school authorities often give the Pill to girls eleven or twelve years old and promote the condom, and so Organon will profit from extra sales of Pills. Profamily leaders and doctors assured me that most young people are fornicating by age fourteen, with the usual consequences. The "alternative lifestyle" that we used to call "shacking up" is common. So is divorce: in "Catholic" cities in south Holland, 70 percent of all couples divorce at least once.

---

*It's a total lie that Holland has the
lowest abortion rate in Europe.*

THE DUTCH ABORTION HOAX

The pro-aborts say over and over that Holland has the lowest abortion rate in Europe. It's a total lie. Most abortions aren't even counted. The Dutch use "overtime treatment," elsewhere called "bringing on the menses" or "menstrual regulation." When a girl misses a period or two, the "doctor" destroys her pregnancy by "D & C" or mini-suction without first verifying it with a test. The state pays him handsomely; the taxpayer foots the bill. (Many Indian and Pakistani Moslem "doctors" love the blood money.) There's never any mention of abortion.

Approximately 60 percent of all Dutch abortions are performed on the babies of unmarried mothers. The best estimate of children killed is 50,000 per year, not counting very early abortions caused by Pill/IUD, the morning-after dose, and Depo-Provera ("the Shot"). By one vote, Parliament legalized virtual abortion-on-demand in 1980. Today it's even advertised as a means of contraception.

A doctrinaire feminist heads the Ministry of Health. Thanks to her and her kind, Dutch law protects the money-greedy killers, not the unborn babies. Two years ago a committee of the Dutch Medical Association proposed that killing babies born with defects was a form of medical treatment! Recently, the Dutch Pediatric Association declared that "in rare cases mercy killing was better than treatment" of babies with severe handicaps, to "reduce suffering." You see the hypocrisy of our times in the Dutch, who protest the earmarking of calves yet remain undisturbed by the mass killing of preborn children.

LET'S KILL OUR PATIENTS

Thanks to decisions of the Supreme Court and other courts, Holland "leads" the world in euthanasia killings. Killer "doctors," relying on case law to avoid prosecution, currently operate in a legal gray area. But the center-left government is preparing new legislation to legalize euthanasia, starting in 1993.

The "doctors" kill an estimated 20,000 patients yearly, among them an alleged 7,000-8,000 victims who have not given consent. It's against the law, but the Dutch don't want to take a stand or appear harsh, and so the police overlook much, as long as the doctors report the killings and "don't go too far." No wonder "doctors" do the immoral in-vitro fertilization (IVF) procedure at the medical school of the "Catholic" Pontifical University of Nijmegen, which has removed the crucifixes from every classroom.

It's astonishing that a nation that's so progressive economically, so creative in many ways, and so clean (at least externally) should be so morally obtuse, wallowing in affluence. Remember, it was the Dutch medical profession that heroically resisted the Nazis' euthanasia program.

Thank God for *real* doctors, such as HLI's friend Karl Gunning, who've steadfastly defended patients' rights.

Leading Holland's moral/religious decline were Dutch theologians such as the Dominican Edward Schillebeeckx, with the blessing of the weak Cardinal Bernard-Jan Alfrink of Utrecht, who died in 1987. The infamous *Dutch Catechism*, never approved by the U.S. bishops, produced indifference to and ignorance of the faith. Holland's many homemade canons of the Mass led to many liturgical abuses.

While in Holland, I and forty other priests concelebrated a Mass for the annual Catholic Day with HLI's friend Cardinal Adrianus Simonis, who was homilist and chief concelebrant. (Alas, one "girl altar boy" slipped in.) On hand were 4,000 people; the schismatic 8th May Celebration this year drew 8,000. Cardinal Simonis greeted me with, "You are an archangel; never give up, never give up" (our *benefactors* deserve that compliment). I pinned a gold precious-feet pin to his lapel, at his request.

Rare in Holland is the truly Catholic school. Home schooling hasn't caught on yet. Appearing twice weekly is a good national Catholic paper, *Katholick Nieuwsblad*, with 18,000 subscribers. Religious/clerical scandals in the past and present are shocking.

HOLLAND'S PROLIFERS

The Netherlands' national prolife organization, "Vereniging Bescherming Ongeboren Kind" (VBOK) or Society for the Protection of the Unborn Child, has 80,000 members. Like some U.S. right-to-life groups, it opposes only one symptom of sex run loose—surgical abortion—and never gets at the roots of baby-killing: fornication, adultery, contraception, pornography, immodesty, "education" in the mechanics of sex and lust, and godlessness. Dutch right-to-life leaders don't yet see, or don't want to see, how foresight contraception leads to hindsight abortion; they're deathly afraid to tell people that the Pill and IUD are abortifacients. We have evidence that VBOK kept my interviews out of Catholic and other newspapers. Its members love their contraceptives and abortifacients and want no one to upset the apple cart.

Allegedly, VBOK has saved 1,500 babies through counseling. But it also refers women for abortions, in collaboration with the government, which gives it grants! The Catholic Church contributes 40,000 guilders (about $24,000) to VBOK.

Bishop Austin Vaughan and other Americans have introduced rescuing to the Dutch. HLI hopes to organize a prolife/profamily movement from the bottom up, using our total approach, now increasingly adopted by prolife groups worldwide.

BELGIUM'S NATIONAL SUICIDE

Two years ago the Belgian Parliament legalized abortion-on-demand in the first three months of life. If the preborn child has a handicap or if the "doctor" foresees that the baby may have serious defects after birth, he may kill his little patient any time during pregnancy.

"Doctors" kill an estimated 18,000 preborn children yearly in this country of ten million, which is home to 1.2 million immigrants, many of whom are Moslems. Brussels is 14 percent Moslem.

The ancient University of Louvain was once the most prestigious Catholic university in the world. Today, like Notre Dame and Georgetown, it's no longer a Catholic force. Louvain runs one of three "Catholic" medical schools in Europe that defy Rome by doing the immoral in-vitro fertilization procedure and performing abortions for several "indications." Where are the Catholic alumni of these and other "Catholic" universities, who should all be pressuring the administrations?

About five years ago, I witnessed how Louvain's medical school let drug companies use it to introduce the abortifacient, triphasic "birth control" Pill. At their news conference, I upset the Pill promoters greatly by reminding them of the abortifacient character of their new potion.

> ***Once-Catholic Louvain University***
> ***performs in-vitro fertilization***
> ***procedures and selected abortions.***

A colleague embarrassed the lay head of the medical school by asking how a pontifical "Catholic" university could lend itself to a meeting totally opposed to Catholic teaching. Like the presidents of the several U.S. Jesuit universities, he replied that universities must look at all sides of a question; besides, Louvain would soon sponsor a conference on NFP. Later he asked my help in securing NFP experts, which I provided. The conference never took place. When I sent a report of the shameful Louvain meeting to the U.S. bishops' National Catholic News Service, the bureaucrats there refused to publish it.

PROLIFERS FIGHT ON

Belgium's Flemish population fought abortion with a very good program in the schools, thanks to the leadership of Dr. Charles Convent and school teacher Gilbert Sprengers, whose Pro Vita—"Gezin en leven" (Flemish) or Life and Family—is the only effective prolife group in the country. But very little was done by the French-speaking Walloons, who, along with 60,000 German-speaking Belgians, comprise 37 percent of the nation.

The clergy are very anti-*Humanae Vitae*, thanks to the dissent of the Belgian bishops to *Humanae Vitae*, under the dissident leadership of Cardinal Leo Joseph Suenens. And with the exception of Monsigneur Van Peteghem, Bishop of Ghent, the bishops have been scandalously indifferent to the war on preborn children. Accordingly, NFP has made little progress. At Vatican II, Cardinal Suenens, along with Cardinals Alfrink (Holland), Leger (Canada),

Döpfner (Germany), and König (Austria), questioned the immorality of contraception. Today their countries are dying. Divine punishment?

If the Walloons had been as ready and as educated for the baby-killing onslaught as were the Flemish, the Parliament would never have been able to impose abortion-on-demand on the nation in April 1990. Today the typical married woman has a catastrophic 1.4 children, and this statistic includes the children of the many immigrants!

Pro Vita has just become an autonomous branch of HLI. To foster the prolife work further, we also established HLI-Belgium, under the sterling leadership of the Sprengers family. Now we can work in all of Belgium, which is nominally 90 percent Catholic. Only about 15 percent of Belgian Catholics attend Mass regularly. Please pray for Belgium and Holland.

TOP KNIGHTS OUT OF STEP WITH HOLY SEE ON UNICEF

Report by HLI staff member Jean Guilfoyle, editor of our Population Research Institute Review: Robert Wade, supreme treasurer of the Knights of Columbus, has attacked the credibility of HLI's Population Research Institute (PRI) in an official K of C newsletter. According to Wade, "We find no basis in fact...for the allegations made [concerning UNICEF and population control] or the accuracy of the Population Research Institute." His article has appeared in Canadian diocesan newspapers and in K of C periodicals such as the *Ontario State Bulletin* (Pentecost 1992). Wade and the Knights are dead wrong.

Operating out of the office of Supreme Knight Virgil Dechant, Wade claims to have "investigated the matter in the U.S. capital of Washington, D.C., and the permanent Mission of the Holy See to the UN."

Why would Wade leave K of C headquarters in New Haven, Connecticut, bypass nearby New York with its UNICEF offices, and travel all the way to Washington to "investigate" UNICEF? The information would have been his for the asking at UN headquarters in New York.

(Perhaps he just wanted to use some of the travel funds that are on tap for K of C leaders. Last year the Knights' officers spent $2,671,639 on travel—not all of it, we hope, on such misdirected missions.)

And, during his jaunt to the District of Columbia, Wade could have easily satisfied his not-so-insatiable curiosity by visiting the nearby offices of PRI. Here he could have personally examined the largest deposit of documentation on UNICEF's contraception/abortion activities. Not only is the proof available at PRI's offices, but we gladly mail it to anyone who requests it.

UNICEF is deeply involved in depopulation projects in the Third World.

VATICAN SCORES UNICEF

Jean Guilfoyle's report continues: In his discussion of "the matter directly with His Excellency Archbishop Renato Martino, Permanent Observer of the Holy See to the United Nations," Wade failed to note Archbishop Martino's warning to UNICEF's board of directors in April 1990, when His Excellency stated:

> ...the Holy See views with great alarm some repeated proposals to the effect that this United Nations agency, established for the well-being of children, become involved in the destruction of existing human life, even to the point of suggesting that UNICEF become an advocate for abortion in countries whose sovereign legislation doesn't allow it....Moreover, such proposals appear to reveal a dangerous form of neo-colonialism....

If Wade had consulted the United Nations Fund for Population Activities (UNFPA) *Inventory of Population Projects in Developing Countries* at the UN offices in New York, he would have discovered that UNICEF consistently takes part in depopulation projects in the Third World. Even a small selection of examples attests to UNICEF's deep involvement:

—UNICEF received $700,000 from the World Bank for a population project in Kenya that set up an interagency information and education program to promote a small-family norm and provided startup funds for 300 maternal and child health/family planning "clinics." "[T]he project was amended in 1985 to include the establishment of surgical contraceptive [sterilization] facilities in 13 district hospitals and family planning clinics" (UNFPA *Inventory*, 1987/88, p. 292).

—UNFPA provided $5,453,023 to UNICEF in Bangladesh to "support integrated maternal and child health/family planning services and the Population Control and Family Planning Division" (*Ibid.*, 1988/89, p. 28).

—The list goes on and on—UNICEF in Malawi, Nepal, Jamaica, Malaysia, Cape Verde, Burundi, Red China, Tanzania, Uganda, Rwanda, etc. UNICEF's latest project is an "interagency partnership" of the World Bank, UNICEF, the UN Development Program (UNDP), the UN's World Health Organization (WHO), UNFPA, International Planned Parenthood Federation (IPPF), and the Population Council, which has proposed a "Safe Motherhood Initiative" aimed at legalizing abortion within all national maternal and child programs in developing countries.

UNICEF V. THE CHURCH

Jean Guilfoyle's report continues: Years ago IPPF, the world's most notorious abortion/depopulation organization, revealed the truth about UNICEF in a review of its own publication, The Children of the Nations: The Story of UNICEF, in IPPF's People magazine (Vol. 14, No. 3):

As early as 1959, the Swedish delegation to the UNICEF Executive Board had brought up the topics of population and family planning, to be met by general embarrassment and hostility from most Catholic countries. In 1966, Harry Bavouisse put forward to the Executive Board meeting at Addis Ababa, the first, cautious suggestion to be presented formally to the governing body of a UN organization, that multilateral funds should be spent on providing poor mothers with access to family planning [translation: contraception, sterilization, abortifacients, and surgical abortions]. The result was the most bitter and explosive confrontation in UNICEF history.

Slowly, the intransigence of the opposition mellowed, and *family planning has found its rightful place in most of UNICEF maternal and child health programmes*, although the anathema of the Catholic Church on artificial fertility control has acted as a brake and inhibitor to faster progress [emphasis added].

UNICEF loses no opportunity—and now with the help of the Knights—to sneak behind the respectable mask of the Catholic Church in order to mimic and exploit a religious-cultural force that speaks to millions in a language they trust. Further, many of the populations that UNICEF, UNFPA, the World Bank, and others would like to "reduce" live in predominantly Catholic areas such as Latin America, Africa, and the Philippines.

UNICEF assertions that a Vatican gift of $3,000 represents support for UNICEF's depopulation agenda are also contradicted by Archbishop Martino's statement of April 1990. In it, he carefully detailed the limited purpose of the Vatican gift as "...earmarked for the budget for mobilization activities related to the forthcoming World Summit for Children" on behalf of "the Pontifical Society of the Holy Childhood—an agency which aims at forming in children and adolescents awareness of and solidarity for the resources and needs of their fellow children throughout the world."

LAY APOSTLES OR BUSINESS EXECUTIVES?

Jean Guilfoyle's report continues: One has to ask what possible purpose—what vested interest—the highest officers of the Knights of Columbus have in whitewashing the tragic victimization of women and children through UNICEF's imposition of depopulation projects in maternal and child health-care programs and other community health centers.

The women of the developing nations have cried out for relief in the corridors of power at the UN, at the World Women's Meeting in Miami, at the Women's Tent of the Global Forum in Brazil, and within the halls of their own national governments. But Wade and Dechant have turned a deaf ear to their cries and have closed their eyes to the readily available public records of their suffering.

Not only does Wade whitewash the pro-aborts of UNICEF, he also commits slander against his prolife fellow Catholics at PRI. Our purpose, he charges, is "fund raising...which is the real objective of the [PRI] publication" on UNICEF!

This is an interesting accusation, coming from a "lay apostle" whose annual salary is $81,000 plus perks (*National Catholic Reporter*, 3 April 1992). The Knights admit to an "aggregate total" of $1,697,814 in "salaries, compensation, reimbursements and fees" for their ten top directors. Faithful local Knights who "volunteer much time on behalf of the nonprofit organization to raise money for the organization and private charities" (*NCR*, 3 April 1992) have roundly criticized this figure. Supreme Knight Dechant has conceded he's an insurance executive whose salary last year was $455,500 (*NCR*, 3 April 1992) and who rides in a chauffeur-driven car while many Knights are out of work.

We strongly urge Dechant to rein in Wade and to inform his conscience instead of shouting falsehoods from the housetops to 1.5 million Knights.

We also call upon him again to expel the proabortion Knights of Death who are members of Congress and the state legislatures. He should stop hiding behind the bishops and do his duty to God's little babies.

Dear reader, if you spot any attack on HLI's or PRI's work in a diocesan newspaper or a K of C publication, please send it to Father Marx, along with the name and address of the editor or your state's/province's top K of C officer. And please pray for the Knights.

Aussie twins—a double blessing!

Letters

I am forty-two years old, a Catholic nerve specialist living and working in a Romanian town.

As a result of the social democratization, in 1989 we looked at the possibilities in connection with knowing and diffusing Christian views within the framework of medicine. There is a great need for this, because in recent decades the medical instruction has been given only in the spirit of materialistic ideology. The various prohibitions and the dearth of information have had an effect on public knowledge, too. In moral respects, liberty has signified libertinism. Especially nowadays, pornography has had a strong effect on our young people.

Some intellectuals gathered around the ecclesiastical institutions and in 1990 established a society in order to fight abortion. Then, having formed the Society of Christian Medical Persons, we directed the attention of medical specialists to the actuality of the protection of life. We also foster the concept of the protection of life by contacting schools, colleges, and meetings of young people.

In 1991 we will disseminate knowledge of natural family planning and also conduct a three-day prolife seminar for medical personnel and social workers. Thank you for any help you can give us.

Foldes Adalbert, MD
Oradea, Romania

Some months ago we learned about the activities of your organization, and it gave us some hope.

My colleagues and I have set up an initiative group fighting against abortion. You probably know that the political and economic situation in our republic at present is very tense, but all that is nothing in comparison with the fact that in Georgia 70,000 abortions are performed every year.

For obvious reasons our group's possibilities are limited, and so is our experience. We'll be very glad if you contact us and include our organization in the HLI structure.

Akaki Bakradze, MD
Tbilisi, Georgia (formerly USSR)

We, a group of enthusiasts of the prolife campaign in Russia, call upon you to help us to develop this movement in our country.

We are deeply worried about our government's family-planning program, which is based on the International Planned Parenthood Federation recommendations. We want to save our children from aggressive anti-Christian sexual education that pushes them into promiscuity and sexually transmitted diseases. We want to save our children from dangerous contraceptives given without parental consent. We want to have family-oriented politics based on traditional Christian values.

Obviously, Russia is going through a dramatic period and is at the turning point of its history. Hard times afflicted Russia in the past as well, but never before were so many children deprived of life without even being given a chance to be born.

Our Christian duty is to speak out. Our movement cries: "Don't kill! Don't let the future of this great European country perish!"

At the moment, we are few. We lack understanding and help in our work.. We should like to make useful and helpful contacts with Christian organizations dealing with the prolife movement in your country. We would be very thankful for literature and any other assistance and cooperation.

Igor Guzov
Russian Right to Life Movement
Moscow, Russia

*Croatia's tireless Dr. Antun Lisec (l.) and a friend with
one-horsepower transportation (1993)*

Modern apostle reaching thousands through the Polish media

*When the late Cardinal Mindszenty
went home to Hungary,
Church officials found the hero's
body incorrupt*

*Dr. Rene Bulecer in
HLI-Philippines' new office*

*Bishop Enrique Hernan de Rivera of Caguas and Fr. Aurelio Adan of
HLI-Puerto Rico helped lead our first Congress on the island*

Sex Ed and Latin America

No. 94   September 1992

We at HLI are learning much about the total
mess that is "sex ed," in both public and private
schools. From our many contacts, phone conversa-
tions, and incoming letters, it's evident that most Catholic
parents still don't know that almost the entire Catholic
school system has broken down, from kindergarten
through university.

Catholic parents don't realize that their children no
longer learn the Faith integrally in these schools; that in
some Catholic schools non-Catholics teach "Catholic" religion classes; that all too many Catholic-college students
lose their faith, as proven by their failure to attend Mass
later; that some 90 percent of married, Catholic teachers of
childbearing age are contracepting or have been sterilized;
and that it's *impossible* for these so-called Catholics to
teach, generate, or inspire chastity, because they don't
practice it themselves.

What's more, our contacts report that *all* classroom sex
"education" has failed, in every country from pioneering
Sweden to the USA, because it fuels the fires of teen sexual curiosity and activity; that parents have the solemn
right and supreme duty to teach and exemplify to their
children the many-faceted virtue of chastity; that parents
themselves, armed with "the grace of state," are their children's best educators in this delicate area; and that it
would be better to learn the facts of life on the street from
other kids than in a classroom from teachers who are
authority figures to their students but often need moral
and spiritual rehabilitation themselves.

WHAT'S THE BEST SEX ED?

Once again, we shout it from the rooftops: The best sex
education any child can have is a loving set of parents who
were properly prepared for marriage and who obey and
live out the rich and comprehensive teaching on chaste,

loving, fruitful sexuality contained in the total
Christian/biblical message.

**The best sex education any child can
have is a loving set of parents....**

Too few children have such parents, some will argue.
But this argument only proves that a generation of young
people has been mistaught. Planned Parenthood-type sex
ed programs and their offspring, the abstinence/chastity
programs, won't rehabilitate these victims, whether children or parents. Let's make every effort, then, to produce
no more miseducated children. Let's teach children on
every level the entire Faith in a comprehensive catechesis,
supported by integral, orthodox preaching from the pulpit.

Because HLI opposes *classroom* sex education, no matter how innocuous a given program sounds, some naive
parents, teachers, religious, priests, and even bishops
wrongly assume that we're against the teaching of loving
chastity! This assumption proves how little they've
thought about the whole question and how unaware they
are of today's vicious, sin-soaked, pornographic culture and
environment—to say nothing of what's being taught in
"Catholic" schools. They overlook the observation of
Vatican II: "Their [the parents'] role as educator is so decisive that scarcely anything can compensate for their failure in it."

If we at HLI hadn't been enlightened by the best of parents (people whom we know personally), we wouldn't believe
what teachers, some religious, and even some priests are
telling young people in classrooms and elsewhere. They're
violating innocent children during their latency period by
planting all kinds of premature sexual thoughts and questions in their malleable young personalities.

To these teachers, and to all who are interested in sex
ed, we recommend the chapter on sex ed in Marshall and
Donovan's eye-opening *Blessed Are the Barren*, a $19.95
book that you can order from HLI for $13 postpaid. We
also recommend psychiatrist Melvin Anchell's *What's*

Wrong with Sex Education? and Father Vern Sattler's *Challenging Children to Chastity: A Parental Guide,* which you can get from HLI for $8 each. Order any one or all of these vital books and we'll include my reprint, "Sanity, Sex Ed and Chastity," free of charge.

MARIAN CONGRESS GETS COLD SHOULDER FROM BISHOP

On the weekend of 7-9 August 1992, Father Matthew Habiger and I spoke at a Marian congress in Kansas City's municipal auditorium. Entitled "Our Lady of the Americas," the event combined Eucharistic, prolife, and Marian themes. About 2,000 people came from Missouri and surrounding states.

By the end of 1992, thirty Marian congresses will have been held throughout the USA. In a typical congress, noted speakers address real faith problems of the day, hundreds of penitents receive the Sacrament of Reconciliation, local bishops preside at the Eucharist and give homilies, and participants leave with a renewed sense of faith and purpose.

We wonder why only 2,000 people came, instead of 4,000, 6,000, or 8,000. Last year 4,000 attended at nearby St. Joseph, Missouri, and 9,000 at Des Moines. One reason is that the diocesan paper, the *Catholic Key,* refused to carry ads for the event, even though neighboring diocesan papers did.

The local bishop, John Sullivan, thought the congress would be counterproductive. He gave these reasons: (1) The bishops of Mexico and the USA hadn't exchanged proper protocols regarding the traveling image of Our Lady of Guadalupe; (2) if the image were unable to stop abortions, as claimed, the Church would look foolish in the eyes of the secular media; and (3) a Marian congress would set back the ecumenical movement. When Bishop Sullivan realized the congress would go on anyway, he declared that the diocese would neither affirm nor resist it. Two brave old priests attended; some younger ones confided that they would have been punished if they'd come!

It's interesting that Bishop Sullivan raised no

objections to Notre Dame's rebel Father Richard McBrien's speaking at Jesuit-run Rockhurst College on 23 January 1992.

The bishop's *Catholic Key* gave three pages of coverage to this talk, in which Father McBrien said, "Unless the Church changes its current discipline on obligatory celibacy and the ordination of women, and unless a different kind of bishop is appointed, less ideologically rigid and more pastorally open and unafraid, it will be a Church with very few ordained priests who are at the same time healthy human beings." Father McBrien apparently had the approval of the local ordinary.

Several weeks before the congress, the *Key* ran an ad for talks in the Kansas City area by the now-ousted Dominican Father Matthew Fox. Bishop Sullivan voiced no objections, even though Father Fox endorses homosexual acts and travels with a witch. Spokesmen for the *Key* defended their decision to run the ad by saying it wasn't contrary to the principles of their paper.

DEPOPULATIONISTS PUSH LATIN TEENS INTO SEX

From 15 to 19 June 1992, the U.N. Fund for Population Activities (UNFPA), the International Planned Parenthood Federation (IPPF), and the Japanese Organization for International Cooperation in Family Planning (JOICFP)— an IPPF affiliate—held the first Latin American Workshop on Adolescent Health. (They use the euphemism "adolescent health" in Latin America, where "sex education" has become a dirty word.) All of IPPF's Latin American affiliates attended.

Among the goals of the meeting were the prevention of adolescent pregnancy by contraception and the prevention of VD and AIDS by condoms. The assembled "experts" concluded that the best way to influence adolescent sexual behavior is through audiovisuals; that society should change adults' attitudes toward adolescents' use of contraceptives; and that we must inform adolescents about VD and AIDS without producing feelings of fear, while emphasizing and preserving sexual pleasure in all aspects.

The real problem, the workshoppers decreed, isn't the teen girl's having intercourse, but her having it without using contraception. They want to give children information on all contraceptive methods and to make those "plugs and drugs" freely available to kids through many organizations. The bottom line and goal is: make sex recreation without procreation; get the kids to copulate but not populate.

Hirachal Sanchez of Brazil's Department of Health stated crudely that "pregnancy in adolescents is a social disease." Therefore, "health" programs must aim at preventing pregnancy in the young girl, who must learn to use her "true" sexuality, i.e., to realize genuine sexual pleasure. To achieve this end, JOICFP has produced three grossly offensive, full-color pornographic films. These are already corrupting children in Mexico and will soon do the same throughout all of Latin America and the Caribbean.

Two major concerns came out of this five-day meeting: (1) the educational process used must involve personal participation by the children, and (2) it must ensure that the children assimilate the information, to ensure behavioral changes. All opposition must be neutralized. Again, parents' and other adults' attitudes toward children's sex acts must change, and suitable materials must be provided.

International Planned Parenthood exploits Latin America's illiteracy, confused clergy, and often-uninformed bishops.

To encourage children to fornicate, organizations are already launching aggressive adolescent "health" programs that dispense sexual information through pornographic videos that teach kids how to use the freely dispensed contraceptives. IPPF exploits Latin America's illiteracy, confused clergy, and often-uninformed bishops. If there's a more evil organization on earth than IPPF, I'm not aware of it. IPPF is a godless monster destroying youth, family, society, and Church.

MOLESTING COLOMBIA'S CHILDREN

ProFamilia, the Colombian branch of IPPF, has just won
another big victory. The constitutional court has handed
down a decision making sex "education" mandatory from
kindergarten onward in all of the country's government
schools.

This ruling opens the door for this antilife/antifamily
organization to invade every public school classroom, with
the approval of school authorities and against the will of
most parents. At the same time, religious instruction was
removed; it's no longer required in this "Catholic" nation.
Colombia's bishops have unwittingly rolled out the red car-
pet for IPPF by accepting the constitutional provision.

ProFamilia could have achieved no greater victory. A
former IPPF official, Julia Henderson, boasted that when
ProFamilia first arrived in 1965, they "had cooperation
from priests in 15 of the first 16 dioceses to which they
took mobile teams of health [sic] workers. On the whole,
we have not found the Catholic Church to be a big obstacle
to family planning" (*Calypso Log*, October 1988).

Just as with "health" (sex) centers in some U.S. high
schools, ProFamilia's plans for teens thirteen to nineteen
include "offering medical services with an emphasis on
reproductive health....to help information and communica-
tion strategies on human sexuality and family planning
tailored to teens....direct distribution of contraceptives...."

Their plans also include "collaboration with educational institutions for students' and teachers' training programs in the area of human sexuality and family planning," as promulgated by ProFamilia's youth center in
Bogotá. So now contraceptives are freely available in grocery stores, gas stations, and supermarkets. Sound familiar? How long will it be before they're passing out Pills and
condoms in Colombia's schools? And now there's talk of
school sex clinics.

SEX ED: KEY TO ABORTION

Remember that Dr. Alan Guttmacher, the organizer of
Planned Parenthood Physicians and a president of
Planned Parenthood, once said, "The only avenue in which

Planned Parenthood has to win the battle is sex education"
(*Washington Star*, 3 May 1973). Next, legalized abortion in
Colombia? Ana Milena Gaviria, the First Lady, recently
approved obligatory "sex ed" plans for Colombia's children.
She works with IPPF, UNFPA, and the dirty-video-
producing JOICFP. UNICEF is involved, too.

Soon IPPF, UNFPA, and JOICFP will bring together
all the bribed, wined-and-dined first ladies of the twenty-
one Latin American countries and the Caribbean to promote their satanic, incredibly raw sex ed. An IPPF stooge
pleaded IPPF's cause at the first Latin American
Encounter on Adolescent Health (i.e., sex ed and contraception) in Colombia last September.

Nowhere have the contraceptive imperialists been
more successful than in Colombia. In less than thirty years
they've reduced the average family from more than 6 children to 2.5, producing a hellish moral and social after-
math: broken families, thousands of street children,
increasing VD and AIDS, widespread "living together,"
social violence, assassinations, and ever more "no-name
graves" (NNG), to mention a few results.

Meanwhile, some bishops, Catholic movements, and
many of the Catholic laity, led by Sen./Dr. Carlos Corsi,
are battling to restore religious education to the schools.

The birth-controllers have organized similar programs
in other Latin countries, such as Guatemala. Words cannot
adequately describe the foul deeds of IPPF in Latin
America, supported by millions of dollars from the mori-
bund rich countries.

One of the worst offenders is dying Japan's JOICFP,
an affiliate of IPPF. Since 1974, this wealthy organization
has helped promote twenty private "family planning" projects in twenty-four countries. Japan also donates one-
fourth of UNFPA's global budget. Why? Because Japan
fears government instability in the developing countries,
which could mean the loss of raw materials, markets for
cars, etc.

Meanwhile, thanks to her low birthrate (only 1.53 children per family), Japan is enduring a serious labor shortage. The desperate government is luring Japanese-

Brazilians to Japan for employment and so far has succeeded in bringing 160,000 of the 1.1 million Japanese-Brazilians back to Japan. We live in an age of madness and contradictions—a new paganism.

We live in an age of madness and
contradictions—a new paganism.

I.P.P.F. V. MEXICO

For years MEXFAM (Mexican Foundation for Family Planning), an IPPF offshoot, has been spreading its evil tentacles throughout the country. In 1979, working with the U.N.'s World Health Organization (WHO), MEXFAM introduced "family planning" and "reproductive health" programs side by side with programs combating intestinal parasites!

Officials of MEXFAM boldly say, "Birth control continues to be an operational point of entry which MEXFAM uses to increase coordination with health and educational institutions in extending the methods of family-planning [sic] programs to areas that are difficult to reach."

MEXFAM struck early and broadly. In this country of eighty-two million people, fully half—forty million—are under nineteen years of age. In 1990 there were twenty-nine million Mexicans between fifteen and nineteen—almost one-third of the population. Thank God, Mexico has the highest proportion of priestly vocations in Latin America.

WE HELPED BEAT ABORTION IN HONDURAS

Good news! We (helped by our friends' gifts and prayers) defeated legalized abortion in Parliament for the second time! Our campaign included a life chain of 3,000 young people, many carrying HLI's aborted-baby posters. Our people debated the enemy on radio and TV, using our posters everywhere, even inside Parliament!

CONTRACEPTIVE IMPERIALISM IN NIGERIA AND BRAZIL

More good news! Because of documentation provided by our Population Research Institute, Rep. Chris Smith (R-N.J.) will call for a hearing on U.S.-financed, forced birth-control practices, including massive sterilization, in these two countries.

H.L.I. AIDS SEYCHELLES & ALBANIA

IPPF extends its dirty tentacles everywhere. Most Americans don't even know where the Seychelles are. But IPPF is there in full force! Their bishop wanted HLI to come. We've only been able to comply with his desperate request for prolife materials.

And now Albania: Our man there writes, "I think now it is high time for Albanian doctors and people at large to make their choice. But, firstly, they are unaware of the risks of contraception and abortion promoted by IPPF." He pleads for aborted baby photos, videos, films, tapes, and any other materials that might help Albanians resist the onslaught of "Planned Hell."

UPDATE ON POLAND

Abortion is a never-ending controversy in this country, where the Communists legalized it on demand in 1956. Some four years after the start of the emotional public debate on abortion, the Sejm (lower house of Parliament) recently rejected a bad new law and the possibility of a referendum on abortion. According to polls, only 10 percent of the voters support a total ban on abortion, and so the pro-aborts' suggested referendum would be very dangerous to the babies. On July 24, lawmakers debated two abortion proposals: one a proposal to give preborn children good protection, and the other an open-season-on-babies bill from the Women's Parliamentary Caucus.

Some months ago the Polish Medical Society decreed that it would allow abortions only in cases of rape, incest, and (alleged) life of the mother; "doctors" who performed them for other reasons would be suspended. This decree and the pope's urgent pleas have reduced the number of abortions. Parliament will take up the whole problem again this fall.

A letter from Andrzej Winkler, the head of HLI's branch in Katowice, will give you some insights:

> "Condomology," the new rhetoric of "safe sex" brought to us by the U.S., is flourishing in Poland. Of course, the preachers of condomology tell us that they want to implement the most proven methods in the areas of sexual behavior which have been worked out in the U.S. for "protecting people against the HIV virus."
>
> As a matter of fact, anything that is American or comes from America is unconditionally accepted. It looks as though we are now having the Americanization of our lifestyle (a counter-reaction to forty years of Communism). People in the media, particularly TV, repeat stupidities about "safe sex" in order to protect (!) young people, telling us it is the best way to avoid AIDS.

As in other countries plagued by abortion, the baby-killing habit is now a deeply rooted part of Polish sexual life. It'll take a long, long time to uproot that habit.

Letters

Enclosed are the reports of some of my prolife activities and copies of two letters.

Today I spoke with Rev. Majstorovic by phone. He told me that today I must not come to help with the prolife counseling, because Slavonski Brod was the victim of a big shell attack. One person was killed and ten wounded. Rev. Majstorovic hasn't time to write you, but he asked me to say thanks for your precious help.

Tomorrow in the morning I shall travel to Zagreb and to Zabok, near Zagreb, to give a prolife interview for the local radio station.

Antun Lisec, MD
Croatia-Hrvatska

I have received and read you *Special Report. No. 94.* Thanks for your insightful analysis of our diocese and bishop.

Any diocesan paper (such as the *Catholic Key*) that carries Father Richard McBrien as a regular columnist should arouse trepidation about its sponsorship.

Thanks also for your many years of heroic effort for the unborn. Please give my best wishes to Father Matthew, whom I have never met but who is from my *alma mater*, St. Benedict's of Atchinson, Kansas.

Francis M. Whitesell
Kansas City, Missouri

TV interview in abortion-ravaged Hungary

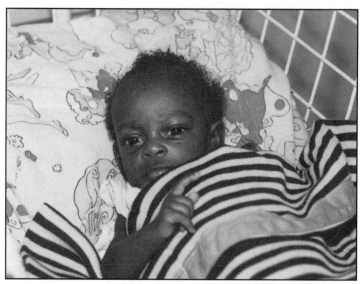

IPPF's target: the African baby (Kenya)

S.V.D.'s Moral Theology for Waffle-Lovers

No. 95 October-November 1992

I touched some raw nerves when I reported, after our last mission journey to the Philippines, that seminarians there are "victimized by rebel theologians, the worst being the Jesuits and the Divine Word (SVD) Fathers, both of whom reject *Humanae Vitae* brazenly" (*Special Report No. 89*, April 1992).

Correspondence with complaining SVD superiors then revealed more: *Christian Ethics*, a dangerous textbook on moral theology, is published in the Philippines for seminarians. The author is Father Karl H. Peschke ("peshkee"), SVD. The publisher is Divine Word Publications, Manila.

Ironically, most of the two-volume text constitutes perhaps the best systematic and comprehensive course on moral theology written for seminarians since Vatican II, and its pages testify to an astounding amount of research and hard work by the author. But the section on abortion and contraception in volume 2 is a catastrophe.

The section on abortion and contraception in volume 2 is a catastrophe.

The dissenters quoted on these pages leave little room for the pope. The author mobilized a Lilliputian army to shoot arrows at *Humanae Vitae* (*HV*): theologians B. Häring, C. Curran, R. McCormick, F. Böckle, J. Gründel, P. Schoonenberg, G. Lobo, J. Dedek, G. Postrana, J. Donceel, and Georgetown professor of OB-GYN A. Hellegers—in short, name a dissenter and you'll probably find his opinion hallowed here.

SPREADING POISON WORLDWIDE

Father Peschke taught in the large Tagaytay Seminary near Manila during 1968-1974. Volume 2 of his *Christian Ethics* has sold more than 28,000 copies worldwide, a measure of its popularity in seminaries and also of the enormous harm it's done. Examine this book to learn what many new priests think.

Father Peschke's work evidently had the approval of his SVD superiors during all these years; they appointed him to form SVD members at major seminaries in Brazil, Germany, and the Philippines. More recently, he achieved the high honor of being appointed a professor at the Pontifical Urban University in Rome, whose chancellor is president of the Vatican's Congregation for the Propagation of the Faith.

The text appeared in various editions in England, Ireland, India, the Philippines, and Italy. In December 1990 a newsletter featured the author as a courageous theologian "following the steps of the moral theologian Häring." Father Bernard Häring, the loudest dissenter, had lectured (by invitation) at the SVD house of formation in Nemi, near Rome, and harmed many a nun and priest in the USA with his summer courses in theology.

Then came the Manila incident, on 2 February 1992, when an SVD seminarian argued with HLI's Father Matthew Habiger at our Asian-Pacific prolife conference. This incident led to my exposure of SVD's theology; what HLI works for, Father Peschke's text works against.

Since February, things have been breaking fast. A critique of the book went to the cardinal chancellor of the Pontifical Urban University. A reply stated that Father Peschke "is no longer a professor at the Pontifical Urban University." But HLI isn't finished. We ask you to read this *Report* and then work with us until the poisonous text is either made orthodox or banned from all seminaries.

WAFFLING ON ABORTION

Of course, we shouldn't reject the book just because the author presents the views of adversaries. Major seminarians must become professional theologians of sorts and

should know what the opposition says. This is standard
preparation for future priests whom the Church will send
to hear confessions, preach, teach, counsel, and inspire.
The first task of the morals professor, then, is the apostolate of forming faithful priests who'll point the way to
Heaven, whether the message is politically correct or not.
The priest's first duty is to be faithful to the Church that
sends him.

But this book's section on abortion and contraception is
worm-eaten with compromises. It almost makes the Vicar
of Christ appear to be a lone dissenter against an army of
self-appointed infallibles. In the pages about abortion, for
example, the Magisterium gets 10 lines, but the dissenters
get 500 lines—a ratio of one to fifty! Let's look at some of
the compromises.

B. Häring reports the case of a pregnant woman who
suffered from a uterine tumor that caused profuse bleeding. In order to prevent the woman from bleeding to death,
the attending physician decided to open and empty [!] the
uterus. Thereupon the uterus contracted and the bleeding
ceased. Yet (Häring continues) according to the principle of
directly and indirectly willed evil effects, this procedure
must be considered illicit. The expulsion of the fetus from
the uterus constitutes a direct abortion, which is unlawful.
The argument that in this way the uterus could be saved
for this childless woman is not a reason that could justify
the procedure. But (Häring continues) it would be considered licit to remove the whole uterus as a sick organ,
together with the child, because this merely is indirect
abortion. Häring justly doubts whether this reasoning is
sound morality (p. 362).

And so the author lets Father Häring sow doubts about
clear Church teaching against direct abortion by using an
outlandish case, the authenticity of which cannot be examined. The case obviously is phony; why didn't the doctor
save both the mother *and* her child by better medical practice? Today, a doctor who kills a baby to save the mother
may be sued for malpractice.

Father Peschke then proposes that direct abortion is
sometimes permitted (never mind that God and His

Church forbid this "abominable crime"!):

> The anticipated death of a fetus constitutes a lesser evil and offends against a lesser right than the death of mother and child together.... In view of such considerations J. Dedek judges that a sufficient reason for a therapeutic abortion "would be to save the physical life of the mother or, what I would think equivalent, her mental sanity." A similar view is held by C. Curran....

Note that the text gives the place of honor to sundry famous (notorious?) dissidents, yet fails to counter them with direct quotations from the pope. After conceding that we really shouldn't kill a child just for the mother's mental health, the text continues: "Other recent Catholic authors who consider therapeutic abortion permissible in order to save the mother's life are R. Springer, J. Noonan, B. Häring, the Belgian bishops, W. May [now back to orthodoxy], J. Stimpfle, H. Rötter, L. Janssens, F. Böckle, J. Gründel, and L. Cornerotte" (pp. 363-364). Where is the pope among these preferred authorities? Should seminarians be taught to be loyal to a counter-Magisterium?

The author grasps at straws of doubtful evidence to erode the Church's clear condemnation of direct abortion.

The assertion that 40-50 percent of "fertilized ova" (early embryos) are lost and naturally expelled (p. 354) is just plain wrong; 8-12 percent is closer to the truth. The author grasps at straws of doubtful evidence to erode the Church's clear condemnation of direct abortion. At any rate, there is clearly a big difference between letting things happen and *making* them happen.

HEROIC MOMS V. FLACCID THEOLOGY

Father Peschke's acceptance of the "mother or child" dilemma is antique. If a doctor wants to save both patients, he can do so in almost every case. The correct answer to the "mother or child" dilemma is, almost always, "If your doctor can't save both of you, find another doctor." As Dr. Hymie Gordon, the famous Mayo Clinic geneticist, has said, "A doctor who kills a preborn baby to save the mother should surrender his license."

When a gynecologist at the central Red Cross Hospital in Tokyo wanted to abort a mother who was bleeding, a head nurse was present who had attended our profamily conferences. She put her foot down and said, "NO!" to the doctor: "We're going to save this baby!" (The baby's father had been at our HLI gatherings, too.) So the doctor prescribed medication and bed rest instead of a child-killing. When the bleeding stopped, the mother returned home. The subsequent birth was routine.

I once held little Akira Saito in my arms and told him to be a good boy. He's blessed to have escaped the gloomy, outdated, and deadly heresy of this "Catholic" textbook. Akira, now in grammar school, can thank God that we at HLI don't use the SVD *Christian Ethics* text at our conferences.

For genuine mother-or-child cases—if such still exist—the book would do well to cite the holy and heroic example that Pope Pius XII related to the audience of the Family Front on 26 November 1951. An expectant mother was told that an abortion was necessary without delay to save her life. She answered, "I thank you for your merciful advice, but I cannot suppress the life of my child! I cannot, I cannot! I feel it already throbbing in my womb; it has the right to live; it comes from God and should know God so as to love and enjoy Him."

She bore the child, but her condition worsened. As her death neared, she once again saw her little child, who was growing healthily under the care of a robust nurse; the mother's lips broke into a sweet smile and she passed away peacefully. The child later became a nun who, remembering her mother, dedicated herself to the care and education of abandoned children. The strength and heroism of

these women stand in vivid contrast to the flaccid theology
of the SVD-sponsored textbook.

DELAYED HOMINIZATION?

The text, pathetically warming an old chestnut, says the
idea of delayed hominization—fourteen days after fertiliza-
tion/conception—"has indeed much in its favor" (p. 355).
"This view has been adopted by Schoonenberg, Donceel,
Gründel, Curran, Häring, Lobo, Postrana." (St. Jerome
chose caustic words for a text glittering with famous
names: "An ugly crow trying to adorn itself in borrowed
plumes.")

The SVD author concludes that "one could not speak of
abortion in the strict sense before the elapse of a period of
about fourteen days. Consequently one could also not simply classify the IUD or those medicaments and pills that
possibly or certainly hinder the fertilized ovum [sic] from
nidation as 'abortive means,' as J. Gründel rightly
observes" (p. 355). This is scientific nonsense, as you know
from other HLI reports, e.g., the testimony of famed
geneticist Dr. Jerome Lejeune that the baby who's alive on
day fourteen was already alive on day one.

The Church teaches that the life of a human being is
inviolable from the beginning: "From the moral view-
point...it is clear that, even if there be some doubt whether
the entity conceived is already a human person, it is an
objectively serious sin to expose oneself to the danger of
committing murder: 'He who will be a human being is
already a human being' [words of Tertullian]" (*Declaration
on Procured Abortion*, no. 13). To do the author justice, he
admits that the *Declaration* "advances that interruption of
a pregnancy even during the first days after fertilization
was nevertheless always considered a grave offense by
Catholic moral teaching" (p. 356).

But then he adds a grossly erroneous statement,
putting into the mouth of the Church the very opposite of
what she proclaimed: Father Peschke says the same
Declaration "admits the possibility that the state may
refrain from legal sanctions in certain instances of interruption of pregnancy." *That is untrue.* Such a statement

absolutely cannot be found in that document. On the contrary, the *Declaration* forbids working for a law that approves abortion in principle.

CONTRACEPTION "NOT GRAVELY SINFUL"

"Artificial contraceptives [sic] are not necessarily gravely sinful," intones the author (p. 476), before he wades through reams of quotes from dissidents who waffle on contraception. In this section, the author concedes the pope 14 lines before awarding about 400 to the dissenters. Such cavalier treatment of official teachings is hardly the way to teach malleable seminarians to honor the Magisterium. Incredibly, Rev. Thomas A. Krosnicki, SVD, director of the Divine Word Missionaries in Techny, Illinois, and other SVDs tell me that the SVDs and their theologians are simon pure.

If the author doesn't approve of contraception, why does he say the following? "Contraceptives which prevent a fertilized ovum [sic] from nidation cannot simply be put on a par with other contraceptives. There is greater reason to avoid them" (p. 356). Greater? May we then allow other contraceptives (*true* contraceptives, perhaps) with *lesser* reason? That conclusion, which seems inescapable, can certainly confuse seminarians.

We look in vain in this text for the in-season and out-of-season teaching of Pope John Paul II against contraception, e.g., "Contraception and sterilization for contraceptive purposes are always gravely illicit" (Caracas, 17 January 1985). And nowhere do we find these words of his:

> It is sometimes reported that a large number of Catholics today do not adhere to the teaching of the Church...notably about sexual and conjugal morality, divorce and remarriage. Some are reported as not accepting the Church's clear position on abortion.... It is sometimes claimed that dissent from the Magisterium is totally compatible with being a good Catholic and poses no obstacle to the reception of the sacraments. This is a grave

error [to the U.S. bishops, Los Angeles, 16
September 1987].

Ignoring this serious warning, the SVD author casually serves seminarians what the Austrian bishops once
said, namely, that people may receive Holy Communion
while contracepting (see below). The Austrian prelates
later withdrew that statement, but this text brazenly continues to use it in the face of the pope's many admonitions.
When the worthy reception of the sacraments and the eternal salvation of souls is in question, we expect moral theologians to be humble enough to teach faithfully what the
Church teaches.

The universal pastor of souls also warned that contraception leads to abortion: "The invitation to contraception...promotes in the last analysis that mentality out of
which abortion arises and from which it is continually
nourished" (to the Austrian bishops, 19 June 1987). The
text fails to teach this warning to seminarians.

***Many priests naively expect that the
next pope will permit contraception.***

A "PEOPLE V. THE POPE"
MAGISTERIUM?

Many priests miss the point that because God's law
against contraception is made in Heaven no pope can
change it. They naively expect that the next pope will
permit contraception. Some priests reach the devilish
conclusion—tragically dangerous for the eternal welfare of
souls—that "what the next pope will allow, we can permit
in anticipation." Father Peschke's text by no means
discourages such dreaming, and Father Krosnicki and
other SVDs defend it.

Page 473 serves up another chapter from the unholy
gospel according to Father Häring:

> Only a couple who act out of egoism in refusing the
> service of life without any reasonable motive can
> be compared with Onan whose sin God punished
> with death (Gen. 38:9f). A great injustice would be
> done to married people who follow the fundamental
> principle of responsible parenthood with the great-
> est generosity, if in their case an interrupted inter-
> course were to be called "onanism." [Read: Just
> find a reason; then it's all right.]

Far better than Father Häring's erring is this passage
from *HV*: "Similarly excluded is every action that, either in
anticipation of the conjugal act or in its accomplishment or
in the development of its natural consequences, would
have as an end or as a means, to render procreation impossible" (*HV*, no. 14).

Father Peschke subtly hints that the law against contraception is now controverted, or even changed, by
popular vote:

> Until recently [!] the use of all artificial means of
> birth control was—supported by the magisterium
> of the popes [as opposed to the "magisterium" of
> the theologians?]—judged gravely sinful. But since
> these means are of rather recent origin, this moral
> doctrine does not look back on a long tradition. The
> encyclical *HV* simply states that they are illicit.
> The number of theologians and bishops rejecting
> the traditional qualification—namely that the use
> of all these means without further distinction is
> gravely sinful—is at any rate very considerable
> today [p. 473].

But truth isn't determined by the ballot. When "Aaron
had let the people get out of control" (Ex. 32:25), God didn't
change the Ten Commandments.

After raising questions about the morality of contraception and then leaving them unsolved, the author moves on
to medical indications. Some contraceptives, he says, are
contraindicated medically. "In principle the sterilizing

drugs should not be taken without previous consultation of a physician. All these factors have to be considered in a moral, psychological and medical evaluation [sic] of the various artificial means" (p. 474). Should both priest *and* doctor be consulted about the use of contraceptives and abortifacients? Has the teaching of moral theology come to this?

Page 474 dredges up the obsolete theory that the Pill may be used to regulate the menstrual cycle, a notion medically disproved long ago. Then the book discusses using the Pill during lactation to supplement nature's tendency to make the mother infertile during this time. The text *should* state: "Doctors advise against using the Pill during lactation for medical reasons, and God forbids contraception during lactation as well as at other times." Nature itself discourages the production of both estrogen and progesterone during lactation. If a mother nurses her baby day and night according to the baby's needs and without the use of supplements, ovulation is suppressed for ten or more months. The Pill's chemicals are somewhat poisonous to the nursing baby.

LET'S SUBVERT *HUMANAE VITAE*

The author continues:

> The encyclical *Humanae Vitae* received a very divided echo and is probably the most controverted encyclical ever written.... Many theologians and lay people are convinced that at least under certain circumstances their use (artificial means of birth control) is not contrary to moral law. They find themselves in conflict with the teaching of the encyclical. How is this conflict to be resolved [p. 475]?

The text proposes, incredibly, consulting the 12 dissenting bishops' conferences (there are 100 conferences worldwide). First comes the Austrian bishops' later-retracted advice:

> The Holy Father does not speak of mortal sin in his

encyclical. If therefore someone should offend against the doctrine of the encyclical, he need not necessarily feel himself separated from God's love and is therefore also allowed to receive Holy Communion without previous confession.... However, if somebody excludes offspring from his marriage for fundamentally egoistic reasons, he cannot consider himself free from grave sin [quoted on p. 476].

The text informs us that the bishops' conferences of Italy, England, Brazil, and Japan followed the same line of teaching (note the collapse of religious practice and family morals in these nations).

Next comes a citation of the French bishops' conference about "choosing the lesser evil in conflicts of duties" (p. 477). On pp. 478-479, the author cites the bishops' conferences of Belgium, Germany, Austria, England, Canada, and Scandinavia on a "right to follow one's conscience if it dissents for weighty reasons." The last line is from the Scandinavian bishops: "In such an instance perhaps [!] no sin is committed which must be confessed or which excludes from Holy Communion" (p. 479). After reading this, will seminarians still support *HV*? (And do the SVDs deserve *your* support?)

Actually, many more bishops' conferences *supported* the pope fully than didn't. Why did the author quote only the wavering responses and omit the supporting ones? What is he trying to teach the seminarians? Father Thomas Krosnicki—you who accused me of false generalization and unsubstantiated accusation—please tell us.

Instead of waving the red flag of dissenters before the seminarians, the author might well have quoted Father Marcellino Zalba, SJ, who gives a balanced picture of the responses of bishops' conferences to *HV*:

The great majority of conferences stated either explicitly or in a manifestly implicit way their total agreement with the Pope. Some also expressed their profound gratitude for the support he gave to their concerns (Latin America and the Third World in general). Others assured the Pope of their firm support and urged the faithful to do so (United States, Mexico, Poland, East Germany, southern Europe). Others were concerned about restraining and remedying the resistance they feared would follow, without, however, calling in doubt the validity of the papal document (Belgium, Austria, Scandinavia, England, Canada). Some were at least ambiguous or confusing on certain points, but without claiming to disagree (France, Austria, Indonesia, South Africa)....

In fact, some conferences (Canada, Australia, Indonesia, Mexico and, at a later date, add Austria) subsequently explained their thinking when faced with mistaken interpretations....

If we look at the number of pastoral letters and of bishops, the group openly declaring that they support the encyclical is by far the larger [M. Zalba, in *Natural Family Planning: Nature's Way—God's Way*, DeRance, Milwaukee, 1980, general editor Anthony Zimmerman; pp. 217-218].

Page 468 argues for artificial birth control in view of "national needs conditioned by limited resources." This is not only a slap in the face of parents of large families in general, it's also contrary to Church doctrine, which approves large and well-ordered families (*Gaudium et Spes*, no. 49). The test here is a falsification of Church teaching, apt to nudge seminarians to agree with Planned Parenthood. Very dangerous!

In the 1970s I lectured at SVD-run San Carlos University in Cebu City in the Philippines. I was told beforehand that there was a PP unit functioning on campus. I discovered it. I cannot get assurance from SVD superiors that it has been shut down.

WHAT THE S.V.D.'S MUST DO

The generalate of the Society of the Divine Word has no choice but to suppress Father Peschke's book in its present form. And it has an obligation to minimize scandal. In 1985 the Vatican compelled the society to withdraw a pro-contraception booklet printed in Japan under SVD sponsorship. But the society didn't do much to correct the scandal, which continues to trouble undecided confreres and to corrode family morals in Japan. The SVD leadership may in fact be divided on the issue of contraception. At its last general chapter, for example, the generalate and delegates opposed abortion but were silent on contraception.

The Society of the Divine Word must suppress Father Pesche's book in its present form.

The scandal induced by the 28,800 copies of Father Peschke's book must be enormous. To undo the scandal at least partially, and to show seminarians that the society condemns contraception as the Church does, a symbolic "book burning" of all remaining copies is in order.

AFTER THE BOOK BURNING

HLI has contacts with moral theologians and specialists in almost every field of concern to students studying moral theology. We'll offer the hand of friendship and cooperation to Father Peschke and the SVDs to negotiate a joint venture to produce a revised issue of *Christian Ethics* if and when the present problems with the text are cleared away.

At least until this cleanup is certain, *please give no contributions to the SVDs.* Never waste your God-given money on bishops, priests, and religious who, in disobeying the Vicar of Christ, mutilate Catholic truth. If and when the SVDs withdraw or correct Father Peschke's book, HLI will inform you and then will give a substantial gift to their 57-country missionary work. Meanwhile, we shall continue to support orthodox individual SVD missionaries with our prolife materials.

Letters

Your *Report No. 95* went directly to the heart of the Catholic problem that has caused me so much grief and anger over these years of fighting for true Catholicism.

Now that you have taken on that corrupting legion of theologicans, I feel much safer in this Catholic world! Your masterful job of "putting down" those intellectual traitors is a great piece of work.

> *Perry Walsh*
> *Sacramento, California*

I just came across an issue of your *HLI Reports*. What a fund of information and inspiration! The work your organization does in terms of action and education is amazing.

When I read the encyclical *Humanae Vitae* for the first time in 1988 (twenty years after the fact), I realized how beautiful and true the teaching is, and I became convinced, after years of wandering, that the Catholic Church teaches God's word "in season and out."

And now I am in the seminary, studying for the priesthood for the Archdiocese of New York. We have begun a prolife committee here at St. John Neumann and already have had Msgr. William Smith lecture on the Catholic conscience and the presidential election.

> *Brian Caulfield*
> *Bronx, New York*

I'm applying for entrance into the seminary of the San Bernadino diocese and am going through interviews, recommendations, and college-entrance applications.

HLI has had a large impact on my decision to enter the seminary. I hope to be a strong voice in the future of the Church in exposing the crime of abortion and the reality that contraception is against what the pope and the Church teach.

May God bless you for all you've done to enlighten our feeble minds, and may your reward in Heaven be as great as your sacrifice on earth.

Joseph Borba
Upland, California

Dr. Lawrence Adekoya leads 35 HLI chapters in Nigeria

Nigerians need development; IPPF offers them sterility

Down Under and a Little Over

No. 96   December 1992

At the invitation of our two branches in Australia, the Australian Catholic Pro-Life Association and Endeavour Forum (a prolife, antifeminist women's group), I spoke two or three times daily for nine days in October, in every major city except Perth.

In August 1971 I'd given thirty-one talks in Australia to counter the legalization of abortion. The State of South Australia had passed the country's first law allowing abortion. After addressing a medical meeting in New Zealand in 1976, I did another lecture tour Down Under. Australia is surely the most USA-like foreign country I've visited, and it's truly a fascinating place.

Did you know Australia has more kangaroos than people? That destructive animal (the kangaroo!) comes in all sizes; in rural areas, cars have "bull bumpers" to lessen damage from collisions with kangaroos. The loveable koala bear isn't a bear but, like the kangaroo, a marsupial.

WOMBATS AND DINGOS

Also unique to Australia are the gentle, furry, bearlike wombat (another marsupial), the dingo (a wild dog), the Tasmanian devil (a raccoonlike marsupial), the emu (a large, flightless bird), and the barking and frilled lizards. So is the platypus, which incorporates the features of four animals in one. Pious Australians say the Lord had leftovers and so He created the platypus. Less pious Aussies say He got confused and made a mistake when He created this strange animal.

Captain Cook discovered this continent Down Under in 1770; the first settlers, mostly English and Irish prisoners, came in 1788. Australia is the driest continent on earth, being two-thirds desert and only 9 percent arable. Almost the size of the continental USA, Australia numbers just 17.1 million people and is one of the most urbanized nations on earth.

Modern Australia is a mixture of nationalities: aborigines (1.5 percent), English, Scots, Italians, Greeks, Germans, Latin Americans, Vietnamese, and others, with the Irish being the largest single group. Strict racial policies excluded oriental immigrants until 1973. In 1991-92, there were 107,291 immigrants.

Just north of this island continent lie the 13,500 islands of Indonesia. The largest Moslem country in the world (190 million people), Indonesia is an ominous, potential enemy. Already the oil-rich Indonesians have swallowed Catholic East Timor, killing at least 100,000 people.

Practically everything grows in Australia, including bananas, coffee, and citrus fruit; it's a very self-sufficient continent. Unfortunately, the country has found only a limited market for its abundant wheat, barley, oats, corn, beef, lamb, wool (30 percent of the world's output), sugar, fruit, nuts, steel, and other products. Totally sufficient in natural gas, Australia does import some oil.

The Aussies boast a per-capita income of more than $15,000, but almost 12 percent are unemployed. The nation and the Church have suffered from decades of socialist government. After WWII, the Communists infested the unions, but they've been contained since then.

TROUBLED CHURCHES

In 1986 the Catholics (26 percent) surpassed the Anglicans (24 percent) in numbers; the latter arrived first but now are in decline, beset with debates over women priests and with some clergy sex-assault cases. The Uniting Church ranks third. The rest of the country is made up of many Protestant groups, with Mormons and fundamentalists arriving lately. A serious shortage of priests afflicts virtually all thirty-one Catholic dioceses; the median age of priests is almost sixty.

Informed Australians told me that, unlike the USA, their country lacks strong Protestant denominations. As early as 1974, the Australian Presbyterian Church ordained women. When the Uniting Church emerged in

1977, many of the female Presbyterian ministers joined it, along with about half of the congregations.

On Sunday, 28 September 1992, the 700-member synod of the 1-2-million-strong Uniting Church shocked Australia when it supported legalized abortion-on-demand. The disuniting Uniting Church has become an amorphous amalgam of Methodists, Presbyterians, and Congregationalists.

Earlier this year, Anglican Bishop Owen Dowling of the Diocese of Canberra-Goulburn was charged with male sexual solicitation. His plan to ordain women was litigated in a New South Wales court. Bishop Dowling expects to ordain twelve priestesses around Christmas.

The three Catholic major seminaries in Sydney, Melbourne, and Adelaide are virtually empty.

The three Catholic major seminaries in Sydney, Melbourne, and Adelaide are virtually empty. Corpus Christi Seminary in Melbourne canceled my talk because the co-sponsoring Endeavour Forum opposes women priests. Sydney's archdiocesan St. Patrick's Seminary in Manly has only twenty major seminarians and only two applicants for the coming year. The seminary is rumored to be closing and moving to one of the campuses of the Australian Catholic University, a collection of mostly undistinguished former Catholic teachers' colleges. St. Paul's National Seminary in Sydney has a number of late vocations, students studying theology, and some seminarians from the various dioceses.

TWO SHEPHERDS STAND FIRM

Because the theology taught in the major seminaries is questionable, 52-year-old Bishop William Brennan of the small Diocese of Wagga Wagga sold the bishop's mansion and this year built his own seminary, Vianney College. Vianney has seven seminarians, room for ten, and twenty applicants for the next school year. Bishop Brennan will soon have to enlarge the seminary, which is Australia's hope.

Bishop Brennan underwent fierce persecution, both locally and nationwide. One Australian bishop called the new seminary "a medieval adventure." I spoke to the seminarians and was much impressed. Bishop Brennan has also taken great steps toward working up an impressive, orthodox catechetical program, so lacking in other parts of Australia. Sadly, we didn't meet. No bishop impressed me more than Perth's Archbishop Barry Hickey, who tells it the way it is. He pickets the abortionists with his people.

Another new seminary in Melbourne, named Christ the Priest, was started by a farseeing Redemptorist, Father John Whiting. In 1954 he founded a religious order known as the Confraternity of Christ the Priest. Because it's orthodox, the seminary is flourishing with vocations. Outstanding Catholic lay people told me again and again that Australia's seminaries were so poor intellectually and so radical theologically that they feared for the future of the Church in Australia.

In this country, general absolution goes unchecked; liturgical directives and canon law are often ignored; contraceptive education is taught in "Catholic" schools; altars and statues are destroyed at the whim of pastors; and priests are free to openly contradict Church teaching on the ordination of women. It galls faithful Catholics that their money goes to sponsor what they call "Church Wrecks."

Archbishop Leonard Faulkner of Adelaide has gone overboard with "inclusive language" in the Mass. He even tried to change the wording of the Creed but had to back off because of opposition, particularly from Archbishop Frank Little of Melbourne. Hundreds of Catholics picketed Archbishop Faulkner, holding several prayer vigils for him.

Reportedly, he acquired his mania for "inclusive language" while on retreat in Canada last year. When Catholics United for the Faith wrote to his priests for support, he resented it deeply. The archbishop, say his faithful, is too much impressed with feminists. His leadership against and resistance to abortion has been little more than tokenism, although he *has* prayed before an abortion mill.

In Brisbane's *Sunday Mail*, auxiliary Bishop James Cuskelly boldly predicted that the growing involvement of the laity in parish administration was preparing

Queensland for a time when a future pope would approve the ordination of women or married men. The bishops of Queensland moved to formalize feminist power with a new position right at the top: women's advisor to the archbishop.

The Movement for the Ordination of Catholic Women began in 1983. Their bible is *Changing Women, Changing Church*, which rejects (among much else) God the Father. The Sisters of Mercy and the Brown Josephite Sisters seem the most confused. Lecture tours by American feminist theologians such as Monika Hellweg and the lesbian Mary Hunt have added fuel to the fire. The ousted Dominican Father Matthew Fox is scheduled to return to Sydney next year for a second round of mischief-making.

IF YOU THINK IT'S BAD HERE...

While I was in Australia, a clergy conference in Sydney dealt with environmentalism. Every abuse that plagues the Catholic Church in the USA also plagues the Church in Australia—only worse. However, in speaking to two meetings of the Confraternity of Catholic Priests in separate cities, I was impressed. Infected by radical feminism, Australian nuns have abandoned the schools to do "pastoral" work; they're dying out fast—"the sooner the better," commented a good pastor. The Brown Josephites of Victoria and New South Wales actually asked the bishops to let them anoint the sick and hear confessions!

The state pays 45 percent of Catholic school-building costs and teachers' salaries. The diocesan central office, usually in the hands of liberal, dissenting lay people with little orthodox clergy supervision, runs the school system; local pastors have virtually nothing to say. For example, Sydney's central education office recommended condoms as a way to avoid AIDS. The infiltration of New Age philosophy, "values clarification," and "nondirective counseling" in Catholic schools is perhaps even worse than in the USA.

Because of state support, about one-third of all Catholic students attend "Catholic" schools, now taught mostly by lay people since the nuns went off to do "meaningful" work and live in apartments. The decimated

Christian Brothers still run six "Catholic" high schools in Sydney, with mostly lay faculties. A gathering of eighty students from these schools reacted well to my talk on chastity.

Militant homosexuals aren't as loud as in the USA. But the Labour government has decided to force the armed services to accept homosexuals. Last June, Dennis Stevenson, MP, observed, "Figures from Interpol show that Australia has the fourth highest rate of sex offenses in the world" (the USA is twenty-fifth).

Drug use, alcoholism, prostitution, and pornography are huge problems Down Under. Among fifteen-year-olds, suicide is the chief cause of death. Biological/physical sex education, involving little Catholic doctrine and more likely to promote fornication than chastity, is rampant. Drs. Lyn and John Billings and Dr. Kevin Hume of natural family planning (NFP) fame have come up with a good alternative Catholic program, now used in some schools but resisted in others. I've never heard more complaints from good Catholics about immoral teachers in the schools. Nor have I heard more complaints about priests, in any country. Sunday Mass attendance ranges from 21 to 25 percent.

Several lay people told me the Church should do more to educate everyone in basic morality, especially in chastity.

Several lay people told me the Church should do more to educate everyone in basic morality, especially in chastity—a rare virtue, as Australia's teen pregnancies and dangerously low birthrates indicate. About ten lay people told me they'd never heard a priest preach on contraception and sterilization, which are pervasive.

Australia does support one of the world's finest Catholic magazines, *A.D. 2000*, edited by the great layman and newspaper columnist, Robert Santamaria. Also, Father B. J. H. Tierney has done impressive, pioneering catechetical work, although with much opposition. Sadly, Australia "leads" the world in *In Vitro Fertilization* (IVF) research and "success." And its divorce rate is like the USA's: one out of three; every year, divorce semi-orphans 150,000 children.

EMPTY COUNTRY, EMPTY CRADLE

In 1969 the State of South Australia deprived preborn children of most legal protection. In the following years, failure to legalize abortion through the legislatures led corrupt judges in the other five states to "interpret" the law, thus imposing abortion-on-demand throughout Australia. Token legal protection for babies evaporated, as happens always and everywhere. As in the USA, every third preborn child is killed, an estimated 80,000 annually.

The number of births per completed family is 1.9, slightly above that of the USA. The Pill, the IUD, Depo-Provera (all abortifacients), and sterilization are the main means of birth control, besides abortion. Norplant hasn't arrived yet. Current studies reveal dire consequences from Australia's nonreplacement birthrate. The country has a good NFP program, but the bishops promote it so little that few people practice NFP.

The Australian hierarchy came out at first with a somewhat equivocal statement on *Humanae Vitae*, and then with a much better one. The bishops have spoken out against abortion now and then, but none more than Archbishop Hickey. However, they exhibit the usual inability to engender bold, effective prolife programs. The prolifers' latest goal is passage of Alastair Webster's reintroduced Abortion Funding Abolition Bill.

Archbishop Little of Melbourne, the city of four seasons in one day, has invited Milwaukee's rebel Benedictine Archbishop Rembert Weakland to lecture to his priests and faithful next year. Confronted with a large file of documentation on Archbishop Weakland's abuses, Archbishop Little said Weakland would talk only on music and liturgy! Some years ago, Archbishop Little involved himself in a doctrinally unsound statement on euthanasia. While I was in Australia, the State of South Australia was discussing a seemingly innocent, palliative euthanasia bill.

Australia has a variety of prolife groups. They're divided and beset, in part, by personality conflicts. Perhaps the best group overall is the Australian Catholic Pro-Life Association, led by Bede McDougall and Gail Instance and founded in 1986. They take a total approach to the whole antilife problem, work with everyone, and distribute our HLI materials far and wide. Allied with them is Endeavour Forum, led by the tireless Babette Francis, an international authority on radical feminism, which her group opposes intelligently.

Pray for Australia, her prolifers and her Church!

NEWS FROM NEW ZEALAND

After Australia, I made my third visit to the most beautiful country in the world, New Zealand; there I spent a busy three days.

This nation of 3.4 million people lives on two large islands, each about 500 miles long and separated by thirty miles of water, with small Stewart Island at the bottom. In 1642 the Dutchman Abel Tasman stumbled upon New Zealand. In 1769 Captain Cook rediscovered the islands, but it was only on his second voyage that he charted the whole.

A few English settlers came in the early 1800s. General settlement by the English began after the Treaty of Waitingi, which England made with the indigenous Maori in 1840. The Maori are a dark-brown-skinned Polynesian people, generously tattooed. At one time they were cannibals. Once almost extinct, today they make up 10 percent of the population, about 300,000 souls. The New Zealanders are 73 percent Caucasian, 10 percent Maori, 4 percent other Polynesian, and 13 percent Indian, Vietnamese, or other nationalities. If the Aussies seem very American, the Kiwis are much more British.

The country's economy is largely agricultural, with some manufacturing. Tourism is the second source of income. New Zealand is known for its wool, meat, dairy products, livestock, and wood products. The kanoi trees of the Waipona Forest are thirty-six feet in circumference and are more than 1,000 years old. The country has count-less deer and seventy million sheep, twenty-four for every human.

The per-capita income is $8,390. The government has succeeded in reducing inflation from 18 percent to 1 per-cent in five years, but 12 percent of the people are unem-ployed. Because of emigration and a low birthrate, there was actually a small decrease in the population last year.

THE VASECTOMY CAPITAL OF THE WORLD

The birthrate stands at eighteen per thousand. The average family size is just under two children, and therefore nonreplacement, although it's one of the highest in the Western world. The Pill and the IUD are used widely, as is sterilization; New Zealand reports the highest number of vasectomies per capita in the world, according to the infamous Family Planning Association (Planned Parenthood). Earlier, the country held the record for Pill use. Twenty-three percent of all married men had been neutered by 1986. Today, the number is thought to be about 30 percent, and a huge number of women have

---

New Zealand reports the highest number of vasectomies per capita in the world.

---

undergone tubal ligations.

On Christmas Day, 1977, abortion became legal *via* court "interpretation" of the law. Today, New Zealand has virtual abortion-on-demand. I recall testifying against legalized abortion with Dr. Jerome Lejeune in 1976.

In 1991, New Zealanders aborted 11,590 babies, for a ratio of one baby killed for every five born (the U.S. ratio is one for every three). In 97 percent of the cases, the medical reason given for the abortion was "serious danger to men-tal health." Psychiatric services must be rather poor in New Zealand! Seventy-nine percent of the abortions are performed on the babies of unmarried women. The abortifacient Depo-Provera injection seems to be widely used. Norplant hasn't arrived yet. Just as I was leaving, New Zealanders (with good episcopal cooperation) were planning a massive life chain to take place soon.

Catholics, mostly Irish, make up 15 percent of the nation, with Anglicans (20 percent) predominating; 16 percent are Presbyterian, 8 percent Methodist, and 1 percent Jewish. Mass attendance has fallen steadily and now hovers around 22 percent.

Rare is the priest who preaches against contraception and sterilization. Biological, "organ recital" sex education has invaded the schools. Two years ago, the Catholic school system, abandoned by the vanishing nuns, was absorbed into the public school system after much haggling; the government agreed to pay teachers' salaries.

According to Auckland's diocesan paper *Towards Tomorrow* (September 1992), Mercy Sister Aileen Martin teaches the occult Enneagram at the Mercy Spiritual Life Centre in Auckland: "This psycho-spiritual tool enables growth in understanding self, others and God; there will be presented an opportunity for one to journey towards self-discovery." When nuns lose their faith, they often end up with a substitute pseudo-psychologism, or worse.

FIGHTING AIDS THROUGH SODOMY

"Homophobia" and a new menace, "heterosexism," are hot topics at various meetings involving nuns who've deserted their classrooms to do "pastoral" work in various self-chosen "ministries." The national Catholic Women's League proposed offering money to the AIDS Foundation, which pushes "safe sex" via condom. Hypocritically, the AIDS Foundation promotes homosexuality! A certain Father Michael Bancroft works with the "gays." He played an active role in the national Gay Christian Conference, which decried "homophobia" and preached loudly about being "compassionate," being "nonjudgmental," and "practicing unconditional love."

As in other countries, the bishops, overall, seem unduly influenced by radical feminists. Pedophilia has surfaced among the priests, who are in short supply.

Priestesses and married clergy are discussed openly. In fact, Dunedin received the second female Anglican bishop months ago, with much feminist fanfare and wide acclaim from rebel Catholics. Bishop Basil Meeking of Christchurch seems to be the most orthodox of the bishops. Good Catholic lay people complain much about their shepherds' lack of leadership in serious matters. The bishops' National Justice, Peace, and Development Commission gave $30,000 for the study of "sexism" in 1989; like the U.S. bishops, they seem to have been taken in by battalions of wild feminists. The title of the report, "Made in God's Image," appeared in 1991; the document, written mostly by a certain Christian Cheyne, provided little substance. The bishops then put out a second report featuring their theological reflections. This didn't set well with thinking Catholics.

Thanks to a former cardinal who cultivated and educated New Zealand's doctors in ethics, the country has one of the world's best-organized Catholic doctor groups. Known as the Guild of St. Luke, SS. Cosmas and Damian, the organization sponsors frequent and impressive medical meetings emphasizing medical ethics and new developments. The theme of this year's gathering is "The Care of the Dying." Among New Zealand's great, pioneer prolife Catholic doctors have been the retired author Pat Dunn and the internationally active John Bergin.

In short, New Zealand is more conservative both politically and religiously than Australia, the USA, and most of the West. But New Zealand's Catholic Church suffers from all of the problems that afflict the Church in the Western world today. Parents assured me that their children no longer learn their faith in "Catholic" schools. Home schooling hasn't caught on yet.

Marvelous Catholics asked me what they could do to move their priests and bishops to greater leadership and orthodoxy. I told them that U.S. Catholics were years ahead of them: Yanks don't believe they were baptized to financially support bishops and priests who don't teach the whole truth. This information pleased some and stunned others.

Stunned, too, were some fifty priests from the Diocese of Auckland and their bishop, for whom I described the worldwide sex/abortion mess. New Zealand has a number of prolife groups. At a public meeting, we launched a new branch of HLI under the able leadership of Colleen Bayer, leader of the Company of Peace, a budding lay-religious community in Auckland.

Because of a visa mix-up in Washington, I missed a scheduled day of rest on arriving in Australia. After thirty-five hours with no sleep, I charged immediately into a nine-day lecture tour, speaking two or three times daily. Never was I interviewed more by radio, TV, and newspapers. I came back jetlagged and exhausted. But now I'm ready for my postponed mission journey to Russia.

Pray for New Zealand, her prolifers and her Church!

Letters

Thank you for sending me a copy of your latest book, *The Apostle of Life*. Cetainly the Holy Father was right in giving you this title. I do not think that anyone has worked harder in our country and across the world to promote the prolife cause than you have.
 Please keep up your fine work.

> *The Most Rev. Daniel E. Sheehan*
> *Archbishop of Omaha*
> *Nebraska*

Today a friend of mine loaned me a copy of your book *The Apostle of Life*. My wife and I were not familiar with HLI, and we are very excited to see this book in print. We should like to have many more copies of this book for some of our friends and family who claim to be both anti-abortion and pro-choice.

> *Eric Michael Woolhiser*
> *Billerica, Massachusetts*

I think the John Paul II Fellowship Program deserves enthusiastic support. Please keep up the good work. Requesting your prayers, I wish you and all your co-workers God's abundant blessing.

> *The Most Rev. Francis Arinze*
> *Cardinal*
> *Vatican City*

European prolife leaders meet in Croatia

With Fr. Anthony Zimmerman, SVD, and Kinji Nishimura, inventor of the L-Sophia fertility awareness device

Planned Barrenhood at work in Nigeria

With Irish leader John Little

Fr. Matthew helps to form the next generation of prolifers (Philippines)

Alfonso Cardinal Lopez Trujillo
brings the Vatican's blessings to
HLI's World Conference
(Houston)

HLI's generous family gave
$15,000 to "the world's greatest
beggar," Fr. van Straaten,
in Houston

Magaly Llaguno, the Cuban-born dynamo who heads HLI's huge Latin
American outreach

The Legacy of Communism in Poland and Belarus

No. 97   January 1993

Because **Ireland, Poland,** and the republics of the former Soviet Union have become the latest targets of the baby-killers and family-destroyers, I spent several weeks in these countries recently—in Poland and Belarus first (October 5-19), then in Ireland (October 22-November 2), and again in Poland (November 26-30).

I don't remember how many mission journeys I've made to Ireland. These were my third and fourth trips to Poland, and my second trip to Belarus, formerly ruled by the USSR.

COMMUNISM'S LEGACY: 20 MILLION DEAD BABIES

The enemies of life and family are always the same: feminists, Freemasons, Communists, secular humanists, and the ubiquitous International Planned Parenthood Federation (IPPF).

In Poland, IPPF operates through its affiliate, the Polish Family Planning Association (PFPA). The PFPA, already active in the 1950s, is little known to the Poles even today, although Mikolay Kozakiewicz, the first premier of post-Communist Poland, was president of PFPA from 1960 to 1980. PFPA publishes a sophisticated monthly magazine, *Developing the Family*, and has infiltrated Polish society and the media with little opposition. HLI is now publishing Polish-language exposés of that wicked organization, which is funded by foreign money.

In WWII the Soviet and Nazi invaders killed six million Poles. During the German occupation, the Nazis performed forced abortions on Polish mothers so that their pregnancies wouldn't interfere with their slave labor. Thus was this Catholic country introduced to massive abortion. Poland's Red regime legitimized baby-killing in 1956.

Since then, the Poles have killed twenty million preborn babies.

Poland is unique in that married women obtain the most abortions. It's estimated that 40 percent of women thirty-five and over have aborted at least one child. These women suffer in silence; postabortion counseling is just beginning.

You can see the importance of having laws that protect preborn children when you examine the sad situation in Poland, one of the world's most staunchly Catholic nations. Despite two great cardinals, Stefan Wyszynski and Karol Wojtyla (now Pope John Paul II), a loyal hierarchy, abundant priests and religious, and many Catholic institutions, many Polish babies die through abortion—at least 500,000 in 1991 alone, according to one bishop.

After forty years of baby-killing and antilife "medical" training, few gynecologists are prolife today (this situation is now changing among young doctors).

Today the climate for baby-killing has definitely changed, and the number of abortions is declining sharply. Bishops, the pope, and an active prolife movement, organized into a national prolife federation last June, have helped bring about this decline. Today, abortions are performed in doctors' private offices, often after hours, or only at certain clinics. I'm happy to report that of all the foreign prolife groups, HLI was the first to enter Poland. None has contributed more videos, films, audiocassettes, literature, money, and know-how, thanks to our friends' unfailing generosity.

Ingeniously, the bishops turned the parishes into centers of Catholic education and catechizing.

PUBLIC SCHOOL KIDS NOW HAVE A PRAYER

The Communists, of course, destroyed or took over all Catholic institutions except parish churches. Ingeniously, the bishops turned the parishes into centers of Catholic education and catechizing, with every priest teaching religion twenty hours each week. Thus did the Church survive—aided by prayers, tears, and the blood of martyrs.

In 1990, religion classes for all denominations returned to the public schools, authorized by law. Students in all grades may take classes on religions other than Catholicism, take no lessons on religion, or take ethics instead. Parochial and other private schools are gradually reopening.

In 1991 the bishops snuffed out a bad sex-ed course—sweetly called "Preparation for Family Life"—foisted on them earlier by the Reds. When Catholics and others complain about the Church's "undue" influence on education today, the bishops remind them that the Church stood by them through the worst times.

Another toxic by-product of Communism is divorce: one out of five couples divorce (in the USA, it's four out of ten). Easy divorce and alcoholism produce many single-parent families. Still, Poland reports the lowest divorce rate in Eastern Europe. Since 1984 there's been a constant decline in marriages and births, but deaths have increased. Poland also has one of Europe's highest infant-mortality rates, 19 per 1,000 (v. the USA's 11). There's comparatively little VD or drug abuse (people can't afford drugs) but much alcoholism in this nation of forty million. There are 1.5 million confirmed alcoholics and some 5 million abusers.

MATERIALISM: THE NEW SLAVERY

Several pastors told me that many brides are already pregnant at marriage. They blamed it on pornographic TV, the biological sex education, the influx of dirty films and videos from the wealthy West—and the general secularization of society, including the invasion of Freemasons, humanists, and the common, false idea of freedom as license to do anything, now that people are suddenly free from Red oppression. Early on, the pope warned the Poles against shedding one form of atheism under Communism only to embrace another—the godless, hedonistic consumerism of the capitalistic West.

I saw sex shops and plenty of pornography. The Polish edition of *Playboy*, printed in Austria, hit the newsstands last November with a print run of 100,000 copies; it sold out in two days. The editors predict that within a year they'll be selling 200,000 copies every month. *Penthouse* appeared two years ago.

Since the political upheaval of 1989, lawmakers have made various attempts in Parliament to curb or outlaw abortion. The baby-killers—former Communists who now call themselves radical socialists, and new leftists—know they cannot get abortion-on-demand legalized, and so they're using the old tactic of promoting exceptions for "hard cases," and even a national referendum. Polls show that a proabortion referendum could succeed. The alert bishops have rightly fought the idea, reminding people that morality isn't decided by vote. President Lech Walesa said he wouldn't tolerate a referendum. The prolifers have only a small majority in Parliament.

Now in Parliament is a bill to outlaw abortions. It would punish the abortionist with two years in jail—ten if the woman dies. Sadly, the Sejm (lower house) has riddled the bill with loopholes. I met twice with members of the Sejm. In many news conferences and talks I exposed the real enemy, IPPF, and its feminist hangers-on.

Last February, the USA's "Catholics for a Free Choice" (CFFC) gave Poland's radical feminists ("feminazis"!) $15,000; IPPF gave even more. When the Communists lost control in 1989, they gave a large sum to the feminists. These possessed women went house to house, gathering signatures for a referendum on the prolife bill; they claim to have gathered more than a million signatures. Last February, CFFC trained them in a four-day workshop. The feminists told housewives that the government and the Church want to punish them, a lie also spread by the pro-abort and viciously anti-Church media, which "former" Reds still control.

Meanwhile, shelters for lonely, abandoned women and Birthright-type centers are springing up; in fact, I sat in on a spirited, three-hour session with fourteen counselors (mostly women) at Czestochowa to describe what prolifers do in other countries. I answered endless questions.

In May 1991 the Polish Medical Association revised the medical ethics code to permit baby-killing only in cases of rape and danger to the physical life of the mother, after preliminary counseling; a doctor who kills indiscriminately can lose his license. The new code has put some doctors in a dilemma, what with the old law's freely permitting abortion and their professional association's condemning it.

CONTRACEPTIVE IMPERIALISM AT WORK

Last January the well-heeled radical feminists launched *Society*, a sophisticated, bimonthly magazine subtitled *Bulletin of Member Organizations*. They receive financial and other help from the abortion-and-euthanasia favoring European Economic Community. Others taught them how to proceed legally; how to use polls, the media, and naive Catholics; how to oppose the Church; etc.

Meanwhile, it's astonishing that the Poles hardly know who IPPF and its cohorts are—even though the antilifers have been subverting Polish society for some twenty-five years. The pro-aborts get plenty of money from foreign proabortion organizations. The latter, of course, are funded by U.S. nonprofits such as the Packard Foundation (Hewlett-Packard computers) and the Rockefeller Foundation.

Unfortunately, the bishops control none of the TV channels, have no access to TV, and have no national Catholic newspaper or radio network, although there are Catholic radio stations in several dioceses. The Polish bishops asked their U.S. counterparts for $7 million to build a media network to refute the lies of the enemy; the Americans have yet to pay the $500,000 they promised. The Polish prelates will, however, launch their own news agency by the end of this year. Poland's youngest ordinary, Bishop Jozef Zycinski of Tarnow, is in charge of the project. When the Reds were still in the saddle, the people rejected media propaganda, knowing from whom it came; today they fall for it easily.

The impoverished bishops have done well in fighting

the abortion monster, goaded on by the eloquent pleas of the pope during his third visit to Poland. A Bishop Bronislaw Dabrowski, head of the Polish hierarchy, assured me that the bishops value HLI's international experience and our materials, provided, as always, by our benefactors.

"DON'T IMITATE THE U.S.A."

We have received an invitation to found a prolife center in Lodz; this centrally located base would serve not only Poland but also the whole Eastern world. Lacking financing, we've tentatively decided to shore up our branches in Katowice, Poznan, and Gdansk more and more. HLI has a chance to do cheap printing in Poznan. Now is the crucial time!

I gave more than fifteen talks to prolife groups, parishes, etc. (I also did a TV program.) People responded eagerly, asking many questions. It was a joy to speak twice to the 3,000 students of the Pontifical Catholic University in Lublin, where the pope once taught moral philosophy.

In these talks and meetings, we described our U.S. and global experience. Too many Polish Catholics say, "I am a Catholic, but..." or "I am against abortion, but..." (sound familiar?). Many support exceptions, naively thinking these concessions will hold the line against massive abortion.

The bishops of Poland like HLI's total approach of dealing with every problem from contraception to euthanasia.

In talks to many groups in various cities, I emphasized the folly of such thinking, judging from Western experience. Thanks be to God, the bishops of Poland, unlike those of Louisiana and unlike the National Right to Life Committee, see the inconsistency and the dangers of allowing "a little" killing (the so-called incremental approach). And they like HLI's total approach of dealing with every problem from contraception to euthanasia.

Like some of the Irish, many Poles foolishly think Poland must become "modern," "progressive," and "European" by embracing (among other things) a Western European-style abortion law. I told both groups to be proud of being Polish or Irish and Catholic. I told them that the Germans, Americans, and others who call them "backward" and "medieval" are dying out. The "progressive" West is full of VD and AIDS, enslaved by contraception, pornography, prostitution, and abortion, misled by rebel theologians and plagued by divorce and other family-destroying ills.

HOW HEALTHY A CHURCH?

Poland's forty million people include thirty-six million Catholics, more than 60 percent of whom attend Mass weekly. The percentage is declining, though, because of the influx of Western secularism. During the Communist era, people flocked to the churches to stand up to the enemy. At every daily Mass I saw more than 200 people, often singing beautifully to an elegant organ accompaniment. They receive Holy Communion on the tongue, there are no liturgical aberrations in the "spirit of Vatican II," and you see no "girl altar boys."

Poland has forty dioceses, each with its own seminary. Recently the pope created thirteen new dioceses; all plan to establish their own seminaries. The Poles have some 24,000 priests and three times that number of nuns, all in habit. The nation ordains more than 1,000 priests annually and sends out 200 missionaries every year; today, it's the only major source of missionaries in the West. Also, a growing number of Polish priests and religious now work in the former USSR. Poland's beautiful, huge new churches are impressive. This country is frightfully important to the Church right now, and we must do all we can to help her bishops and the prolife federation. Meanwhile, the incoming sects are now joining two million other Protestants, mostly Lutherans.

Thanks to Krakow's Cardinal Karol Wojtyla (now Pope John Paul II), Poland may offer the best marriage-preparation course of any country; six of its twelve sessions are taught by priests and the rest by other professionals. Almost every parish has a marriage-counseling center. These centers emphasize natural family planning (NFP), condemn contraception and sterilization, and present a positive theology of marriage inspired by Cardinal Wojtyla. An estimated 15-20 percent of Polish Catholics practice NFP, compared with 3-5 percent in the USA. NFP literature abounds.

The main contraceptive method is probably *coitus interruptus*; an estimated 3 percent of all Poles use the Pill; more use suppositories. The diaphragm, the cervical cap, and the new "female condom" are also available. There's little sterilization, as of now. Direct advertising of contraceptives is illegal, but druggists must sell them. Norplant and RU-486 haven't invaded yet. Condoms "to prevent AIDS" can be obtained everywhere. At 2.05 children per family, Poland has the highest birthrate in Eastern Europe, although it's not at replacement level. Homosexuals are somewhat active but less conspicuous than in the USA. There are some 2,000 known cases of AIDS, but the real incidence may be much higher.

Poland is far ahead of other former Communist countries in political and economic recovery.

POLAND STRUGGLES TO REFORM

Unfortunately, too many Communists still occupy high places in government, business, and society, having ensured their positions before the anti-Red upheaval of 1989; naturally, they appoint their fellow Bolsheviks wherever they can. There are twenty-nine political parties, the Red-dominated party being the largest, claiming 11 percent of Parliament. A coalition of the Christian National Party and the Democratic Union form the government. The highly competent premier is Hanna Suchocka, the Polish "Iron Lady" and a prolife Catholic.

Poland is far ahead of other former Communist countries in political and economic recovery, although it has a long way to go. Production and exports are up, but living standards are still declining, unemployment is 13.5 percent, and inflation is still 40 percent. The average salary of a professor or a general is only one-seventh that of a Western company's junior executive; businessmen told me virtually every contract with a Western company involves much bribery. Even so, Poland is on track this year to become the first ex-Red country to record annual economic growth.

Driving through the countryside, you see primitive farming methods alongside modern equipment. Horse-drawn carts are a common sight on the highways. Agriculture has recovered the most, because the Communists were never able to deprive farmers of private ownership. Foreign companies are helping bring Poland from a centrally planned economy to one of free enterprise. Shops are filled everywhere, but prices are high. As the saying goes, the shops may be full, but the goods have to be paid for at inflated Western prices by people on Eastern wages. Those living on pensions are severely pressed.

One thing seems certain: the healthily stubborn Catholic Poles will succeed as no other ex-Red nation, thanks to their pride, their good bishops, their many vocations, their national suffering through the centuries, and Our Lady of Czestochowa. They need and deserve your prayers.

PROLIFE PRIESTS FOR BELARUS (WHITE RUSSIA)

Bishop Alexander Kaszkewicz of Grodno invited HLI to do a seminar on the weekend of October 16-18. Dr. Antun Lisec and Bernice Kowalik accompanied me. We were astonished to see how Grodno's twenty-four seminarians had grown to eighty-two since Father Matthew Habiger and I spoke there two years ago. The bishop told us he'd turned away several qualified seminarians for lack of room. What a tragedy! Some 400,000 of the 10.2 million citizens of Belarus are Catholics, many Polish in background.

Three-quarters of the Catholics live in the Diocese of Grodno, which has 800,000 people. There are three dioceses. Grodno has 140 parishes but only sixty-seven priests—half of whom are Polish missionaries and the other half old survivors who were often beaten up in Red jails. There are eighty-two nuns and a remnant of staunch, once severely persecuted lay people. The faithful occupied Grodno's huge, ancient rococo cathedral day and night for forty years to prevent the Communists from closing it! How's that for a rescue?!

The seminary, now being repaired somewhat, is in terrible condition; six long-suffering seminarians occupy each room, with no desks and no drawers. The young priests were impressive. We did a weekend seminar in a neighboring public hall. Enthusiastic, responsive crowds attended, including the genuinely pious seminarians.

There are now five seminaries in the former USSR—one in Latvia, two in Lithuania, one in Belarus, and the biggest in Ukraine, with 350 seminarians; in Ukraine, the bishop had to turn away fifty qualified young men for lack of room. Father Werenfried van Straaten's great organization, Aid to the Church in Need, is building a seminary for 400 in Lviv, where we're founding a branch. Bishop Kaszkewicz was delighted to have HLI coming to his diocese, especially because he wants to build a family center.

Our opportunities in the former USSR are truly mind-boggling. If only we had more money!

Seven different institutions work out of Grodno's huge old monastery, of which the diocese owns only a third (the government has the rest). Catholics hope to get more of the building back under their control. With their great young bishop, the Catholic people work together as well as they can with what little they have. Sadly, the abortionists kill one-third of all preborn children in Belarus, and the birthrate is at a nonreplacement level.

Croatia's unbelievable Dr. Antun Lisec, who gave up

surgery to work full-time for HLI, also spoke on prolife themes in three huge hospitals in Belarus and saved several babies by counseling their mothers. Our opportunities in the former USSR are truly mind-boggling. If only we had more money...!

ANTILIFE "MISSIONARIES" INVADE

Dr. Igor Guzov, an educator, flew in from Moscow to talk with me about founding an HLI branch there; with him was a woman prolife apostle. I was appalled when they told me IPPF has been in Russia for years, although it was formally organized only recently. IPPF is designing "health" programs for all the newly free republics and is shaping the curricula for student obstetricians and gynecologists in the medical schools and institutes. Just as here, IPPF is always in the media, promoting sex ed, contraception, sterilization, and abortion.

Moscow TV airs programs teaching schoolchildren how to use contraceptives and abortifacients. One program shows a beautiful home in Holland with well-dressed parents and one or two children; the caption says this pleasant, luxurious life is possible only with contraception, sterilization, "good" sex ed, and abortion. Always, the pitch is: if Russia wants to recover and to enjoy affluent living like the West, it must realize zero population growth. (Never mind that the country already has *negative* population "growth.")

Dr. Guzov and his friend stressed that from adolescence to menopause, the typical Russian woman undergoes five to ten abortions. Another mind-boggling statistic: 60 percent of Russian hospitals have no running water.

Pointing out that Russia already has vast empty areas, Dr. Guzov warned of a bleak future if IPPF succeeds. Because of the present political and socioeconomic chaos, even the Moslem birthrate in the six Islamic republics is low, although it's markedly higher than that of the other republics.

From another authentic source we learned that more than two years ago the UN's World Health Organization (WHO) and IPPF met in Tbilisi, the capital of then-Soviet

Georgia, to plan the systematic distribution of contraceptives and abortifacients, backed up by sterilization and abortion, and to prepare for immoral sex ed.

Meanwhile, doctors from Columbia Medical School in New York are already in Russia, training medical students and doctors to perform sterilizations and "menstrual extractions," i.e., early suction abortions. Dr. Guzov and his colleague, converts to the Orthodox Church, begged for all possible help.

According to Dr. Guzov, European Russia officially kills 3.5 million preborn babies annually, but he believes the true figure is twice that. Women often become sterile or sick because of repeated abortions. The killing and suffering stagger the imagination.

H.L.I. COUNTERATTACKS

We left Dr. Lisec behind to lecture in Russian medical schools and hospitals and to take the first steps toward founding HLI branches in the various republics, in Ukraine first of all. Dr. Lisec and I found so many needs and opportunities that we plan to spend a month in Russia and the other republics next summer. I promised Dr. Guzov that HLI would sponsor a mini-conference in Moscow as soon as we can raise the money. Dr. Lisec just sent me a small avalanche of addresses of interested doctors, lawyers, professors, priests, heads of medical schools, etc.

Chaotic socioeconomic conditions only lead to more and more abortions. Meanwhile, sex shops and the rawest pornography have moved in from the West; even children sell smut on the streets. Because the people don't know their enemy, HLI will launch a program to teach the citizens of Russia, Ukraine, Belarus, and other countries about the evil plans and insidious machinations of IPPF and to educate them for a better day.

Translated into Ukrainian, Russian, etc., our little best-sellers—*This We Believe* and *A Practical Guide for the Sacrament of Penance in the 1990's*—are just what people need, along with basic prolife/profamily literature. Labor costs for translaters, printers, and other workers are only a fraction of what we pay in the West; in Russia, the average wage is $10-15 per month! Imagine what $1,000 would do for the prolife cause! Please pray for our efforts. We're now sending as much literature and as many videos as we can afford, while preparing basic items in local languages. Dr. Lisec found endless opportunities to speak to medical staffs in huge hospitals.

Letters

I continue to be impressed at the depth and extent of your knowledge as reflected in your special reports. The information about Australia (No. 96) and Poland (No. 97) was tremendous. The media seldom present us with such a range of information and—as with AIDS—they continue to try to hide the facts.

Now, with the new president, I expect that we will be sinking into the morass of humanism at an accelerated rate. I won't dwell on all the new evils that continue to penetrate our belief.

It is difficult to find words that give a true picture of the range of your good works. I wish you all the best—you are going to need all the energy you can summon, especially in view of the Clinton election. It looks as though people are getting just what they asked for, but little did they fathom the implications.

> *Lee A. Blaske, PhD*
> *Center for Planning and Evaluation*
> *St. Cloud, Minnesota*

I write to you with the hope that you'll help me in the cause of the struggle with abortion. I learned recently that you, Father, are a great member of the Catholic Church and are waging a great struggle with this devilish business of killing unborn children.

As a member of our Ukrainan Catholic Church and a first-year seminary student, I want to dedicate myself to this very important affair and hope that you'll help me in it. You'll help not only me but those Ukrainians that care about the future of our Ukrainian nation.

I hope we can join each other, all our forces, against this evil, against these ominous forces.

> *Ivan Gnativ*
> *Ukraine*

ABC's Lynn Sher interviews a prolife apostle for "20/20" (1992)

A warehouse raid by future priests from Mount St. Mary's Seminary,
Emmitsburg, Maryland

*Defending freedom of religion: Fr. Marx and Sr. Lucille Durocher
meet the media outside an Ottawa courthouse*

*"Film at 11:00!" HLI's lawyer, Angela Costigan, defends our right
to pray in public (Ottawa)*

Steel Drums and Elastic Bishops

No. 98   February 1993

L ast November 12-15, HLI sponsored a highly successful mini-conference in Port-of-Spain, Trinidad, in collaboration with the Antilles bishops' conference. The international faculty of ten experts drew some 600 participants from thirteen Caribbean countries. On Saturday an almost completely self-organized youth conference listened to three talks and then swelled to 6,000 as it marched to a park to pray and to sing prolife/prochastity songs, with music composed mostly by the young people. We were impressed and thrilled!

On opening night, Port-of-Spain's dynamic Archbishop Anthony Pantin concelebrated Mass with the papal nuncio, six bishops, and forty priests (yours truly preached). Afterward, 1,900 people gave witness to their faith in a candlelight procession marked by much evidence that the Trinidadians love to sing.

During Columbus's fourth voyage to the Americas in 1498, his sailors were ready to mutiny because they hadn't found land. The explorer promised he'd name the first land sighted "Sanctissima Trinitas." Today, this unusually scenic country has a population of 1.3 million living on two islands, Trinidad (1,980 square miles, the size of Delaware) and Tobago (116 square miles).

AMAZING TRINIDAD

The nation boasts an unusual mixture of races—49 percent African, 40 percent East Indian, and 14 percent mixed—and religions—32 percent Catholic, 29 percent Protestant, 25 percent Hindu, and 6 percent Moslem.

The country is just seven miles from Venezuela at the nearest point. The first rulers were the Spaniards. During the French Revolution, many refugees settled here. Later, many Indians and Hindus were brought in as indentured laborers, with families intact. Many Africans came as slaves, their families disrupted. Portuguese, Chinese, and others came, too, including the first of what are today 70,000 Moslems. Britain took over in 1802. In 1834 slavery ended. Trinidad and Tobago became an independent parliamentary democracy in 1962.

Trinidad invented the steel drum, played wonderfully to the calypso beat in local music and songs at the closing Mass.

Trinidad invented the steel drum, played wonderfully to the calypso beat in local music and songs at the closing Mass that the archbishop offered—an experience we'll never forget. The Trinidadians love celebrations so much that the Hindus and Moslems celebrate Christmas and Easter! Every October there's a national Moslem holiday.

Trinidad is not Latin American but English-speaking and USA-oriented. Seven million people, including two million Catholics, live on the twenty-three island-nations of the Caribbean. Trinidad is the wealthiest.

INSIDE TRINIDAD'S CHURCH

More than 100 priests, many from foreign countries, care for the spiritual needs of some 400,000 Catholics. There are more than 200 nuns, mostly in habit. Vocations are few. Some years ago, because of Masonic intrigue, the government took over all Catholic schools. Religion is still taught for one hour a week, but good Catholics claim that children don't learn their faith. Church leaders cannot hire, fire, or decide the curriculum; only sometimes does the government hear their complaints.

Pope Pius XII asked the archbishop of Port-of-Spain to build a regional seminary. It has room for forty future priests; Father Matthew and I addressed the mere fifteen seminarians who actually are there. The school's library is loaded with questionable theological books such as those written by the non-Catholic theologian Father Charles Curran. This situation is common in developing countries, and it's why HLI ships orthodox theology books to seminaries around the world.

For years I've corresponded with the likeable Archbishop Pantin. He's as healthily ecumenical as can be, and he enjoys the finest relations with the media I've ever seen in any country. (As he told me, "They can make you or break you.") For six years he's sent delegates to our world conferences; this practice explains, in part, the huge success of our three-day mini-conference in Port-of-Spain.

Trinidad's industries include oil products, cement, rum, and tourism (the latter mainly on Tobago, because the island of Trinidad has always shied away from the corruption of tourism). The chief crops are sugar, cocoa, coffee, citrus fruits, and bananas. Pitch Lake, one of the wonders of the world, is the source of the finest asphalt on earth. Sadly, some 20 percent of the people are jobless. Meanwhile, the archbishop and other authorities believe Trinidad could support three to four million people if properly organized.

ATTEMPTING NATIONAL SUICIDE

Since 1960 the government has committed itself to reducing population growth. The usual foreign money is at work, mostly handled through the government health department and the Family Planning Association of Trinidad and Tobago (FPATT), whose centers perform most of the abortions.

The antilife National Population Council appeared in 1967; in 1986 the national "family planning" program, typically, was taken over by the newly formed Ministry of Health, Welfare and the Status of Women. The usual propaganda linked population and community development, in order to hide massive distribution of birth-control paraphernalia, including the subtle promotion of abortion. The UN's World Health Organization (WHO) has called Trinidad's abortion law "broad" because it allows babykilling for the mother's physical or mental health. Through this loophole the "doctors" refer mothers to FPATT's two urban killing chambers.

The gynecological department of almost every large hospital maintains a unit that completes abortions started by quacks and others. Nurses told me the hospitals some-times finish as many as fifteen baby-killings in one day.

Strangely, even educated Trinidadians think abortion is illegal! We disabused them of this idea with the facts; Catholic leaders told us Trinidad will never be the same. By the way, sterilization is illegal, but it's often performed on women, with spousal consent.

Archbishop Pantin guessed there were 15,000 abor-tions yearly; some doctors estimate 30,000-40,000 and oth-ers, still more. We hope the likeable Trinidadians will heed our advice and start picketing the abortuaries and the abortionists.

Thirty-three percent of the people of this young, rather happy nation are under thirty-three. Forty percent of the babies are illegitimate, with many common-law marriages, many single-parent families, and much divorce. Fifty-eight percent of couples use contraceptives. The infant mortality rate is high, 24 per 1,000 (*vs.* 11 in the USA). The reported birthrate is 27 per 1,000, with six babies dying, for a natu-ral increase of 2.1 percent, but we found conflicting figures. Emigration is high. Three percent are illiterate. Trinidad supports one university with three campuses. The nation suffers its share of drug problems, alcoholism, and AIDS, and endures a bad distribution of income.

HLI has known for a long time that the International Planned Parenthood Federation (IPPF) has invaded the Caribbean nations full force. IPPF's affiliate, the Family Planning Association, is very active. We exposed their sin-ister, secret work via many radio and TV appearances and, as much as possible, in the reluctant press. Their leader, Emile Elias, refused to debate me on TV. A TV program presented during our last evening was completely rigged against us.

Please pray for Trinidad, her babies, and her prolifers.

BISHOPS LET CATHOLICS ELECT "BLOODY BILL" AND "GORY AL"

The election of Bill Clinton and Al Gore was an unmiti-gated, total disaster: millions more preborn babies will die in the developing countries, not to mention our own. The

Reagan and Bush administrations denied tax dollars to "birth control" groups that performed abortion overseas, but now these depopulation imperialists will get millions of your tax dollars to kill preborn children. The USA supplies an estimated 40 percent of all depopulation funding worldwide.

My friend Virgil Blum, SJ, used to call U.S. Catholics—especially the bishops—"political pygmies."

My friend Virgil Blum, SJ, the founder of the Catholic League for Religious and Civil Rights, used to say U.S. Catholics were "political pygmies" despite their large numbers, today 55 million. I once asked him whether his term applied to the bishops, too. "Especially them," he answered. I thought of that during the 1992 election campaign, which our shepherds virtually "sat out." Few bishops gave their flocks moral guidelines for voting, and one rebuked a good pastor for saying it was a mortal sin to vote for abortion-promoting candidates. (Send $1 to HLI for Pastor D. James Kennedy's most insightful article, "The Separation of Church and State," that explains how the Irreligious Left has systematically destroyed our religious liberties.)

Yet the Church never had more at stake in any election. Archbishop Daniel Pilarczyk of Cincinnati, then president of the U.S. hierarchy, said the policies of the past were quite sufficient. Oh? A few years ago, in true seamless-garment fashion, one bishop cited fourteen issues for voters to consider, of which mass baby-killing was only one!

Monsignor Eugene V. Clark, the great pastor of New York City's St. Agnes' Church, told his parishioners via his parish bulletin:

> In the United States hardly anyone practices the separation of church and state to their disadvantage, except Catholics. Baptist ministers rally

Baptists to place them in public office. Jewish communities, wisely, demand Jewish cultural courses in local schools. WASPs vote against sharing tax revenues with Catholics in education. And thousands of churches and temples are sounding boards for the right to choose abortion. In all these places, political opponents are named for their opposition.

Both Bush and Clinton politicked in Protestant churches. Clinton flaunted his victory two Sundays after the election when he attended Sunday Mass in Little Rock; to rub it in more deeply, he received Holy Communion. Pro-abort Jesse Jackson preached!

UNCERTAIN TRUMPETS

To 1,700 Catholic parishioners in Florida, I preached, "I have never discussed politics in the pulpit in forty-five years of priesthood, and I won't start here. But if not a hair falls from your head without God's knowing it, then surely no vote for a proabortion politician will go unrecorded—and you will be answerable." Did I tell anyone specifically how to vote? No! After Mass, many thanked me profusely. No one objected. Why didn't our bishops say something like this?

They could have quoted from Pope Paul VI's *Declaration on Procured Abortion* of 1974: "It must...be clearly understood that a Christian can never conform to a law which is in itself immoral, and such is the case of a law which would admit in principle the liceity [legitimacy] of abortion. Nor can a Christian take part in a propaganda campaign in favor of such a law, or vote for it...[No. 22]."

The bishops of Dublin and two other Irish bishops told the media they wouldn't vote for last fall's proabortion referendum. This swung the vote. Why couldn't our bishops, as citizens, have told the people that in conscience they couldn't vote for Clinton, and have given them the reasons?

Our timid bishops—there are exceptions, of course—harbor an almost obsessive fear of losing their tax exemption (the Protestants don't), even though years ago the federal courts ruled that the Church's political activities were legal. Unlike bishops of the past, people tell me constantly, many bishops today are afraid of "bad publicity," of a hostile reaction if they teach an unpopular truth. But as Cardinal Joseph Ratzinger has said, "It is necessary for bishops to risk being unpopular because of the truth. In the deepest sense of the word, the evangelist must also be a martyr."

> *The bishops of the twelve most "Catholic" states must ask themselves why their people chose as president a baby killer, a fetal experimenter, a promoter of homosexuality, an adulterer.*

The bishops of the twelve most "Catholic" states must ask themselves why their people chose as president a baby killer, a fetal experimenter, a promoter of homosexuality, an adulterer. Perhaps here we see starkly what Cardinal Ratzinger has called "a catastrophic collapse of modern catechesis." Most Catholics voted for Clinton or another pro-abort, Perot. May God forgive us all.

PAGANIZED CATHOLICS

If this election proved one thing, it proved that the USA and the whole dying Western world have fallen into a new paganism. Ours really is worse than the old paganism, because global television makes every home a potential strip show instead of a little church (ecclesiola). In a culture of death, self-indulgence, and instant gratification, heathens usually consider only materialistic issues. So most "Catholics" based their votes on material, monetary concerns, not on grave moral issues such as abortion, homosexuality, and fetal cannibalization.

Sunk in a sex-sick culture, shallow Catholics, like their pagan fellow citizens, don't realize that a healthy socioeconomic life is impossible without a healthy, well-ordered, sex-controlled family life. Remember, 90 percent of our affluent, fertile Catholics have been sterilized or use abortifacients or contraceptives and, therefore, are (objectively) sexually immoral.

Our teenagers fornicate as never before, VD and AIDS are out of control, abortionists kill one out of three babies, one out of four births is illegitimate, 2.5 million couples are "shacked up," and single-parent families are mushrooming in record numbers. Why? We can blame the Pill, pornography, and a dozen other evils, but I lay much of the blame for the sexual anarchy of the Western world at the feet of the theologians who dissent to *Humanae Vitae* and the bishops who let them teach false sexual doctrine. As Cardinal Ratzinger observes, "In many parts of the world, theologians have taken the place of bishops as teachers, engendering insecurity and disorientation [among the faithful]."

The new *Catechism of the Catholic Church* thoroughly explains orthodox teaching on sexual morality, condemning contraception, sterilization, and abortion as grave sins. Will our theologians, bishops, priests, and religious obey, teach, and preach accordingly? Don't bet on it. And don't share their guilt by supporting them financially.

Many Catholics kill their preborn children and don't even know it, because virtually no bishops, priests, religious, or Catholic doctors have warned them about the abortifacient nature of Pills, IUDs, the morning-after Pill (widely used on college campuses), and now Norplant and Depo-Provera.

DISLOYAL THEOLOGIANS

St. Paul once defined lust as idol worship. Sex has become a god in the West. Make no mistake, we live in a pagan country, in a time of total crisis. We can no longer follow or trust many (most?) bishops, priests, religious, or "Catholic" teachers.

Was there ever a time when we had more proof that the Church has always been right about sexual morality? Why don't wild, rebel theologians such as Notre Dame's Father Richard McBrien, Father Richard McCormick, and scores of others in high places see what happens when people abandon the perennial Christian morality proclaimed anew in *Humanae Vitae*?

Indeed, God always forgives, men sometimes forgive, but nature never forgives. As Prof. Etienne Gilson used to observe, "The natural law has a way of burying its undertakers." The McBriens, the McCormicks, the Currans, and the other theologians who have discarded the natural moral law are being swept into the dustbin of history.

DID CARDINAL MAHONY VOTE FOR CLINTON?

The election results plunged grassroots prolifers everywhere into a gloom verging on despair; one young woman in the Los Angeles area wept for two days.

But her bishop, Cardinal Roger Mahony, was upbeat. "Now that the... elections are behind us, there is a sense of hope," he rejoiced in his newspaper. "The voters hope that promises made in the political platforms will be fulfilled" (*The Tidings*, 27 November 1992). His column made not one mention of the millions of additional babies about to receive the death sentence from Clinton here and abroad, but it did say "we care for the earth" (the cardinal's column of December 11 informed Catholics that "environmental healing is also a life issue").

These signals were especially disturbing, coming as they did from this new chairman of the U.S. bishops' pro-life committee. But even more alarming were his remarks on January 22, the anniversary of *Roe*.

Addressing throngs of emotionally battered prolifers at the March for Life in Washington, the cardinal said that he was pleased that Clinton had quoted Gal. 6:9 and that we should take that verse as a motto! Just as inexplicable was the prelate's statement, quoted by the Associated Press the next day, that "none of the federal [baby protection] policies reversed today restricted a single abortion"!

"NOT THE ONLY ISSUE"?

But these remarks should come as no surprise. Before last year's primary elections, Cardinal Mahony told his pastors and parishioners that abortion is "not the only issue facing the people" (*The Tidings*, 17 April 1992). Can you imagine a Russian bishop of the '30s, a German bishop of the '40s, a Chinese bishop of the '50s, or a Cambodian bishop of the '70s saying, Sure, millions of innocent human beings are being put to death all around us, but that's not the only issue? And Clinton is even worse than Stalin, Hitler, and Mao, in that those other butchers hid their crimes while he makes ceremonies of his.

> ***Everyone knows the only possible reason for saying abortion is "not the only issue" is to give people the green light to vote for pro-aborts.***

Everyone knows the only possible reason for saying abortion is "not the only issue" is to give people the green light to vote for pro-aborts. That is why, two weeks before the fall election, the cardinal's newspaper ran an insulting, un-Christian editorial attacking Operation Rescue founder Randall Terry for saying it was a sin to vote for Clinton.

The Tidings editorial told Catholics to "consider 'all issues'" and to vote their "individual conscience[s]." The proabortion, anti-Catholic *Los Angeles Times* was so pleased with this advice that it reprinted it for its 3.4 million readers on the eve of the election.

The editorial worked. Exit polls showed that 71 percent of California Catholics voted for pro-abort presidential candidates, and most also voted for rabid pro-aborts Dianne Feinstein and Barbara Boxer for the U.S. Senate. Evangelical Protestants voted prolife two to one.

Judging from his record, the world's Catholics can expect little from the new prolife chairman in terms of efforts to actually outlaw abortion or close the abortion mills. When then-Archbishop Mahony headed the California bishops' prolife committee, their spokesman, Father William Wood, SJ, said their major efforts would be in education and social action because outlawing abortion "doesn't seem to affect people's behavior" (*The Tidings*, 3 November 1989)!

The Vatican displays no such fear of confrontation. It immediately blasted Clinton for embarking on "the paths of death and violence against innocent human beings." The Holy See knows Clinton has dealt a severe blow to babies, not only in the USA but also in Poland, Ireland, Africa, and Latin America, the hottest fronts in the global battle for life.

WHAT THE BISHOPS COULD DO

If the bishops really believe abortion is the killing of millions of innocent human beings in our midst, they'll make abortion a top priority, tell voters they must vote prolife, refuse to be seen with any Clinton administration figures, lead huge marches on our capitals, make heroes of rescuers and visit the prisoners of conscience, protest the persecution of prolifers, make massive efforts to help unwed mothers, get the sex-ed out of their schools, teach their young people chastity, kick the radical feminists out of their bureaucracies, heavily promote the Fatima message, and resolve to close their local abortion mills through peaceful rosary vigils and Eucharistic devotion (there are some 4,000 killing centers in the USA—13 per bishop).

The one good thing the election did was to put the responsibility for saving babies and mothers back in the laps of the bishops. The White House, the Congress, and the Court are lost causes for now. But any bishop can close his abortuaries through the awesome spiritual power he commands.

In the Diocese of Brooklyn, for example, rosary/ Eucharistic vigils have closed eleven mills, driven baby-killing out of several hospitals, saved a thousand babies, and produced several priestly and religious vocations—all without a single arrest (contact Msgr. Philip Reilly, the Monastery of the Precious Blood, 5300 Fort Hamilton Pkwy., Brooklyn, NY 11219, 718-853-2789).

Abortion came in when the rosary and Eucharistic devotion went out. May Cardinal Mahony persuade all of his fellow shepherds to lead their people in these devotions until they exorcise the abortion demon from our beloved country!

Letters

No. 98 correctly summarizes the cowardly actions of the U.S. bishops (as a group) during the recent election. What does it take to "build a fire" under these cowardly churchmen?

Harry Oakley
Holstein, Iowa

I recently spoke to His Eminence, Cardinal Roger Mahony, only to find myself treated not like one of his flock but rather like a wolf!

I commended him on his efforts to alert his diocese about the Freedom of Choice Act. However, when I mentioned *Humanae Vitae* he was most rude. He told me to read the bishops' last pastoral (?) about this topic. I don't know what he's talking about! He very quickly brushed me aside, just as though I were some troublemaker.

It's not surprising any more to distrust your average clergyman. I just can't understand why a cardinal would be so uncooperative with well-meaning people.

Thank you for tackling this problem. Now, if only more priests and bishops would follow suit!

Fernando Cavuto
Rancho Palos Verdes, California

I hope to put some thoughts on paper relative to the world conference at Houston. I wanted to let the euphoria wane, for I thought Houston was one of the greatest experiences in my life. It excites me just thinking back on it. Houston was a masterpiece which, if it could be painted, would belong on the ceiling of St. Peter's in Rome!

I think of HLI as family—you have a wonderful staff.

Hope you're hitting on all eight cylinders!

Richard T. Healy
Hancock, New Hampshire

It is fitting that I write on the feast of St. Gregory VIII, who was a true son of St. Benedict and a fighter. You can take comfort in the fact that he was exiled for his trouble and also in the fact that your patron was beaten, stoned, imprisoned, and finally beheaded—the last fate being one your enemies would rejoice in!

Father James Downey, OSB
Institute on Religious Life
Ann Arbor, Michigan

Thank you for the Houston conference. It was the most spiritually and intellectually satisfying experience that I have had in recent years. You are indeed an Apostle of Life, and I pray that God will continue to bless us through you.

When we packed our seven children into our old van, I was optimistic about the conference. Well, my optimism has been replaced by enthusiastic and rekindled idealism. If I were given to regrets, it would only be to regret that I have not been to any of your previous events.

Vincent M. Polis
Lancaster, California

Let me express my deepest gratitude to you for what has been up to now the most important week in my seven years of priesthood. The week in Houston was an unqualified blessing for me, and I pray that it will be just as great a blessing for those whom God has called me to serve!

I have never before had the privilege of listening to so many excellent lectures in one week! I have never before had the pleasure of meeting so many genuinely good people in one place! I've seldom encountered such deep Christian generosity at one time! It is no exaggeration to say that I experienced at a vital stage of its development the Kingdom of God for which we pray daily. Thank you most cordially, and if I can make it I will certainly be in Irvine, California, next year with (I hope) good news about the struggle in Barbados, where Planned Parenthood has firmly entrenched itself with its murderous policies.

Your latest book, *The Apostle of Life*, is a gem. May God give you the health and strength to continue to be the outstanding apostle that Mary has made you.

Father Leonard Alfonso
Barbados, West Indies

Canada's Queen leads 1,200 praying HLI supporters to Parliament Hill (Ottawa)

"…and bless, Holy Mary, the land of our birth" (Ottawa)

Abortion holocaust survivors: Iyamille and Maggie Munoz, Kristen Pulliam-Campbell, Nathan Post, (Fr. Marx and Theresa Bell), Joshua Vandervelden, Sharon and Mike Post, Gianna Jessen

"Defenders of women's rights" in the Netherlands

Words Less Than Divine

No. 99 March 1993

F**ather Thomas A. Krosnicki,** spokesman at the Chicago Province headquarters of the Society of the Divine Word (SVD) has written a three-page "Response to Human Life International" (write me for a copy if you wish to see it), trying to refute our exposé of the SVD moral theologian Father Karl Peschke, author of the dissent-riddled seminary text *Christian Ethics.* The "Response" is a sad, futile attempt to do the impossible, despite the anxious help of Father Superior General Henry Barlage in Rome; Father Krosnicki refutes *none* of our observations. (Please reread our exposé in *Report No. 95.*)

CAN CATHOLICS TRUST AN *IMPRIMATUR* TODAY?

For example, he says, "Father Peschke has duly obtained the required *imprimatur* for each edition and translation of his work, *Christian Ethics.*" Is Father Krosnicki so unschooled in the present state of theology as to think that *imprimaturs* sanate (cure) the errors of books in which they appear? Philip S. Keane's *Sexual Morality* was published with an *imprimatur* from Raymond Hunthausen, then Archbishop of Seattle. Did that sanate the errors until the Holy See ordered Archbishop Hunthausen to remove the *imprimatur*?

Another example: Archbishop Peter Gerety of Newark gave the *imprimatur* to Paulist (and now ex-priest) Father Anthony Wilhelm's *Christ among Us*, which contained a total dissent to *Humanae Vitae* (*HV*). After 168,000 copies were sold, the Holy See ordered Archbishop Gerety to withdraw his *imprimatur*, whereupon some theologically fuzzy Paulist gave the book to a secular publisher for further distribution!

Is Father Krosnicki suggesting that *Christ among Us*, which was used widely in convert instructions, where it misled many, was correct until the *imprimatur* was withdrawn? Perhaps Krosnicki's professional training should have been in logic instead of in liturgy.

Then there are Father Charles Curran's books, published mostly by "Catholic" publishers, which contained seven major moral errors. He taught these seven errors for eighteen years at the Catholic University of America, a pontifical university owned and controlled by the bishops of the USA, until the Holy See finally declared him unfit to teach Catholic theology. Would Krosnicki claim that because his publishers were mostly "Catholic" and his teachings had the approval of the bishops, Father Curran always taught and wrote Catholic truth?

Father Charles Curran taught seven major moral errors for eighteen years at the Catholic University of America.

Father Krosnicki argues, "At NO time was Father Peschke's book condemned by the proper and competent Church authorities." Neither were Father Curran's books for eighteen (!) years, or many other error-poisoned theological works.

Krosnicki asserts that Peschke "has discussed his work with Cardinal Ratzinger...." Is Krosnicki suggesting that Cardinal Ratzinger would approve of Peschke's dissent to *HV*, or of the other errors we pointed out?

Illogically, Krosnicki goes on: "At NO time was an order ever given by the competent Roman authorities which prohibited the printing, distribution, or use of Father Peschke's book in Catholic educational institutions or major seminaries." I could list more than ten bad theology books used in "Catholic educational institutions or major seminaries" that the Holy See hasn't condemned, but surely that doesn't make them correct!

A POPE WARNS AGAINST *IMPRIMATURED* DISSENT

At a time of deep crisis in the Church, should Catholics trust an *imprimatur*? We find our answer in Pope St. Pius

X's encyclical, *Pascendi Dominici Gregis (On the Doctrines of the Modernists)* of 1907, in which he warned the bishops:

> Nor are you to be deterred by the fact that a book has obtained elsewhere the permission which is commonly called the *Imprimatur*, both because this may be merely simulated, and because it may have been granted through carelessness or too much indulgence or excessive trust placed in the author, which last has perhaps sometimes happened in the religious orders [No. 51].

In *Pascendi*, the pope warned the Lord's flock about the many "enemies of the Cross of Christ who, by arts entirely new and full of deceit, are striving to destroy the vital energy of the Church" (No. 1).

"Partisans of error," the saint called them, and they lurk in "the very bosom" of the Church. He found "Modernists" not only among the laity, but even among "the ranks of the priesthood itself." He characterized them as "animated by a false zeal for the Church," "thoroughly imbued with the poisonous doctrines taught by the enemies of the Church," and "lost to all sense of modesty," having "put themselves forward as reformers of the Church" (No. 2).

"There is no part of Catholic truth which they [the Modernists] leave untouched, none that they do not strive to corrupt," His Holiness observed (No. 3). Although the Holy See does try to remove writings of this kind, he said, as if living today, "Their number has grown to such an extent that it is hardly possible to subject them all to censure." (If this situation prevailed in 1907, imagine what it is today!) As a result, "the remedy arrives too late, for the disease has taken root during the delay" (No. 51).

Father Krosnicki argues that Father Peschke "taught moral theology at the Urbanianum, a Pontifical University in Rome, for six years (1984-1991). He was not dismissed from that position." A colleague wrote to the rector, Cardinal Jozef Tomko, who is also prefect of the Sacred Congregation for the Evangelization of Peoples, to ask about Peschke's position at the school. Cardinal Tomko quickly replied that Peschke no longer taught there. Why not?

I suggest that Father Krosnicki submit to Cardinal Tomko the serious theological errors I pointed out in Father Peschke's book (especially his dissent to *HV*) and ask him for a reply. The answer, I think, would be very interesting. Let Krosnicki ask also why Peschke didn't continue to teach theology at the Urbanianum. Perhaps Krosnicki can also tell us the details of Peschke's reported summons to the Vatican several years ago over what he wrote in Volume II.

Monsignor Gerhard Fittkau, a well-known, orthodox German theologian who read *Report No. 95*, comments, "The disastrous book of Peschke is indeed well known to me. I had already protested against it at several places in Rome, where it is even being used as obligatory reading at some of the pontifical faculties" (I have documentation). We trust that because of his protests and our exposé, other pontifical universities will finally discard Father Peschke's book.

From verifiable sources I've learned that SVD officials were warned about the heresies in Peschke's two volumes as early as 1975.

"HÄRING'S ERRINGS" SURFACE IN S.V.D. TEXT

No theologian has blasted *Humanae Vitae* around the world more than the Redemptorist Father Bernard Häring. He's known as the father of dissent to *HV* and as the guru of the contraceptive movement within the Church. People say that through his seminars he spoiled a continent every summer. Yet he wasn't dismissed from the Alfonsianum! Were/are Father Häring's errors, therefore, acceptable?

I could mention at least ten others who teach at pontifical universities in Rome (such as the former Jesuit professor Josef Fuchs at the Gregorianum), and many more who teach at "Catholic" universities throughout the world, who taught or teach theology not fully Catholic.

In a sophisticated German theological review, *Theologie der Gegenwart*, Häring, who isn't a scientist, wrote pseudoscientific but scary nonsense asserting that natural family planning (NFP) produced miscarriages and defective babies. This assertion misled many German priests, who read mostly German theological literature. Later, with some modification for the USA, the Jesuits' *Theological Studies* published the piece also.

Häring had not a shred of valid scientific evidence, as international scientists confirmed at a global seminar on NFP that I held at St. John's University in Minnesota in the '70s. I'd invited Häring to defend his thesis in the presence of world-famous scientists, even offering to pay his way. He refused to come. I then floated an international news release, written mostly by renowned scientists, refuting Häring. Peschke, however, is still impressed with Häring.

Consider part of the foreword to Father Peschke's first volume of *Christian Ethics*, published by C. Goodlife Neale, Alcester and Dublin, 1975, with an *imprimatur* dated 1973. Note how much he was influenced by the heretical Father Häring:

> Not least, this book owes its publication to the interest, encouragement and support of several good friends and advisors. First of all, the author wishes to thank most sincerely Professor B. Häring, CSSR, who took the pains to evaluate parts of the manuscript and who appreciated it for its biblical orientation and solid, constructive exposition. Prof. Häring is certainly the authority from whom the author *has learned most and from whose writings and ideas he has profited very much* [my emphasis].

For years I've heard about the questionable theology at Nemi, the SVD formation house outside of Rome. I know that a high Vatican official observed some time ago that the teaching at Nemi was notoriously out of line with the Church's teaching. The rebel Father Häring, mentor of the dissident Father Charles Curran, taught his many standard errors there—dissent to *HV*, Holy Communion for divorced and remarried Catholics, fornication for couples who are truly committed, etc.

Father Krosnicki should read Father Häring's heretical "Law and Gospel" in the dissident London *Tablet* (9 January 1993), in which he defiantly writes, "The oath of fidelity must be taken by all those called to function 'in the name of the Church.' I would not be able to swear this oath, nor would I in conscience be able as a bishop to request it of others." Three cancer operations have taught this Redemptorist nothing. The orthodox and incisive Auxiliary Bishop John R. Sheets, SJ, of Fort Wayne-South Bend wrote of him:

> He has no metaphysical depth. There is little or no evidence in his writing of knowledge of Catholic tradition. There is little sense of the cost of discipleship of Christian morality. Through the principles of his moral theology Häring has been one of the major figures in the formation of what can be called today the "para-Church," or the "super-Church." Some call it the Smorgasbord Church. It is a Church which sees dissent as an equally valid way of belonging as assent. It is a Church made up of those who claim a magisterial authority which is above and against that of the Magisterium as we traditionally know it [*Homiletic and Pastoral Review*, November 1992].

And if you think Bishop Sheets or I exaggerate, read Häring's articles in the German SVD family magazine *Stadt Gottes* and in the Italian *Famiglia Cristiana*, published by priests of the Society of St. Paul.

ERROR AND MORE ERROR

We know of other theological deviations and errors promoted at Nemi. One Redemptorist theologian who taught there and exercised a big voice in the curriculum once said that if he were to teach his students that contraception is an intrinsic evil and a grave matter, they'd lose all confidence in him and in the pope (I have the documentation). People often ask us why priests and bishops don't preach against contraception. Well, one big reason is the more than 28,000 copies of Father Peschke's book that have have been sold, a huge number for a seminary text. In the last two decades, the book has malformed thousands of seminarians who are now priests.

By what right, we ask, did the SVD leadership impose the shallow, heretical teachings of Häring upon SVD members who came to Nemi for renewal? And by what right do the SVD leaders today smuggle his "para-Church" teachings into seminaries throughout the world via Peschke's book? If Häring is an arch-elder of a "super Church," does the SVD leadership really want its members to follow him? And to have thousands of other seminarians do the same?

Father Peschke recommends the Pill
"to regulate the cycle." For more than
twenty-five years, top gynecologists
have told me this idea is hogwash.

On p. 474 of his book, Peschke recommends the Pill "to regulate the cycle." For more than twenty-five years, top gynecological doctors have told me this idea is hogwash. Likewise, he exaggerates the incidence of spontaneous fetal loss, as if to imply that abortion isn't so bad. The evidence shows that only about one of seven pregnancies miscarries (after implantation).

Krosnicki reports that Peschke's forthcoming second volume omits the errors we exposed, and that he'll speak "still more clearly" against abortion; this report is an admission that our objections were valid. But what of Peschke's dissent to *HV*?

In his sad attempt at a defense, Krosnicki professes his loyalty to the Holy See and its teachings (including *HV*) and then says, "No staff person or president of Human Life International ever discussed with Krosnicki his positions on abortion and/or *HV.*" Why should we? We never accused him.

We did bring *Father Peschke's* errors to the attention of Father Krosnicki and three times to Superior General Barlage in Rome before going to press, but we got no satisfactory response. All either one had to do was to assure us that he'd look seriously into our findings, promise correction, and give us a report. Sadly, we couldn't get this assurance from either man. Frankly, Krosnicki protesteth too much.

In 1974 I began trying to update the NFP program in Japan, where NFP is practiced more, perhaps, than in the USA. I never received any support from the SVDs except one, even though our Japanese conferences for laity, nurses, and doctors were the largest such gatherings I've ever seen.

About 1974 I discovered a Planned Parenthood (PP) unit operating on the campus of the SVD San Carlos University in Cebu City, Philippines, where I lectured. Neither Krosnicki nor the superior general has been able to assure me that this PP unit has been closed.

There's much more. Let's go back to the beginning. Reactions to my statement that seminarians in the Philippines are "victimized by rebel theologians, the worst being the Jesuits and the Divine Word Fathers, both of whom reject *HV* brazenly" (*Report No. 95*) have now spread from Manila to Rome, Vienna, Washington, Chicago, and all the states and countries where people read our *Special Reports.*

"What a terrible book [is Father Peschke's]!" confided a veteran NFP teacher while in Rome in December 1992, where he was attending a Vatican-sponsored conference of NFP leaders. He'd read *Report No. 95*, which blew the whistle on this disloyal activity in SVD and other seminaries. He was appalled by the contents of that book, published by the SVDs in Manila.

Likewise, a seminarian in West Africa wrote to thank us for our "X-ray" of *Christian Ethics*, which helped him to see its errors.

FATHER PESCHKE'S PARTIAL REMEDY

But a light may be appearing at the end of the tunnel. Father Krosnicki's three-page "Response to Human Life International" indirectly admits past wrongdoing and promises correction.

Directly, it's an involuted and understandably loyal defense of the SVDs. A curious declaration heads the "Response": "Father PESCHKE IS PRO-LIFE—Father Peschke has stated clearly in writing to the superior general of the Society of the Divine Word that he is 'decidedly against abortion'." So what else is new? Do we expect less from a Catholic professor who educates future priests and bishops?

The "Response" continues, "Father Peschke has duly obtained the required *Imprimatur*...." Earlier in this *Report* we looked at *imprimaturs* in general. Note, too, that the *imprimatur* is not that of Cardinal Jaime Sin of Manila, where Divine Word Publications prints the book. Instead, it's that of Monsignor D. Leonard, vicar general to the bishop of faraway Birmingham, England. But not even the bishop of Birmingham, Maurice Noel Leon Couve de Murville, signed the *imprimatur*; he delegated the work to his vicar general, a usual procedure. Therefore, we cannot tell whether any bishop, anywhere, ever *personally* approved the text for use in seminaries.

Let's hope that the promised new edition of Father Peschke's book will be 100 percent orthodox, so that Cardinal Sin himself will be able to grant the *imprimatur*.

An SVD spokesman informs us that Peschke has stated in writing to his superior general that in the coming edition "I have entirely omitted the comments of the bishops' conferences [dissenting to *HV*] in the main text of the book and only make reference to them in a footnote of 12 lines. On the other hand, the teachings of Paul VI and John Paul II receive much broader attention in the body of the text."

Thanks be to God! This statement partially remedies what HLI had criticized, but only partially. Perhaps Peschke can find room to mention that the bishops' conferences of 103 countries did *not* dissent, and that the dissenting bishops' countries now have empty seminaries and too few babies for national survival, with Germany having more coffins than cradles.

Word leaking from one SVD source says the Father Peschke scandal has become so serious that Father Henry Barlage, the superior general, has personally taken up the matter. The "Response" likely reflects directions he gave. But nothing in it opposes contraception. Not a word. Does this omission imply, perhaps, that the superior general himself may not want to take an open stand against contraception?

IS THE S.V.D. AGAINST CONTRACEPTION?

The "Response" vigorously waves a decoy flag when it says Peschke is "decidedly against abortion." What HLI wants to know is whether he's also "decidedly against contraception." If not, we're determined to track down and raise a ruckus about every seminary that uses the text. One, allegedly, is Cardinal Joseph Bernardin's Mundelein Seminary in Chicago—a commentary in itself about that heterodox institution.

The last summit meeting (chapter) of the SVDs, at which Father Barlage presided, passed a resolution condemning abortion; but there was no resolution against contraception. Ditto for the last local summit of the Chicago Province. If the highest superiors of the SVDs condemn abortion but not contraception, and if they allowed the publication of the views of Father Peschke that contradict *HV* on contraception, then their fidelity to the pope on a grave moral issue is now open to question.

The "Response" names Cardinals Tomko and Ratzinger as persons who have *not* condemned *Christian Ethics*. As we commented earlier, we're not impressed. We all know how patient Church authorities are with theologians; how much time passed, for example, before even Father Hans Küng and Father Charles Curran finally received a sentence of disapproval. The "Response" shouldn't insult our intelligence by hinting that either Cardinal Tomko or Cardinal Ratzinger would agree with such outlandish assertions of Peschke's as "Artificial contraceptives are not necessarily gravely sinful" (p. 476).

The cardinals are certainly not in the habit of learning their moral theology from the dissenters whom this book showcases for seminarians, e.g., Häring, Curran, McDonagh, Callahan, McCormick, Böckle, Gründel, and virtually every other dissenting theologian of note. Rather, these cardinals are guardians of the Magisterium, which clearly condemns contraception. *Humanae Vitae* states that the law of God prohibits

> ...every action which, either in anticipation of the conjugal act, or in its accomplishment, or in the development of its natural consequences, proposes, whether as an end or as a means, to render procreation impossible.

HLI showed that Father Peschke's text waffles on contraception:

> The encyclical *HV* received a very divided echo and is probably the most controverted encyclical ever written.... Many theologians and lay people are convinced that at least under certain circumstances their use of [artificial means of birth control] is not contrary to moral law [p. 475].

The deadly dissent to HV has confused many priests and couples worldwide, paving the way to massive contraception, sterilization, and abortion everywhere.

There you have the deadly dissent that has confused so many priests and couples worldwide, paving the way to massive contraception, sterilization, and abortion everywhere. What HLI wants to know is whether Peschke, his helping confreres, and his SVD superiors are now among these "many theologians" who still undermine *HV*.

There's evidence that they are. For example, Father Albert Van Gansewinkel, a senior SVD confrere, wrote in the July 1992 *Anzeiger für die Seelsorge (Guide for Pastoral Care)* that *HV* was built upon a "fundamental error" (p. 320); he thus accuses the papal encyclical of being wrong from start to finish.

God made it possible for humans to separate love from procreation by means of the condom and the Pill, the priest writes; but the Church forbids this act that God allows (p. 327). Anyone, he continues, who thinks using condoms is gravely evil thinks in the pagan categories of the ancient stoics (p. 322). The priest even justifies using the abortifacient Pill! And much more drivel follows (write me for a copy of the article).

Father Van Gansewinkel's advice was meant for every pastor in Germany, to whom the heretical Herder publishing house sent the article. The author invoked the SVD name at the beginning of the article, trying to add authority to his writing; so far, not a word of protest from the SVD leadership has come to our attention. We can only pray that this leadership will demand more discipline among the members from now on.

DISSENT AT AN S.V.D. SEMINARY

Catholics have a right to expect future priests, nuns, brothers, and teachers to receive an education that values both premarital and marital chastity, so that they can lead their people one day to trust this magnificent promise of *HV*:

> This self-discipline...brings to family life abundant fruits of tranquility and peace. It helps in solving difficulties of other kinds. It fosters in husband and wife thoughtfulness and loving consideration for each other. It helps them to repel the excessive self-love which is the opposite of charity. It arouses in them a consciousness of their responsibilities. And finally, it confers upon parents a deeper and more effective influence in the education of their children. For these latter, both in childhood and in

youth, as years go by, develop a right sense of values as regards the true blessings of life and achieve a serene and harmonious use of their mental and physical powers [No. 21].

Will Father Peschke's new text train seminarians in this spirit, or will it continue to downgrade *HV*? Recall all the evidence we've given in these *Reports* over the years, showing that foresight contraception leads to hindsight abortion, dangerously low birthrates, and massive sterilization; that it increases fornication, adultery, VD, divorce, AIDS, etc. As Pope John Paul II has pointed out, contraception feeds the mentality "out of which abortion arises" (to the Austrian Bishops, 19 May 1987).

And now, concerning the "Manila Incident," in which an SVD seminarian questioned *HV* before 1,600 people at our international prolife/profamily conference there in early 1972: A priest who was present wrote to me that "I...personally spoke to the seminarian after his interview at the conference.... I asked the seminarian whether his morals professor at Tagaytay [the SVD seminary] adheres to *HV* as binding, especially in regard to contraception. He responded that his professor is not absolutely supportive of *HV*." (We must withhold the seminarian's name to protect him from what happens too often in cases such as this.)

An SVD priest who was there, but doesn't want to be named, wrote to a confrere, "I also asked Bishop Jesus Varela about the teaching on contraception at Tagaytay. According to my notes, Bishop Varela responded that 'they are liberal on contraception.'" Bishop Varela is head of the Commission on Marriage and Family Life in the Philippines.

A Filipino theologian has complained to us that the nuns who operate many of the country's Catholic colleges have been misled by a glowing review that Peschke's book received.

Concerning the statement in the "Response" that "professors in Tagaytay [seminary] are respectful of the Holy Father and submissive to his teaching authority": we expect no less, but the proof must be deeds, not mere words.

The smooth words of the "Response" will be verified by deeds if and when SVD superiors resolve at their summit meetings and through internal SVD media to oppose contraception as well as abortion; instruct Divine Word Publications in Manila to stop selling Peschke's textbook and to discard the remaining copies; send an apology to seminaries that used the book, in order to undo the fifteen-year scandal; eject from San Carlos University the PP unit (if it's still there); and admonish confreres in Japan that the pro-contraception sex-ed pamphlet they once published (see our comments below) was thoroughly wrong. Meanwhile, potential benefactors should give no money to the SVD.

We advise Father Krosnicki again that this book wasn't his work; there's no need for him to soil his moral integrity by trying to defend the indefensible.

MORE S.V.D. DISSENT

In 1979 the SVD Province of Japan sponsored a most offensive sex-ed book that was a best seller in Catholic bookstores for six years, until the Vatican ordered it withdrawn. The author was George Nuerenberger, who came to Japan from Germany as an SVD priest, was laicized, and then married a Japanese woman. (This is another indication that laicized priests shouldn't be given positions of responsibility as teachers, as the Vatican has said more than once.) The booklet was published with impeccable Catholic credentials involving doctors and several SVD professors at the SVD Nanzan University in Nagoya. The infamous booklet more than waffles on *HV*, and charts all of the sinful methods of birth control.

Some excerpts: "The choice of methods employed to prevent conception should emerge from the mutual love which marriage partners have for each other." And, "It is a mistake, then, to say that, when selecting the method of contraception, love should not be taken into consideration." Further, "The couple must decide about the choice of method of contraception...." It then displays a smorgasbord of "approved" choices—Ogino rhythm, temperature method, mucus method, condom, pessary, abortifacient

IUD, abortifacient Pill, jelly, douching, and withdrawal.

I've made six missionary journeys to Japan. This deplorable booklet expresses the mind of most lay people there, and most priests and bishops. It says much about the attitudes of the victimized Church in that country and about the theological negligence of the SVDs, who, grasping at straws, are now trying to support the unsupportable. We look forward to a friendly association with loyal SVD superiors who oppose not only abortion but also contraception.

Recently, we were gratified to hear from a loyal SVD priest that the superior general is urging obedience to documents from Rome. Another loyal SVD priest says no SVD superior general has written such a directive in the past twenty-five years.

Let us pray and hope that HLI can soon urge you to financially assist the SVDs once more. We want to be the first to do so.

Some of the nuns in the Sparkill congregation are reviving an interest in witchcraft.

A WITCH'S BREW OF ERROR

Last June, this newsletter reported on some Dominican nuns at Sparkill, New York, who were publicly endorsing pro-abortion politicians through local newspaper advertisements, and who hosted a "homophobia" conference to give homosexuals and lesbians a forum from which to rail against the Catholic Church because she won't sanction their perversions (*Special Report No. 91*). Now we've learned that some of the nuns in the congregation are reviving an interest in witchcraft—and that one recently authored a book ludicrously entitled *Christ, Our Mother of Mercy*.

As if that weren't bad enough, Sparkill also is hosting the likes of pope-badgering feminist Sister Theresa Kane, RSM, and Church-bashing Father Michael M. Crosby,

OFM, who travels about ridiculing "patriarchal clerical-
ism," denouncing celibacy, and counseling priests and religious to engage in "intimate relationships" with others. He
thinks that practicing homosexuals should be allowed to
receive the Eucharist and that guilt feelings are wrong and
should be eliminated.

Sister Kane's most memorable performance came in
1979 when she publicly confronted Pope John Paul II and
demanded a priesshood. She was scheduled to speak at
Sparkill on February 27 on "The Challenge of Commitment
Today," which the printed program describes as "A presen-
tation/discussion on our call to be faithful women of the
Church and how that call relates to personal, congregational and church [sic] authority."

The sacrilegious outrages of Father Crosby were the
subject of a long story in the 4 February 1993 issue of *The
Wanderer*. His March 27 talk is entitled "Images of the
Heart: Inner and Outer Compassion." Besides Sparkill,
seventeen congregations are listed as sponsors of his
appearance.

The Sister Kane-Father Crosby visits are the latest
exhibits in an ongoing series of abominable doings at
Sparkill.

Anyone who cares to read the congregation's October
newsletter, *Update 1992*, will find a page-long paean of
praise to witches. The poem "Fire Tenders" by Pat Boyle,
OP, glorifies witches as martyrs and even blasphemously
suggests that, collectively, witches are the very source of
wisdom—a role theologically reserved in New Testament
times for Jesus Christ.

A footnote contends mournfully, "During a period of
300 years, 9 million were burned as witches. All were
women—a litany of nameless saints." (*Of course* they were
all women; male "witches" are called "warlocks.") But the
radical feminist "pain lobby" is always scrounging for
something to be sorely offended by. The incredible figure of
nine million isn't referenced; nor does Boyle justify using
the term "saints."

The poem contains verses such as: "O men and righteous ladies/ fire quenchers, fire bankers/ not even baker's
dozen will suffice/ to stem your fears/ so you hounded down

the witches/ hurling curses in God's name/ 'you'll no longer make your magic/ we'll break you on the rack/ then your fire will consume you/ and the fire will fall dead!'/ They're burning witches/ do you hear, they're near!"

The poem says the witches' collective name "was Sophia, breath of God!" and asks those "wisdom makers" to "pour your mercy and forgiveness/ on the righteous fallen low" so that there will be no more burning of witches "WHICH IS SUCH ABSURDITY/ for Sophia tends the fire/ she is whispered sigh of God!"

Several priests who read this poem offered the opinion, independently, that its contents are "demonic."

THE VATICAN STEPS IN

A month earlier, the Sparkill newsletter celebrated Sister Margaret Ann Palliser's book, subtitled *Divine Mercy and Compassion in the Theology of the Shewings of Julian of Norwich*. "Julian's image of Christ as the compassionate 'mother' of mercy represents her mature theological vision of divine mercy," says the brief review. "It is with great pride that we congratulate our author, Sister Margaret Ann Palliser, and thank her for her hard work and sound scholarship," the newsletter article gushes breathlessly.

We tried unsuccessfully to obtain a review copy of the book through the Walter de Gruyter & Co. publishing house. The title makes it clear that the work seeks to "feminize" Our Lord, a goal shared by the radical-feminist/goddess-worship set. (Talk-show personality Rush Limbaugh calls such people "feminazis," which certainly conveys a sense of what they're all about.)

Julian was a 14th-century holy woman in Norwich, England, who, after her miraculous cure from a life-threatening illness, experienced a series of visions ("shewings") that, for the most part, presented various aspects of Our Lord's passion. In *Butler's Lives of the Saints*, her account of the visions repeatedly uses the male personal pronoun to refer to Jesus and, of course, makes no mention of His alleged "motherhood."

A decade ago, Sisiter Margaret Ann was quoted in a lead article in the *National Catholic Register* that dealt with the emergence of witchcraft (Wicca) in certain Catholic circles. The 15 May 1983 *Register* story says she reported in the upcoming Sparkill congregation's newsletter a "recent interest in witches as spiritual leaders." She wrote that "many theologians are taking a serious look at witchcraft" so that they can "assess the feminine religious scholarship as it relates to Christian theology."

That newsletter also was to contain a reprint of a speech on witchcraft by New Age witch "Starhawk," a kindred spirit to and fellow traveler with the far-out former Dominican theologian Father Matthew Fox. (Do you suppose he was one of the theologians referred to above?)

In our earlier *Report* on the ungodly shenanigans at the Sparkill motherhouse, HLI added its voice to those calling for the Vatican to send someone to New York to straighten out the mess. Perhaps that's now being done.

An article in the September 1992 issue of *The New York Guardian* says the Sacred Congregation has decided to investigate the "numerous alleged improprieties that have taken place at the Archdiocese's second-largest religious community."

The *Guardian* says allegations made over the past two years include reports of a manipulated election process within the order; the advocacy of an anti-papal "Woman Church" that involves "brainwashing" techniques and liturgical abuses; the questionable sale of congregational property; the "homophobia" gathering; and the political endorsement of the proabortion candidates.

We want to emphasize again that we don't mean to criticize all Dominicans in the Sparkill congregation. Most are loyal to Christ and to His Church and are deeply grieved over the situation, as all true Catholics must be. Join us in praying that right order and sound doctrine will be restored at Sparkill.

(The author of this report on Sparkill is Vernon Kirby, HLI's director of publications.)

Letters

I wish to express my thanks for the report on *Christian Ethics* by Father Karl H. Peschke, SVD.

The only local review that I saw about the book was highly favorable, enough to allay all suspicions and make one desire to have a copy. You can imagine that, with that kind of laudatory review, the book would be highly acceptable, especially with the religious sisters who conduct many Catholic colleges in our country.

But I had my misgivings. I acquired a copy of each of the two volumes; after a perusal, I was not satisfied with the philosophical approach and manner of discussion.

Father Manuel Pinon, OP
Quezon City, Philippines

I was always under the impression, as a lay Catholic, that when the word *imprimatur* appeared on any Catholic book, that book had been reviewed by the Catholic hierarchy and found to be void of errors, as well as being true to the Catholic principles advocated by our Church and approved by the Holy Father.

But, according to your report, the *imprimatur* has little or no meaning at all. In fact, it seems to be a big joke, since the bishops and cardinals spend minimal time perusing any Catholic writings before the *imprimatur* is stamped on the book.

Where does that leave us Catholic people? I thought that the word stood for validity and that I was safe in reading and quoting the text to which it applied. But now we are like a bunch of lost sheep without a shepherd.

What can we do? Must we just rely on our intuition? It certainly is a shame that we who are supposed to look to the hierarchy as the stalwarts of the Church have turned out to be stranded and abandoned.

A.J. Kabat
Chicago, Illinois

Dissenting theologians have done their work well

The gates of Hell did not prevail: our opposition in the Netherlands (1992)

Marxist defends the worst of capitalism: the abortion industry (Ottawa)

Why don't the taxpayers *ever get a choice? (Ottawa)*

"Satan was a murderer from the beginning" (Ottawa)

If you don't pray for their souls, who will? (The Netherlands)

HLI-Canada's Theresa Bell visits our world headquarters in "G-burg"

Irish Mist and Foggy Things

No. 100   April 1993

I n 1983 I was deeply involved in the campaign for Article Eight, the prolife amendment to the Irish Constitution. It reads, "The State acknowledges the right to life of the unborn and with due regard to the equal right to life of the mother, guarantees in its laws to respect, and, as far as practicable, by its laws to defend and vindicate that right."

After a bitter nationwide battle, the voters approved the amendment, two to one. Once for all, the Irish thought, they'd be spared legal abortion. But they underestimated the machinations of Satan and his co-workers, the Family Planning Association-Planned Parenthood (PP)—which had moved into Ireland in 1969.

In early 1992, an anonymous fourteen-year-old Irish schoolgirl alleged that she'd been raped. The police were informed. Because abortion was illegal, the attorney general filed a motion to keep her from going to England to abort her baby.

JUDICIAL TYRANNY

Eventually the case, dubbed "The X Case" by the media, reached the Supreme Court. Using strange, devious reasoning and voting four to one, the Court decided on 5 March 1992 that because the girl had (supposedly) threatened suicide, her life was in danger, and that therefore she should be allowed to go to England to have her baby killed.

Before this, the proabortionists had trumped up a gigantic international campaign to arouse sympathy for the girl and to bemoan the "stupidity" and "unfairness" of Article Eight. Irish prolifers, by now armed with HLI's prolife literature, aborted-baby postcards, and posters, demanded another national referendum to repair the hole smashed into the Constitution by the Court; the government said no.

Meanwhile, prolife and proabort forces began to march, demonstrate, and clash. Finally, the devious Prime Minister Albert Reynolds submitted a three-headed referendum to the voters: (1) every citizen would have the "right" to travel abroad to kill a preborn baby; (2) abortion "counseling" and "information" centers would be legal; and (3) baby-killing would be allowed in the case of supposed serious danger to the mother's life—a big loophole for escalating future abortions—but not for danger to her health or for threatened suicide.

Now Catholic Ireland will have a chain of abortion sales offices to steer colleens to baby-killing mills in England!

The voters approved the first two proposals handily and rejected the third by a wide margin. Now Catholic Ireland will have a chain of abortion sales offices to steer colleens to baby-killing mills in England!

Because the issue was highly complicated, and for other reasons, the bishops seemed confused and paralyzed. They ended up making no united, national statement and ultimately leaving each bishop to handle the problem in his own way, in his own diocese. What saved the day concerning the third proposal, which would have allowed countless abortions, was that Dublin's Archbishop Desmond Connell and four other bishops told the media that they couldn't in conscience vote for it. Their move proved decisive.

Meanwhile, the government fell; the election produced a liberal coalition government and threw Ireland into political turmoil. Events are moving quickly. Reynolds and the labor leader, proabortion Dick Spring, have agreed on a five-year blueprint for a change in Ireland, creating jobs and altering the social face of this conservative and Catholic country.

Ireland now records her worst-ever unemployment rate, 20 percent or 300,000 out of 3.5 million people. The politicians will create three new ministries, increase child allowances, reduce classroom sizes, and launch an ambitious road and railway program.

THE SNAKES RETURN TO ERIN

They also pledge to legalize sodomy; debate over homosexuality is now raging in the Dail (parliament), and a referendum on divorce is in the works—never mind that the Irish already rejected divorce two to one in a referendum in 1986. Instead of creating a ministry for the family, Reynolds appointed a minister of equality, a gift to the feminists!

Prolife leader Dr. A. Kennedy of Cork describes the situation: "We in Ireland now have a new government dominated by socialists with the full agenda for 'the enlightenment' of the Irish people. We are to have decriminalization of perverted sex. New school programs to encourage all types of permissiveness. We even are promised 'limited abortion'."

In early March 1993 the Irish Medical Council issued its *Statement on Guidelines re: Abortion*, declaring that doctors who perform abortions are acting unethically. After extensive research, the council concluded that there's no evidence abortion is a necessary part of medical treatment and that pregnancy had a "protective element" because pregnant women were twenty times less likely to commit suicide than other women. (Research in the USA also shows that pregnant moms very rarely commit suicide.)

On 1 April 1992, the four top professors of OB-GYN in Ireland issued this statement: "We affirm that there are no medical circumstances justifying direct abortion, that is, no medical circumstances in which the life of a mother may only be saved by directly terminating the life of her unborn child."

The Irish Medical Council's well-researched *Statement* and the Doctors for Life's booklet, *Current Controversies in Abortion*, prove how completely flawed the Court's ruling was and demolish any grounds for the liberal government's likely plan to draft a law to widen the legal reasons for abortion, based on the ruling.

Meanwhile, prolife groups have stepped up their demands for a referendum to repair the damage the Court did. If wide-open abortion comes to Ireland, it'll be against the will of the nation and the best judgment of the most eminent doctors.

BEATING UP A WEAKENED CHURCH

As expected, most of the Irish media's coverage of the Statement has been hostile, giving more space to pro-abortion views and trying to undermine the report. Catholic Ireland has the most vicious anti-Catholic media in the world—even worse than Poland's. Once more we see that we no longer live in democracies but are ruled by corrupt politicians propped up by immoral, brainwashing mass media and value-free, "pro-choice" educational systems.

Because the coalition government is denying the nation an opportunity to ban abortions totally through another constitutional amendment, there's great danger that the Dail will pass laws exploiting the loophole created by the Court's decision. So the International Planned Parenthood Federation (IPPF), headquartered in nearby London, may destroy another Catholic nation through its affiliate, the Irish Family Planning Association. In 1972 I warned the Irish bishops about what was coming, but to no avail (see *Report No. 90*).

Reynold's tyrannical handling of the abortion referendum indicates that he and his new socialist colleagues are ready to destroy Catholic Ireland. Tragically, the Catholic Church is already weakened greatly because the bishops didn't enforce *Humanae Vitae* and failed to actively promote natural birth regulation despite the availability of generous government grants. They've also allowed a bad, mandatory marriage-preparation course that says contraception is an option.

And they let the Catholic school system decline through a Carl Rogers-style smorgasbord of "life skills," "learning for life," "encounter groups," "development and self-actualization," "assertiveness training," etc.—and through the usual destructive, post-Vatican II elements such as the collapse of religious discipline in many Catholic schools, seminaries, and high schools, not to mention the subsequent scandals among priests and religious. Not helping the situation is "Catholic," feminist, pro-abortion/-homosexuality/-contraception President Mary Robinson, whom some U.S. bishops wined and dined during her visit to the USA.

The future of Catholic Ireland doesn't look good. What the Government will do about abortion is anyone's guess. Ireland already has a birthrate that's below replacement level. Other destructive evils are at work, one of the worst being secular feminism. Building on HLI's successful conference in Cork last fall, we hope to launch a total-approach, prolife/profamily educational program with various Irish groups. We've tentatively scheduled a weekend seminar for Galway this fall.

Today Malta remains the only country in Western Europe that still legally protects her preborn children. Please pray for Ireland!

CAN A CATHOLIC NATION DEFEND HER BABIES?

Poland first experienced abortion during the Nazi occupation of 1939-45. In 1956 the Communist regime completely legalized prenatal infanticide, and since then the Poles have killed an estimated twenty million preborn babies. After the fall of Communism, efforts to protect Poland's babies began immediately, thanks to the Catholic hierarchy.

Some 100 prolife groups soon organized themselves in a federation. Because of the habit of using abortion as birth control, polls showed that most citizens favored a proabortion law. Fueled by much foreign money, feminists and other proaborts went door to door, gathering 1.3 million signatures demanding a referendum for abortion-on-demand. This referendum probably would have passed, but the bishops bravely fought the idea, saying that moral issues aren't decided by vote.

On 2 May 1992 the Polish Medical Association decreed that its members would lose their licenses if they performed abortions, except in cases of supposed danger to the mother's life. The number of surgical abortions, estimated at 500,000 per year, began to decline, partly, also, because of the pope's frantic pleas during his visits to Poland.

The battle over various bills raged in Parliament for three years. Finally a member introduced a bill to protect all "conceived life." After a fierce debate, President-elect Lech Walesa signed a law that bans abortions except in cases of rape, incest, supposed danger to the mother's life or health, or irreparable damage to the preborn child. Babies may be killed only in public hospitals. In the case of the mother's "health" and "life," three doctors must concur. This kind of law has never worked in any country.

> *President-elect Lech Walesa signed a law that bans abortions—with the usual exceptions. This kind of law has never worked in any country.*

Of course, the measure pleased no one. Bishops and prolife parliamentarians debated whether Walesa should sign it. One prolife leader argued that abortion is war, and in war you grab any territory you can get, even if you have to allow some abortions. (By now, even the USA's National Right to Life Committee could explain eloquently that this "incremental approach" isn't effective.)

Prolifers and proaborts both vowed to fight on, with the latter promising to work for a referendum to bring back wide-open abortion. The health minister naively said the new law would "protect conceived life in 98 percent of pregnancies." Obviously, he knows little about how these "restrictive" abortion laws inevitably stretch to allow abortion-on-demand.

Walesa has long made known his opposition to abortion. Some prolife politicians had hoped he'd veto the bill and press Parliament for a total ban. He signed it because, he said, "In this state of quarreling and emotions, the best solution is to cut off the matter." The law went into effect on March 16. Doctors who break it can go to prison for up to two years (if the mother dies, up to ten years). Mothers go unpunished.

Under the new law, the state must still allow the sale of contraceptives/abortifacients. The law also obliges the government to prepare sex-ed programs for the schools. PP is prepared to move into the schools with its pornographic, "value-free" indoctrination. Prolifers are desperately searching the world for a good sex-ed program and, in fact, have asked HLI for help.

WHICH WAY "POLONIA SACRA"?

Like many of the Irish, many Poles want to be just like other pagan Europeans, not to be Polish and Catholic. Thus, outlawing abortions was called "un-European." Supposedly, banning all abortions would prevent Poland's entry into the European Community (EC); Poland would be branded a backward country; it would create a dangerous medical underground, etc., etc.

Private travel agencies are organizing and advertising to funnel Polish mothers who want abortions to nearby Slovakia, Ukraine, the Czech Republic, Russia, and the Netherlands. We're working with prolife groups to get our antiabortion films shown on Polish TV.

Masonry was a rather large influence in Poland during this battle. The foreign-financed feminists will continue waging their shrill campaign, using their 1.3 million signatures for an abortion-on-demand referendum. IPPF's Polish affiliate, active for years under the Reds, will continue spreading its deceptive propaganda. The antilife media will continue pushing for Poland to become "modern." The pornographic magazines, videos, and films of Western Europe are now ruining lives in Polish cities.

The battle for life will go on fiercely for many years as countless babies are killed in this, the most Catholic nation on earth. Thank God, the Catholic bishops, goaded by the first Polish pope, are fighting nobly.

BISHOPS' PROLIFE CHAIRMAN FINDS "COMMON GROUND" WITH CLINTON

In *Report No. 98* I told you that Cardinal Roger Mahony, the U.S. bishops' new prolife chairman, had indirectly told his flock it was all right to vote for proabortion candidates such as Bill Clinton. I also reported other apparently soft-on-Clinton words of the archbishop of Los Angeles.

Cardinal Mahony wrote me one of his famous "midnight missiles," a long, angry letter (with copies to six other cardinals) accusing me of making "unrelenting attacks" upon our bishops that are "divisive," "reprehensible," "devious," etc. He also charged that I took his remarks out of context, etc. In a subsequent letter, he accused me of causing "scandal" for "good people."

I sent a detailed rebuttal to him. But meanwhile, he came out with more overtures to the Abortion President, in a 27 February 1993 interview in the *Los Angeles Times*.

Asked whether he was "writing off" Clinton, the cardinal replied, "No! Not at all. In fact, I'm looking forward to having a meeting with the President." Will abortion "add a certain amount of strain in trying to work with the President on other issues?" "I don't think so....The President has said some good things. It strikes me that they serve as common-ground themes....And I really look forward to pursuing those with him. Because...he said while [he was] pro-choice, [he was] not pro-abortion....I'd like to know what that...means...." (We'd like to know, too!)

He continued, "There are many issues in which we [Catholics] have a very vital interest and, we hope, a common interest with the Administration and with Congress. So we see ourselves as very much participants—active participants—in a lot of these areas. [In] health care reform we have a very vital interest. We have 900 [it's actually about 625—*P.M.*] Catholic hospitals. So these are issues [in] which we feel we're a pretty significant player and we would like always [to be] as close as we can with the Administration and the Congress on these issues."

It was interesting that a Prince of the Church found "good things" in Bill Clinton and uncommonly "common" ground in their interests. One week later, *The New York Times* (4 March 1993) quoted former Communist dictator of Poland Gen. Wojciech Jaruzelski as saying, "In Clinton's program I see elements I like a lot." Last year Clinton told Italian journalist Antonio Socci that the Communist cooperatives of Italy were "absolutely" his economic prescription for the USA (*Il Sabato*, 8 August 1992).

I truly hope Cardinal Mahony, behind the scenes, can convert Bill and Hillary away from helping to kill millions of preborn babies, including thousands of would-have-been priests. But if the bishops' prolife chairman meets *publicly* with a president who actually believes in sucking the brains out of living preborn babies, it'll be a dark day in the history of the Catholic Church.

Pope John Paul II has likened abortion to the Nazi death camps (*The New York Times*, 5 June 1991). In September 1974 then-Bishop Mahony himself compared proabort politicians to Nazi war criminals. Let Cardinal Mahony take as his example Pope Pius XII, who, when Hitler came to Rome, left town and ordered every church locked shut.

JESUS BLASPHEMED AT CARDINAL MAHONY'S RELIGIOUS-ED MEETING

The cardinal's allegation that I give scandal is interesting, too. Perhaps he should tend to his own archdiocese first.

Let's look at just some of what was said at his religious-education congress—billed as the world's largest—at the Anaheim Convention Center, 19-21 February 1993.

The tape reveals that Father Juknialis spent ninety minutes denying the Resurrection, the Real Presence, and the historicity of the gospels.

Cardinal Mahony's staff brought in Father Joseph Juknialis from rebel Archbishop Rembert Weakland's St. Francis Seminary in Milwaukee for two talks. One was "The Resurrection—What Really Happened?" The tape reveals that Father Juknialis spent ninety minutes denying the Resurrection, the Real Presence, and the historicity of the Gospels. Some quotes:

"In all probability, His corpse was buried in a shallow grave and eaten by dogs that had picked up the scent from the cross" [quoting a "respected Biblical theologian," Dominic Crossan of the Vincentians' DePaul University].

No "reputable Catholic theologian" would agree that "a dead body came to life."

"He was given a new body, and the new body is us. We are the risen body of Christ....Is there a Risen Christ apart from us? No."

Does Jesus live on "as [Communist priest-murderer] Che Guevara or Martin Luther King lives on?"

"The Catholic Church has never said that the Eucharist is the physical reality of the Body and Blood of Christ."

"To receive ourselves [in Holy Communion] is to receive the Body of Christ."

"Was there a Jesus whose body went up in the clouds?...I don't know and we never will know."

"Was Lazarus really raised? I don't know."

"To be human is what Jesus is all about."

After we die, "We will be all that Christ is."

The account of Thomas's placing his finger in Our Lord's wounds is one of the "stories created by the early community."

Father Juknialis not only denied the Resurrection, which St. Paul says is the bedrock of our Faith, but he tried to make the epistles say as much. He also informed Cardinal Mahony's religion teachers that the gospel writers wrote "stories," not "a newspaper account." He suggested that the early Church is guilty of a "fabrication" of a Divine Jesus.

In addition, Juknialis said Jesus didn't use words after He rose; He communicated intuitively. The priest questioned the infancy narratives, whether Jesus claimed to be the Messiah, and the second coming. Cardinal Mahony's religion teachers applauded this blasphemous talk.

In his letter of welcome to people attending the congress, the cardinal said they would be "enriched" by the talks. Did that include Juknialis's talk? To people who complained about it, the archdiocese replied, "We are...in the process of reviewing Father Juknialis's presentation at congress. Father Juknialis has been a well-received speaker at congress for several years. This is the first time we have had any complaint about his presentations. The Office of Religious Education is very careful in its selection of speakers and receives recommendations from a variety of orthodox and informed sources."

Orthodox? The congress schedule listed nine speakers whose names appear (to their discredit) in Donna

Steichen's *Ungodly Rage*, a detailed exposé of dissent, heresy, lesbianism, and occult practices in the Catholic feminist movement.

Teachers attending Cardinal Mahony's congress were "enriched" by such speakers as Sydney Callahan, who dissents from *Humanae Vitae* and endorsed contraception in her talk; Father Richard Fragomeni, who gave a workshop on the occult tarot cards at the 1989 congress; the antipapal feminist Monika Hellwig; Loretta Jancoski, a follower of the witchcraft advocate Father Matthew Fox; Bishop Raymond Lucker, who copies Archbishop Weakland; graphic sex-educator Patricia Miller (*In God's Image*), who recently discussed "what [Jesus] did with his —"; Sister Carolyn Osiek, who's not sure whether we should pray to a male or a female god; Father Richard Rohr, who promotes the occult enneagram; and many others. I shudder to think what's on *all* of the 111 congress tapes.

Maya Angelou received standing ovations from Cardinal Mahony's religion teachers, according to his newspaper,* The Tidings, *which called her a "preacher."

For keynote speaker, the archdiocese brought in the high-priced author-poetess-actress who has named herself Maya Angelou—the one who read her banal pro-"gay" poem at Clinton's inauguration. Reportedly a Christian, she's described herself as a former madam, prostitute, stripper, and advisor to Malcolm X (*Orange County Register*, 9 February 1993). The archdiocese is millions of dollars in debt, but it paid her a fee it refuses to divulge. Angelou receives an annual salary well into six figures from Wake Forest University but reportedly teaches no classes at this time and has no office on campus, other than a glorified broom closet. She received standing ovations from Cardinal Mahony's religion teachers, according to his newspaper, *The Tidings* (28 February 1993), which called her a "preacher."

The congress schedule also mentioned that at the New-Age-style American Indian liturgy, the drum was the "heartbeat of mother-earth" and that all were invited to "join in the Snake Dance."

Perhaps Cardinal Mahony would like to discuss the definition of "scandal" with Sister Edith Prendergast, RSC, the director of his Office of Religious Education, who organized the congress. Mrs. Steichen says Sister Edith, along with ex-priests, is on the board of Time Consultants, Inc. (now renamed), the for-profit company that organizes radical-feminist, anti-Magisterial conferences across the United States.

Please pray for everyone in the Archdiocese of Los Angeles.

WANTED: PROLIFE DOCTORS & PHARMACISTS

Seeing the Church's needs and watching the devil's conniving worldwide, I countenance endless projects in my head that persecute me day and night.

One of these is to gather and publish *office* addresses and *office* phone numbers of all truly prolife doctors and pharmacists who steadfastly refuse to involve themselves in contraception, abortifacients, sterilization, abortions, abortion referrals, and euthanasia. Some of these souls cannot make a living, or are hard pressed to, because they insist on being Christian in their professional practice. Also, women keep asking us for names of prolife doctors.

If you know any of these heroes and heroines, please send me their full *office* addresses and phone numbers (*not* home numbers). We'll contact them. Eventually we'll go international with this project. The Europe-based World Federation of Doctors Who Respect Human Life seems to have come to a dead end because it officially opposes only abortion and euthanasia, not the sexual sins that spawn and accompany these evils.

YOU READ IT HERE FIRST!

Our Catholic and secular media are finally reporting the terrorist acts and threats of some (not all) of the Moslems who are multiplying in Europe and everywhere; but you read it first in these *Special Reports* years ago. At this writing, five Moslems are accused of bombing the World Trade Center. Get ready for more Islamic terrorism.

In fifteen years there will be more Moslems than Christians in our world. What the followers of Mohammed couldn't achieve through war in past centuries, they're now doing by having babies while the West plays with sex.

More than two decades ago I knew the Pill was an abortifacient and said so in many talks and articles. Most bishops, priests, theologians, nuns, Catholic intellectuals, and doctors still don't know this fact—or act as if they didn't.

They remain silent about the more than twelve million U.S. women, including many Catholics, who induce Pill-abortions every year, and about the three million U.S. women who use the abortifacient IUD—not to mention the more than 500,000 who already use the abortifacient Norplant, the just-approved, injectable abortifacient Depo-Provera, or the abortifacient "Morning-after Pill," so popular with college students.

Why, over all these years, has the bishops' bureaucratic apparatus of 300 workers in Washington, D.C., failed to inform bishops, Catholic educators, journalists, and editors about the abortifacient character of certain "contraceptives"? Not even the bishops' annual October Respect Life literature has sounded the alarm. Even the National Right to Life Committee, which falsely claims to speak for all prolife groups in the USA, opposes only surgical abortions and the always-abortifacient RU-486.

Meanwhile, millions of dollars are pouring into research for new "contraceptives" that will cause early, unnoticed abortions by drugs. The quest for the "harmless," low-dose abortifacient drug of the future is the real reason that "scientists" are doing the costly, painful, relatively ineffective (success rate, about 8 percent) *in vitro* fertilizations. It's also the reason the British Parliament last year legalized fetal experimentation into the four-teenth day of pregnancy. And it's the reason that "scientists" coined the deceptive term "pre-embryo"—a fabrication that even Notre Dame's rebel theologian Father Richard McCormick, SJ, has embraced. The UN's World Health Organization (WHO) is leading the drive for the new baby-death potions.

"PILL 'EM OR KILL 'EM"

HLI was one of the first voices to consistently proclaim that abortion is the fruit of contraception, that foresight contraception often leads to hindsight abortion, and that massive contraception has caused increasing abortion worldwide. Having visited and studied eighty-five countries, I challenge any bishop, priest, professor, or scientist to show me the contrary. Abortion is the end point of the abuse of sex, which begins with the unleashing of the sexual urge by contraception.

According to our studies of the U.S. census and government reports, one-third of all U.S. couples who have two children or who have been married ten years have been sterilized; the figure is far higher for older couples. I've exposed facts such as these again and again—but who cares? What bishop has explicitly spoken out against this calamity?

Again, what is the bishops' 300-person apparatus in Washington doing when it leaves our bishops apparently so uninformed on such vital issues? Think of the "prolife" organizations, "Catholic" universities, "Catholic" seminaries, and "Catholic" officials who are so neglectful (I almost said irresponsible). Do they deserve your financial support? Think and pray about it!

Again, HLI was the first organization to study the relationship between declining priestly and religious vocations and low birthrates, which explains (in part) our empty seminaries and novitiates. Also, demographers now finally speak of the economic and social consequences of "youth deficits" in the populations of contracepting/aborting/neutered Western countries. We at HLI have done so for years.

Some observers are now saying our society has built too many houses, apartments, schools, cars, etc. But would there be a recession if we had with us the thirty million producers/consumers whom we've killed by surgical abortion alone since the fateful year 1973?

For more than two decades we've urgently pointed out the consequences of low birthrates caused by selfish, ill-prepared marital living. But then, none are so blind and deaf as those who will not see and will not hear! Our society's morbid, all-pervasive preoccupation with physical sex makes it impossible for most people, including many Christians, to face reality. History tells us that affluence always blinds its recipients. As Benjamin Franklin said, "A remedy for luxury has never been found."

THE HIERARCHY AND CONTRACEPTION

To my knowledge, only two bishops have issued pastoral letters against contraception— Bishops Glennon Flavin of Lincoln, Nebraska, and Donald Montrose of Stockton, California. Cardinal John O'Connor has publicly decried contraception as a sin that Catholics should confess. Some bishops have assured me they do oppose contraception and sterilization, but their pastoral silence is deafening, their action nil. Why? Some say it's fear of criticism; others, the desire for popularity; still others, the notion that there are bigger moral problems. Which?

When he was appointed archbishop of Hartford, Connecticut, Daniel Cronin thanked Pope John Paul II for his confidence in him and assured the pontiff of his loyalty, observing that the Church has always stood against abortion, homosexuality, and euthanasia. But he scrupulously avoided mentioning contraception. Why?

Archbishop Cronin is the kind of bishop that Notre Dame's rebel theologian Father Richard McBrien has rudely criticized. Has Archbishop Cronin, Father McBrien's superior, thrown the latter's heretical column out of his diocesan newspaper and limited his pseudotheologizing? Last year the arrogant McBrien publicly boasted that he'll never get the Charles Curran treatment because he's so friendly with many bishops.

FRANTIC SINGAPORE: DESPERATE FOR BABIES

Governments, like individuals, "get too late smart." Singapore is a good example of that. The official slogan of the 1960s, "Stop at two," has become the 1980s' "Have three children, or more if you can afford them."

Sin is always costly, even for governments. Singapore officials, who listened too long to the antilife, antimarriage, antifamily, antiyouth, antilove, and antireligion siren song of the Family Planning Association (PP), are now spending millions to recoup.

For example, the government has mounted a million-dollar publicity campaign to sell the joys of marriage and the three-or-more-child family. HLI's collaborators in Singapore doubt whether their country has a secure future, with the island's Moslem Malays (17 percent) greatly out-reproducing the native Singaporeans.

The government has also hired a public-relations company to subtly convey these messages: If you're single, think about getting married; if you're married, don't wait too long to have your first child; if you have only one child, realize that he can be lonely without any brother or sister; if you have two children, why not have a third, if you can afford it?

Singapore's misfortune is the legacy of Planned Parenthood, which is still peddling its school-based sex-education in promiscuity.

The government has mobilized television and newspapers for its desperate drive to sell marriage and children to the Singaporeans, among whom the average wife is twenty-eight when she has her first child. Moreover, 44 percent of all women are now working outside the home. New government regulations: For an abortion to be performed legally, the mother must receive counseling before and after, according to government specifications. She gets a thorough education on the effects that abortion can have on her health, both physical and psychological. She must see an abortion-discouraging video.

Even so, Singaporeans abort more than one-fourth of all their preborn children; the average family has only 1.6 children—far below the 2.2 needed for national replacement. In the last five years divorces have doubled and young people have been fornicating as never before. All of this misfortune is the legacy of PP, which, revealingly, is still peddling its school-based sex-education in promiscuity. HLI's vigorous Singapore branch increasingly opposes PP, thanks in part to our friends' help. PP publications around the world still publicize the Singapore debacle as if it were a great victory! For little Singapore, the handwriting is on the wall. Can it recover? No modern nation ever has.

Letters

Congratulations on the publication of your one-hundredth special report. No human being can persevere on his own with such dedication and devotion. We know you must have divine help!

We are indeed grateful for your continuing assistance to us in Singapore. We thank God for having worked so many wonders through you. God bless you, Father Paul Marx!

John Lim, MD
Singapore

Here in "Liberalville," babies are being killed by intauterine injection of potassium chloride under ultrasound guidance, fetal monitor, and prostaglandins as a practice of the Wisconsin genetics network.

May God bless you at every turn.

Thomas F. Warner, MD
Madison, Wisconsin

Enclosed are the reprimand I got from the dean of the College of Sciences at the University of Maine, my written reply, and my cover letter to all those I named as getting copies of both the reprimand and my reply. As you can see, the reprimand doesn't state what I did *specifically* that warranted a reprimand, because if it did, the dean would become a laughingstock.

There is more to the reprimand than meets the eye. I am the only active prolife member of the faculty at the university, and whenever the administration brings one of the proabortion speakers on campus, I and prolifers outside the university are there to greet them with your enlarged photos of aborted babies. We stand in the lecture hall—off to the sides so that we don't block the speaker from the audience—and pray in silence throughout each talk. Anyone in the audience wanting to see what abortion really is need only turn his head to one side and see the aborted babies.

There is no witness more powerful than a silent, prayerful one, while your photos of aborted babies are being displayed. Prayer and pictures slice right through the proabortion rhetoric about "choice" and "reproductive freedom."

I am convinced the administration is desperate to find a way to fire me, even though I am a tenured full-professor with eighteen years on the faculty. A Catholic is acceptable on the faculty only if he puts his faith in a closet. This is just part of a nationwide attempt to crush the Christian witness against abortion, especially direct-action witnessing. Establishment Liberals today are the New Nazis, and they will do whatever it takes to stifle our witness.

Terence J. Hughes
Orono, Maine

***Ready to make a joyful noise unto the Lord: dancers at HLI's opening
night procession in Houston***

Prolife Knights of Columbus at our Opening Mass in Houston

Conferences in Texas and Holland

No. 101 May 1993

Now that our twelfth world conference on love, life, and the family (Houston, April 14-18) is history, let me offer you some of my recollections and observations about this marvelous gathering, which all our friends helped make possible.

HOUSTON: A PROLIFE "UNITED NATIONS"

The total attendance was more than 2,000 souls, including some 300 prolife/profamily activists from forty-six foreign countries. Alphabetically, those countries ranged from A (Argentina, Australia, and Austria) to Z (Zambia and Zimbabwe), and included newly freed nations from Central and Eastern Europe, among them Croatia, Hungary, Lithuania, Poland, Russia, Ukraine, and the Czech and Slovak Republics.

As you'd expect, large contingents represented the USA's nearest neighbors, Canada and Mexico, but the second-largest foreign group (outranked only by Canada) came from little Costa Rica. The delegations that traveled the farthest included these from New Zealand, India, Japan, Singapore, South Africa, Malaysia, and the aforementioned nations, Australia, Russia and Ukraine.

Among our distinguished guests were His Eminence, Cardinal Alfonso Lopez Trujillo, president of the Pontifical Council for the Family, and His Excellency, Bishop Joseph Fiorenza of the diocese of Galveston-Houston.

Cardinal Lopez Trujillo gave a stirring talk on *Humanae Vitae* (*HV*), in which he said the 25-year-old encyclical is more important than ever in light of the decline of traditional families, epidemic divorce, plunging birthrates, dying nations, rampant abortion, and spreading euthanasia. Bishop Fiorenza, in his homily at our opening Mass, also strongly endorsed and defended *HV*.

Auxiliary Bishop James Tamayo and forty-seven

priests concelebrated this Mass and led hundreds of conferees in an impressive six-block candlelight rosary procession from St. Michael's Church back to our hotel headquarters. The conference attracted fifty-five priests, several brothers, and more than forty Vietnamese nuns, mostly young and all resplendent in beautiful white habits.

A WORLD OF EXPERTS

People tell us that one of the greatest benefits of our world conferences is the opportunity to meet, hear, and confer with outstanding prolife leaders from all over the world. Each year HLI brings together the most knowledgeable, most distinguished, and most brilliant people who labor to protect preborn children and the family.

Among the world-renowned experts who spoke this year were: Dr. Jerome Lejeune, discoverer of the genetic cause of Down syndrome and professor of fundamental genetics at the University of Paris; Dr. Rudolph Ehmann, Switzerland's authority on abortifacient birth control; Dr. Peggy Norris, British medical ethicist, researcher, and TV personality; Dr. Bernard Nathanson, chief of OB-GYN at three New York City hospitals and, in his past life, an abortionist and founder of the National Abortion Rights Action League (NARAL); and Dr. Claude Newbury, deputy public-health director of South Africa's largest city, Johannesburg, who's known as "Mr. Right to Life" of South Africa.

Also contributing were Father Michael Schooyans, holder of three PhDs, prolific writer on depopulation and life issues, and professor of political economy at Belgium's University of Louvain; Dr. Lawrence Adekoya, Nigeria's "Mr. Right to Life," who's president of that nation's Human Life Protection League, HLI's largest branch (fifty-five chapters); Dr. Alice von Hildebrand, noted author, lecturer, and former professor of philosophy at Hunter College; and India's Dr. Marie Mascarenhas, social and medical demographer, expert on natural birth regulation, and founder and director of CREST, the Center for Research, Education, Service and Training for family life.

I don't have space to list all of the esteemed lecturers

who spoke, but we featured some sixty faculty members from thirty different nations.

> ***One of the highlights of the conference was the second gathering of abortion-holocaust survivors.***

MEET THE ABORTION SURVIVORS!

One of the highlights of the conference was the second gathering of abortion-holocaust survivors (the first was in Ottawa last year). This time we were honored to present six abortion survivors and one who'd been targeted for euthanasia. They ranged from 22-year-old pre-med student Sarah Smith, who survived a D & C abortion that killed her twin brother, to almost-one-year-old Iyamile Aviel Aguila, who somehow made it through an attempted D & C performed at a notorious Los Angeles abortion mill.

Other survivors included California's Gianna Jessen, a 16-year-old who survived a late-term saline abortion; 14-year-old Joshua Vandervelden, who escaped during an abortion at a Wisconsin mill and was then diagnosed as a "tumor" when his mother suffered postabortion complications; and three-year-old Lauren Pulliam, who foiled a Texas abortionist at one of Planned Parenthood's eighty-odd abortuaries. Lauren's helpless grandparents—prevented by law from interfering with their daughter's "right" to abort—saw their prayers answered when the abortionist fouled up and "missed" the plucky baby. By the way, Planned Parenthood (PP), by its own admission, killed 130,000 preborn children last year.

All were especially pleased to meet 17-month-old Anthony Joseph Speers, whose mother was "counseled" at a PP killing chamber and set up for an abortion a few days later. But his teenage mother canceled her appointment and let him be born after a friend showed her HLI's famous "Freedom of Choice" photo of the severed head of an aborted baby.

This story was especially sweet to me in light of all the

angry phone calls and filthy letters that my wonderful
staff has had to put up with through the years, as outraged
pro-aborts and feminists vented their spleens over our photos that show abortion as it really is.

Just think, pictures our benefactors paid to print are
saving babies' lives! As an old Hebrew axiom states, "He
who saves one life, it is as if he had saved the whole
world." Such is the worth of one human life!

Our euthanasia survivor was Nathan Post, a 12-year-
old lad twice targeted for infanticide because he had been
born with hydrocephalus. Because of Nathan's condition,
the hospital staff never cleaned him up after his birth;
they simply put him aside, leaving him covered with blood
and amniotic fluid while his mother spent four hours in
the recovery room.

Apparently they wanted to produce a dead baby before
his mother awoke from the anesthesia or, failing that, to
persuade her to agree not to treat him. (The devil is a liar
and a murderer from the beginning, Jesus said!) When
Nathan was three years old and gravely ill with chicken
pox, two doctors refused to treat him because of his poor
"quality of life."

Today, despite all his difficulties, Nathan exhibits a
keen sense of humor and can hold an interesting conversation, all the while racing around in his wheelchair, skillfully maneuvering it about in the smallest of places.

As with our previous conferences, all the workshops
and speakers are available on audiocassettes (except
Father Stanley Jaki). One of my favorite tapes is that of
the abortion survivors—not only for the deeply moving stories of love and courage it contains, but also for the laughter and chatter of the younger survivors, which you can
hear clearly in the background. As each mother tells her
story, you can hear her baby call out as she mentions the
child's name to the audience.

HIGHLIGHTS OF THE TALKS

Because we conducted some sixty different ninety-minute
sessions, plus Youth Day and a World Council meeting, it's
impossible for me to comment on all of the wonderful talks

and speakers. So, with apologies to those I miss, let me describe for you some of the highlights of our Houston gathering.

South Africa's Dr. Claude Newbury gave two remarkable presentations, "AIDS and *Apartheid* in South Africa" and "Life Issues in Africa." He traced the country's history from its discovery and exploration by the Portuguese in the 15th century, through later colonizations by the Dutch and British, and the influence of the Congregational Church, to the incredible system of *apartheid*. Coming to the present, he described a country scourged by AIDS, as the South African Family Planning Association promotes sexual license and the population controllers seek to limit the numbers of survivors.

Monsignor William Smith, assistant professor of moral theology at New York's St. Joseph Seminary, presented typically masterful and insightful analyses of "Theological Dissent and *Humanae Vitae*" and "Conscience and Morality." Frankly, I don't know any theologian who can better cut to the heart of an argument and impart more authentic Catholic teaching—and do so in such a humorous way—as does Monsignor Smith. He is simply the USA's foremost moralist.

Dr. Alice von Hildebrand gave three fabulous talks, "Christianity and the Role of Suffering," "Male and Female HE Made Them," and "*Mea Culpa, Tua Culpa*: Confessions of St. Augustine and J. J. Rousseau," to packed rooms of spellbound listeners. If you've never heard a talk by this remarkable woman, you have a treat coming. Buy her tapes!

STANDING ROOM ONLY

Speaking of packed rooms, you should have seen the crowds for Dr. Nathanson's brilliant talks, "RU-486" and "Fetal Tissue Research." Our Marriott hosts kept carting in additional chairs, but the crowd overflowed the large room. Dr. Nathanson tore through the lies and ploys of the abortion industry and the tissue hunters, who are hellbent on bringing the abortion pill to the USA and "harvesting" the bodies of aborted babies. With an avalanche of facts and research, he demolished their claims.

Dr. Nathanson predicted a dramatic rise in abortions in the developing nations to meet the demand for fetal tissue from patients in wealthy nations seeking cures for their ailments. He foresaw the emergence of a "growth industry," including black-market profiteering, in the inevitable trafficking in babies' body parts.

Father Schooyans, he of the triple doctorates, gave outstanding presentations on the "New World Order and Demographic Security," "The Political Implications of Abortion," and "Doctors and Attorneys: Servants of Life and Liberty." His insightful analysis of the worldwide demographic and political effects of the depopulation and abortion movements—soon to be the subjects of another of his best-selling books—offered much food for thought. We'll summarize Father's talks in a future issue of our bimonthly *Population Research Institute Review*.

Former Presbyterian minister Scott Hahn gave an outstanding and deeply moving presentation, "A Protestant Discovers Catholicism"—the story of his own odyssey from staunch anti-Catholicism to the discovery of the "one, true Church," and his subsequent reception into, and defense of, the Catholic Church. Scott's wife Kimberly, who converted later, gave her own unique perspective in "A Protestant Discovers *Humanae Vitae*" and "The Vocation of Being a Wife and Mother."

This remarkable husband-wife team has brought thousands of lapsed Catholics back to the Faith and has inspired many Protestants to embrace it. Incidentally, the largest Christian body in the USA, next to practicing Catholics, is the "fallen-aways."

Our foreign speakers provided conference-goers with priceless, timely information about the abortion situation in their respective lands and about the antilife forces warring against their people. Dr. Igor Guzov, professor of OB-GYN and a leader of Russian Right to Life, and surgeon Dr. Antun Lisec, who works full time for HLI in Central and Eastern Europe, reported on the inroads being made into their countries and all of the former USSR by the International Planned Parenthood Federation (IPPF), with the conniving of the UN's World Health Organization

(WHO).

As soon as Soviet Communism collapsed, IPPF and its cohorts moved in to peddle their wicked programs. HLI has joined the battle, launching new branches in the former Red strongholds of Russia, Lithuania, Croatia, Hungary, Ukraine, and the Czech and Slovak Republics.

H.L.I. TO RESCUE CHILD PROSTITUTES

Experts participated in similar "Life Issues" panels on Africa, Asia, and Latin America, respectively, and one on "Abortion in Europe." The Asian panel was especially shocking in its revelations about the sex industry and the trade in child prostitutes in various cities of Southeast Asia, where brothels have been turned into sex hotels for the pleasure of foreign visitors.

Many European city brothels, too, offer men dainty Asian girls—particularly in Germany and Switzerland, where prostitutes are examined weekly and pay taxes. It's not surprising that Germany, where prostitution, abortion, and pornography are legal, is the greatest producer of pornography in the world.

> *Our newest project, the Magdalene Rescue and Rehabilitation Fund, is now gearing up to save these young victims.*

Our newest project, the Magdalene Rescue and Rehabilitation Fund, is now gearing up to save these young victims, many of whom are sold or kidnapped into prostitution slavery. In Houston, HLI's friend Edgar Debany outlined his vision and his plans for this new HLI mission. Besides child prostitutes, there are also millions of child worker-slaves, e.g., in India.

The heads of our two Croatian branches, Dr. Lisec and economist Marijo Zivkovic, told me that much of the obstetrical field in Croatia, especially in the most prestigious hospitals and universities, is under the control of Serbs who zealously promote abortion and sterilization among their old enemies, the Croats and Moslems—truly, the ultimate in "ethnic cleansing"! We'll report this shocking story in a future issue of *HLI Reports.*

HOLY PRIESTS AND AN ARMLESS TROUBADOUR

At our Friday luncheon we were privileged to hear Canada's Father Ted Colleton, who passed up a career as an entertainer to become a missionary in Kenya, a heroic prolifer (who has spent months in jail for closing abortion mills), and "the funniest priest on earth."

Father Ted kept us shaking with laughter, tickling us with clever Irish jokes and his own inimitable humor. If he had chosen "show biz," he'd be a millionaire many times over! Woven into the mirth, however, was a beautiful talk on the importance of the family and mothers. Father Ted was the perfect counterpoint to the distressing subject matter that our conference workshops must deal with.

We also enjoyed the beautiful guitar music and singing of Tony Melendez, an extremely talented musician and an amazing and courageous prolifer. When Tony was still in his mother's womb, she took thalidomide, which was later found to seriously affect the limbs of preborn children. Tony was born with no arms and with such serious deformities of his feet that doctors predicted he'd never walk.

But after several operations, much orthopedic care, and boundless love and encouragement from his family, Tony not only learned to walk but became so expert in using his toes that he began playing the guitar with them! Today he's a professional musician and composer who gives concerts throughout the world.

Indeed, his career "took off" when he played for the Vicar of Christ during Pope John Paul II's 1987 visit to California. His Holiness was so moved by Tony's performance and his courage that he spontaneously stepped down from the platform to embrace and kiss him. Tony likewise electrified and touched our luncheon audience, who gave him a thunderous ovation that just went on and on. Next time we'll supply Kleenex for each table!

The incredible speaker for our Saturday banquet was

Father Werenfried van Straaten, known as "the greatest beggar on earth" for his forty-six years of collecting alms for Christ's Kingdom. A confidant of the pope, Father Werenfried describes himself as being "twice forty years young"; he's given an average of three talks daily for the past twenty years!

This amazing Norbertine has collected $2.5 *billion* since 1947. When he walked in, those who knew him held onto their wallets and purses! He humorously demonstrated his begging prowess by holding out the battered old hat he's collected millions with, saying that because it has holes, people shouldn't give mere coins. Our generous audience donated $15,000, half of which he kindly shared with HLI.

Father kept his audience enthralled as he told how, as "the Bacon Priest," he fed millions of refugees in Europe after World War II. When the Iron Curtain descended, he extended his work by founding Aid to the Church in Need, the worldwide relief organization serving the martyr Church in Eastern Europe, the USSR, Red China, etc. The success of his apostolate proves his mottoes: "People are better than you think" and "God is better than you think, too."

In his address, Father Werenfried skillfully analyzed the revelations of Fatima and the collapse of European Communism on one hand and, on the other, the state of the "victorious" yet really godless West, which has embraced antilife philosophies every bit as evil as those of the Nazis and Communists. "If Christ is not heeded," he warned, "the world will run aground. It will be like a decaying corpse, a cadaver which will infect everyone."

MARK YOUR CALENDAR FOR CALIFORNIA

By popular demand, Father van Straaten will address the luncheon at our thirteenth world conference in Irvine, California, April 6-10, 1994. If you didn't come to Houston, make plans now to be in Irvine.

"There's just nothing like the world conference," one participant observed. "It's like a gigantic spiritual retreat where everyone shares and lives the same values," said another. And a third marveled, "Every year I keep thinking you can't make it better, but you do!"

I want to publicly acknowledge our great debt to our conference chairwoman, my longtime friend and a great prolifer, Margaret Hotze of Houston; she and her committee labored long and hard to make the conference the huge success it was.

And thanks to all our dear friends who prayed for the conference, bringing down countless blessings upon it. We're grateful, too, for the generous financial help that enabled us to give full or partial scholarships to some 300 marvelous prolife activists, mostly foreigners, who couldn't have come otherwise.

H.L.I. DEFENDS IRELAND

The Irish are still holding their breath over whether their proabortion coalition government will exploit the hole kicked in the Constitution by their Supreme Court (see *Report No. 100*) and pass laws allowing abortions for "hard cases." These exceptions eventually bring abortion-on-demand, in any country. The pro-aborts ignore the fact that Ireland has achieved Europe's lowest infant- and maternal-mortality rates.

Ireland's anti-Catholic media continue to flail away viciously at the Church and prolifers. Prolife/profamily forces are organized to do what they can against a hostile government and the deceptive media.

The politicians and the media want to legalize sodomy and divorce and to place condom machines all over the country for "safe sex." Of course, these "progressive" measures will hasten the rotting of the Western world, which is no longer replacing itself despite the "copulation explosion." The government has refused to hold a referendum to let the people decide the abortion issue.

Over the weekend of November 5-7, HLI will host another prolife/profamily conference in Galway. At our weekend seminar in Cork last fall, the Irish were so impressed by Dr. Bill Coulson's debunking of Carl Rogers's and Abraham Maslow's "nondirective counseling" and Ireland's value-free "Life Skills" school program that they brought him back this year for a week of talks in various cities and universities.

HOW TO DE-CATHOLICIZE IRELAND

A new version of the "human potential" movement is being pushed in Ireland. Called "Stay Safe," it's a mixture of the ideas of agnostic/humanist psychologists Piaget, Dewey, and Kohlberg. It involves feel-good pseudo-psychology, Dewey's experiential "life adjustment" nonsense, and "values clarification"—the errors that have drained Christian values out of Catholic school systems worldwide and have pushed parents out of curriculum planning. Its backers have infiltrated the health and education departments of Ireland's government and teacher organizations.

Dr. Coulson brilliantly exposed the whole movement as a dangerous and unChristian scheme that has failed everywhere, particularly in the USA (even Rogers and Maslow eventually rejected their own theories). The truth is always hard to take but easy to deny: Irish "experts" heckled, hooted, and hassled Coulson for exposing this perilous, unrealistic amalgam, now aimed at the primary-school children of Ireland. Twenty years ago the "Children of God" program was introduced in Ireland to replace doctrine-oriented teaching.

If you want to know how the modern enemies of God, the Irish Family Planning Association (PP) and its quislings, function in Ireland (i.e., how Satan works day and night), read the eye-opening new book, *The X Case,* published by HLI. One very positive Irish trend, encouraged by Bishop John Magee, formerly the pope's secretary, is that more than 60,000 people now take part in perpetual adoration.

P.P. V. POLAND

Poland's thirty-eight million people had no law against abortion after 1956; Polish abortionists have killed some twenty million babies. But a law passed recently is perhaps a little better than nothing.

It amounts to virtual abortion-on-demand; the one good thing about it is a requirement that all abortions be performed in hospitals (not private "clinics"), and that records be kept. But a new coalition of PP and the feminist

Polish Federation of Women, fueled by foreign money, is fighting even those few protections. They've concocted a four-point plan to oppose the new law.

Their strategy is to challenge it on legal grounds and to find loopholes, to create an international protest against "human rights violations" as was done in Ireland, to promote contraception and sex "education," to lure Polish mothers to abortionists outside the country, and to engage in other devilish tricks.

By the way, the suicide rate in Poland is now 14.3 per 100,000, an all-time high.

HOLOCAUSTS OF JEWS AND BABIES

You've read about the $167 million museum opened recently here in Washington, D.C., to commemorate the millions of people victimized by Nazi barbarism. Truly, this was a monstrous, historic crime.

But there's a far bigger holocaust and crime being enacted every day, one that people hardly think about, or even know about. For example, how many Americans realize that every six months our abortionists are paid to kill more Americans than have died in all the wars we've fought in our 212 years of history? But numerous as these abortion-killings are, they're only a fraction of the total deaths.

The abortion holocaust dwarfs even the Jewish holocaust in sheer numbers of victims.

How many Americans know that the "contraceptive" Pill, the IUD, the new matchstick-like implant called Norplant, the recently-FDA-approved injectable Depo-Provera, and the popular-on-campus "Morning-after Pill" are abortifacients, i.e., that at least sometimes they work by causing early, unnoticed abortions? Including chemical abortions, Bogomir Kuhar, president of Pharmacists for Life, estimates that 9-12 million abortions are induced every year in the USA alone!

What has struck me and many others is that at the slightest mention of the far-greater holocaust of the pre-born babies, many Jews, PP members, and others object strongly. They tolerate *no* comparison—perhaps because the abortion holocaust dwarfs even the Jewish Holocaust in sheer numbers of victims.

But there must be other reasons. In *Report No. 34*, I gave incontestable evidence that, sadly, a certain segment of the Jews leads the abortion movement in the USA and in many parts of the world. I noted that Israel reports one of the world's highest rates of abortions *v.* births. Incidentally, former Communist Etienne-Emile Baulieu, the French inventor of the RU-486 baby-killing pill, was, until a decree of 19 November 1947, known as Etienne Felix Azon Blum.

Israel, by the way, found that female soldiers were no help at the front lines, where the men were distracted with worry about the women; today, Israel's women soldiers serve in other capacities, not at the front. According to reports, they are each allowed three abortions every year, paid for by the government.

In Forteleza, Brazil, some years ago, I was astonished to learn from a high-powered international adoption lawyer that many Israeli Jews come to Brazil to adopt babies; they're particularly fond of babies with German backgrounds, whatever the reasons.

IS FATHER MARX ANTI-CATHOLIC?

The reaction from some readers to our exposé in *Report No. 34* was immediate and angry. But none of the critics disproved what we said, not even the head of the U.S. Bishops' Catholic-Jewish office.

Thank God, there are many notable Jewish prolifers. I think of Dr. Hymie Gordon, former head of the department of genetics at the Mayo Clinic, Dr. Bernard Nathanson, New York's Rabbi Yehuda Levin, California's Kenneth Mitzner, Britain's Rabbi Jacobovitz, columnist Don Feder, and others. After the Supreme Court's Black Monday decision in 1973, activist Mitzner wrote, "It is tragic but demonstrably true that most of the leaders of the proabortion movement are of Jewish extraction."

Be sure to read our May 1993 *HLI Reports* (send me $2 for a copy if you don't receive *HLI Reports*) to see a powerful piece of research by scholar Brian Clowes concerning the involvement of certain Jews in abortion. The proof is abundant. And please don't accuse him or me of being anti-Jewish; someday we may do an article on the key role that many *Catholics* have played in abortion, from Pill developer Dr. John Rock to Supreme Court Justice William Brennan to PP President Pamela Maraldo. (I suppose people will say we're anti-Catholic!)

WITCHES, HOMOS GREET H.L.I.

The Dutch people are known around the world for their civility and tolerance, but apparently tolerance is not a virtue among certain "progressive" elements in the Netherlands.

We gained that impression at the First European Pro-Life Leadership Conference, sponsored by HLI at Emmaus Conferentie-Oord in Helvoirt, Holland, March 11-14. Our gathering was the target of a host of protesters from Dutch sodomite, feminist, transvestite, anarchist, and proabortion groups.

About 100 garishly attired protesters, many sporting multicolored hairdos and black leather outfits, marched on Thursday, March 11, and again on Saturday, March 13, to the front of the conference center, a former SVD seminary on the outskirts of Helvoirt. Partially blocking the entrance and impeding highway traffic, they banged on large oil drums and garbage cans, blew whistles, sounded sirens, and otherwise raised a raucous cacophony of ear-splitting noise for more than two hours.

The group also used a truck-bed stage with an amplifier system to project noise at us. Transvestites and men and women dressed as witches paraded about. Half-naked lesbians made "love" publicly.

Several men with torches and bottles of kerosene spat fire from their mouths; some protesters stood in the driveway with a makeshift banner reading "The Portals of Hell." They apparently wanted to "give us Hell," and in fact we got a good taste of what Hell must be like. Their *demon*-stration was ugly, hateful, and juvenile.

WHO ARE THE REAL BIGOTS?

We came to that lovely place to hold a quiet meeting for prolife leaders from throughout Europe, but those unruly protesters seemed to find peaceful prolifers very threatening. The homosexual-feminist sideshow was superficially entertaining, but participants and others were deeply concerned about what was really taking place there.

The protesters called us "fascists," "anarchists," and "pigs"; but which side was using inflammatory rhetoric and trying to interfere with the rights of others? The demonstration was a disturbing attempt to suppress ideas that the people outside didn't like. It really was a form of antireligious bigotry.

The night before, Cardinal Adrianus Simonis of Utrecht, who favored us with an opening Mass and sermon, told me, "Holland has fallen back into a complete paganism." While we were in the Netherlands we learned that Bishop Ronald Philippe Bar of Rotterdam had resigned after being accused of sexual misconduct.

"What we are seeing is the clash of two cultures," said Father Matthew Habiger, OSB, executive director of HLI. "There is the culture of death—represented by those who pervert and destroy the fruits of human sexuality—and there is the culture of life, represented by those who believe in the sanctity of human life from conception to natural death. The people outside say we are old-fashioned, repressed, and frustrated, but I believe they have it upside down and backwards. Ours is the way of hope and life; it is the way of the future." He called the protest "a prolonged temper tantrum, a childish performance from the theater of the absurd."

The HLI conference drew more than 250 prolife leaders representing some one million people from fifteen European countries to pray, to strategize, and to hear an international faculty on a variety of prolife, profamily topics. Thursday's activities included an outdoor rosary procession.

DUTCH "CATHOLICS" APOSTATIZE

According to national diocesan reports, half of the people in this land no longer go to any church. Fewer than 50 percent of the "Catholics" believe in a personal God. The Netherlands, which once produced many missionaries, has itself become a mission country, said Bishop Hendrik Bomers of the Diocese of Haarlem. He graciously offered our closing Mass and preached tellingly.

Bishop Bomers complained that only a minority of "Catholics" still believe that homosexual acts, abortion, and euthanasia are sins. Contraception? It's taken for granted by Catholics, both married and unmarried; no one even talks about it. "Overtime treatment" (early mini-abortion by suction, paid for by the state) helps the Dutch to lie about the number of baby-killings; it is very high, thanks to sex-ed promoted by Organon, a Dutch Pill company.

One cause of this situation is a deep-seated, comfortable secularization and spiritual lethargy. Meanwhile, immigrants and Moslems are taking over while the Dutch play with sex, resulting in a below-replacement birthrate, like that of the rest of once-Christian Europe. The Dutch have also embraced euthanasia wholesale. Out of 129,000 deaths last year, more than one in five were euthanasia cases, and at least half of these were involuntary!

The pleasant Dutch suffer from a kind of schizophrenic blindness. Thus, the Dutch national prolife society, KBOK, fights only surgical abortion, ignores "overtime treatment," and never exposes abortifacients. The law against abortion is still on the books, but it's not enforced. Euthanasia, too, remains in the criminal code, but it's freely allowed. Dutch government officials were "alarmed" when the Holy See came down powerfully on the latest lowering of barriers against euthanasia.

Joining religious leaders at Assisi recently, Pope John Paul II took the "unpredicted" step of asking all to pray for a "miracle" from God. Only the direct intervention of God, the pontiff declared, can now rescue humanity from its pride, sins, and evils, and save many nations from destruction. PRAY!

Our conference topics included euthanasia,

homosexuality, abortion, sterilization, natural birth-regulation, contraception (especially in relation to the papal encyclical *Humanae Vitae*), feminism in the Church, and genetic engineering. Thanks be to God and to our friends' generosity, it was a huge success. The next HLI-sponsored European prolife conference will take place in Paris, October 22-24.

I unleashed these great prolifers in our warehouse, saying they could take anything they wanted.

H.L.I. WAREHOUSE "LOOTED"!

After our Houston conference, fifteen leaders from HLI's various international branches came to our world headquarters for further information and training. I unleashed these great prolifers in the warehouse, saying they could take anything they wanted; whatever they couldn't carry, we'd ship to them. The saintly "looters" happily took home some $35,000 worth of videos, films, books, literature, rosaries, and fetal models! And someone promptly dubbed me the Warehouse Priest.

I'm delighted that these true leaders will be reaching hundreds of thousands with our materials in Africa, Asia, Eastern Europe, and Latin America. But now I must replace $35,000 worth of stock!

Letters

These letters are typical of those we have received in response to HLI's circulation of pictures of aborted babies, including the graphic representation of an aborted baby's head (captioned "Freedom of Choice?"). The explanation accompanying this last photo reads:

> This baby's head was found in a plastic trash bag outside an abortion mill in Houston. Bodies were found there in the spring and summer of 1987. On August 8, the abortionist denied that he or his staff had thrown babies's bodies out. But three days later, prolifers found bodies there again. The abortionist said that he disposed of bodies according to Texas law. This may be true; it is not clear that tossing babies's bodies out to be eaten by dogs, rats, and mice was illegal.

*   *   *   *

I am writing this letter as a protest/criticism of your movement's part in the January 22 antiabortion march I saw in Washington, DC. As a graduate of the University of Notre Dame, I hope that you will credit me with having both the intelligence and the proper moral upbringing to make fair criticism of the atrocious actions your group is perpetuating.

Let me say that I sympathize with many of the goals of the right-to-life movement with regard to teaching responsible behavior and educating youth to recognize the value of human life. However, I feel that the Washington, DC, march did more harm than good for the antiabortion movement by coming off as angry and morally superior.

What disgusted me most about the march was the posters your movement distributed to the protesters. You might think that confronting people with pictures of aborted fetuses will make them fully recognize what having an abortion means, but, quite frankly, you are *wrong*. The practice of showing these pictures is *grotesque*. You elicit disgust in onlookers rather than sympathy for your movement.

It is my sincere hope that the prolife movement will recognize that abortion is a very complex issue and that more abortions would be prevented if the group changed its tactics. By demonstrating in front of clinics you cause more unnecessary pain and suffering for a woman going for an abortion, but rarely cause her to change her mind.

> *Paul M. Conway*
> *Notre Dame, Indiana*

I was at the March for Life and observed a priest distributing the "Freedom of Choice?" posters. I wish to express my congratulations for your decision to distribute these posters.

I was in New York City during the July 1992 Democratic convention during the rescues, and I personally held the posters. We were surrounded by "pro-aborts" who did not want the public to see these graphic proofs of violence against our unborn.

On the corner of Madison and 55th, the so-called heart of the advertising industry, a man approached me and asked, "What is that?" I said it was a picture of a baby's head ripped off by abortion. He turned to the pro-abort and asked her what she had to counter this picture. She could not respond to his challenge, and I replied that were *was* no answer to the picture, since this was the truth of abortion and they could offer no response to truth. The man said to the pro-abort, "You will lose this battle in the streets of America if you cannot counter this picture."

Father, keep up the good fight! We are presently in "occupied territory," but eventually the truth will shine.

> *Peggy Beirne*
> *Pearl River, New York*

Thank you so much for responding to my last letter. Let me tell you a little about myself. I am twelve, was born March 20, 1979, in San Bernadino, California. I now live in Anaheim and have three older brothers.

I intend to ask my teacher to show the video you gave me to my religion class. After I saw that video I cried for several minutes.

I know that this is kind of stretching it a little, but is there *anything* else I can do? When I saw those pictures I felt like screaming. The pain was even greater when I held my baby nephew and thought of all the futures of those innocent children destroyed, as I looked at his beautiful eyes and laughing face.

I could hardly believe it when I got your response. I really didn't count on it. Thank you again, and *please*, if it is at all possible, write back and answer my inquiry about helping.

> *Ann Halsig*
> *Anaheim, California*

I am fifteen years old. I became pregnant at fourteen and was going to get an abortion until a friend brought me a picture of a baby's head found behind a Texas abortion clinic.

This picture was responsible for my changing my mind about having an abortion.

I should like to purchase some of these to hand out to my friends. Maybe I can make a difference in someone else's life.

I want to thank you for saving my baby's life. At birth he was 9 lbs., 4 oz., 21 inches long. He is Anthony Joseph Speers, and the greatest joy in my life.

> *Shelah M. Speers*
> *Puyallup, Washington*

We have taken your postcards of "The 8-Week-Old Baby" to the doors of abortion mills in Charlotte, and they have been most useful in saving lives. We have given them to people who were lukewarm in defense of the children, and they now understand why we are on the streets and why we rescue.

And now we want to mail them to our state legislature to show them what they are making the taxpayers support. May God have mercy on us!

> *Becky Jamison*
> *Action League for Life*
> *Charlotte, North Carolina*

I sidewalk-counsel at a abortion clinic (Planned Parenthood) and your poster and postcards have already made a difference. At least two women have told me they changed their minds because of my sign. Thank you!

> *Judy Bunnell*
> *Savage, Minnesota*

By bringing down the Iron Curtain, the Polish Pope opened the East to HLI missionaries

"In every country, without exception, contraception has been the gateway to abortion"

Armless troubadour to the Pope and now to prolifers: Tony Melendez in Houston

Sr. Robertilde Vander Meer saves babies and mothers from the anti-lifers in Indonesia

Missionary work is a sure path to holey-ness

Russian prolife leader Dr. Igor Guzov visits HLI's warehouse

Ora et labora—*pray and work*—*is the Benedictine motto*

Doing the Theological Sidestep

No. 102   June 1993

There's an old saying in philosophy that there are no ideas so stupid that some philosopher hasn't voiced or embraced them. That now seems to apply to many theologians as well.

THEOLOGIANS: A SECOND MAGISTERIUM?

This application was evident last February in Dallas, where 130 U.S. bishops and 70 bishops from Canada, Latin America, the Caribbean, and the Philippines held their annual workshop on medical and moral issues. Their speaker was Fordham's Father Avery Dulles, SJ, a dissenter from *Humanae Vitae* (*HV*) who once proposed that theologians be considered a second magisterium (God save us!).

Remember, it was chiefly those theologians who dissented from *HV*, and who bastardized Vatican II (with the bishops' permission), that brought on the present global theological and sexual mess. Father Dulles piously deplored this mess, even though he had contributed to it.

He reflects the present moral climate of his audience more than he tries to point it in the direction of true Church teaching. He wants to bend moral principles to fit the actual practice of Catholics instead of bringing the faithful up to where the Lord is calling them. Of course, no religious order dissented as viciously, as powerfully, and as consistently as did the Jesuits (as individuals), followed by the Society of the Divine Word (see *Special Report No. 99*). (Obviously, I'm not criticizing all Jesuits; let's not forget stalwarts such as Fathers Fessio, Hardon, and Baker.)

Father Dulles correctly observed for the bishops that "the current dissent and controversy over artificial birth control has seriously harmed the Catholic Church." But he said nothing about his own dissent, nor that of fellow Jesuits such as Fathers Fuchs, McCormick, Overbrook,

Rötter, Reese, etc.

He said nothing about how Pope John Paul II repeatedly begged theologians and bishops to stop critiquing *HV*, because the Church's teaching on artificial birth control was a settled matter: "No personal or social circumstances have ever or can ever justify such an act."

THE POPE SPEAKS

"We are not dealing with a doctrine invented by man but one written by the creative hand of God," the pontiff advised 300 moral theologians at the Pontifical Lateran University on 12 November 1988. To cast doubt upon this doctrine would, he said, "render useless the voice of Christ." Not for Father Dulles!

The latter ignored *Lumen Gentium*, n. 25, and other documents that ask for "a religious assent of will and intellect" to repeated, serious teachings of the Church. At Dallas, Dulles mentioned Pope John Paul II only once. He didn't mention that the vast majority of national hierarchies did not dissent to *HV*. The hierarchies of twelve nations *did*, and today all but one of these countries are dying (divine punishment?), and that one, Indonesia, has the largest number of women implanted with the dangerous abortifacient Norplant.

"No one who loves and cares for the Church can be content to see the present state of affairs continue," the hypocritical Jesuit told the bishops. Now that theologians have successfully woven dissent to *HV* into the very fabric of the Church in the West, Dulles has called for dissenters to end their loud campaign for a change in Church teaching!

Then he dropped a blockbuster: Church authorities, too, must ease up and, for example, not make one's stand on contraception (and presumably on sterilization or "surgical contraception") "the sole litmus test" for certain Church appointments. He was disappointed that "priests known to be opposed to the encyclical are...considered ineligible for bishops' appointments."

TRUTH BY VOTE?

Father Dulles seems to think the moral law is determined

by consultation, consensus, majority opinion, and general acceptance by the faithful. At the very least, he cannot understand how *HV* could be true if so many theologians, Catholic and Protestant, reject it. "Possibly the Holy Spirit intends that the Magisterium should learn [!] some lesson from this massive disagreement," he says.

Was Dulles thinking of the incredible, disastrous *Human Sexuality: New Directions in American Thought* (1979), by theologian Father Anthony Kosnik, *et al.*, and of other theological enormities approved by the Catholic Theological Society of America (CTSA), to say nothing of its counterparts in Europe?

According to documents of Vatican II (particularly *Lumen Gentium*, n. 25), it's clear that when a doctrine is taught continuously, emphasized consistently, and repeated firmly, it commands the allegiance of mind and will of every practicing Catholic, and surely of every Catholic theologian with sound principles.

If the Catholic Church is wrong in what the Holy Spirit inspired her to teach for twenty centuries, then we're in a bad way indeed!

If the Catholic Church is wrong in what the Holy Spirit inspired her to teach for twenty centuries—until worldly-wise Jesuits and certain SVD, Redemptorist, and Benedictine theologians came along—then we're in a bad way indeed! More and more people are asking why Dulles and company don't see that in large part they caused this mess, with the help of the bishops.

Dulles, at Dallas, went on to say the purpose of his talk was not to deal with the moral questions surrounding *HV* but to "reflect on how dissent from the encyclical has affected the life of the Church." But he *did* deal with moral questions, again and again. (When I was a young priest I used to admire the Jesuits for their logic and consistency!)

THE REAL PROBLEM: DISSENT

Convert Father Dulles didn't really address the rightness or wrongness of dissent, or whether there's room for it in the areas of contraception, sterilization, abortifacients, and surgical abortion. His only concern was how dissent has affected the life of the Church, or so he said. This manuever is like observing how people infected with AIDS affect their society, while ignoring the more basic question of how they got AIDS.

Preoccupied with proportionalism—a form of relative morality—Dulles seemingly doesn't appreciate the role and importance of moral principles. They seem to be of little importance to him, compared with peace and unity (however achieved) among the ranks of Catholics.

But moral principles—e.g., that every marital act must remain open to life, that the unitive and procreative meanings of intercourse may never be separated, etc.—are moral truths that enable us to know God's moral order for His human universe. Thus, they are terribly important! We guide our lives by them. They're trustworthy and true because they come from our one true teacher, who is the Way, the Truth, and the Life.

If we want good marriages, healthy, happy families, and a mature and loving sexuality, then we must know God's moral truths and choose to live them. When we stand before the judgment seat of God, from which no one is excused, He will judge us worthy to enter His Kingdom only if we accepted and conformed to His moral truths: "If you love me, keep my Commandments."

In a futile attempt at verbal handwashing, Dulles tried to distance himself and other theologians from the dissent over *HV*. He actually had the gall to say that "although the public and highly visible disagreement of theologians is regarded by some as one of the chief causes of the dissent," he questioned that view!

If not the rebel theologians—aided by the current silence of most bishops in the Western world—who is to blame for the confusion of the faithful and for their failure to adhere to *HV*? I'm reminded of Pope Leo XIII in *Satis Cognitum* (1886): "The episcopal order is considered to be in proper union with Peter, as Christ commanded, if it is subordinate to Peter."

Dulles endorsed the "right" of theologians to dissent from *HV*, while admitting they're "disregarding official Church teaching." He admitted that this disregard has disastrous consequences, but he's unclear about the evil of dissent itself.

"LET'S MAKE DISSENTERS BISHOPS"

He deplored using assent to *HV* as a litmus test for selecting new bishops, seminary teachers, and episcopal consultants: "Priests known to be opposed to the encyclical are, I [Father Dulles] am told, considered ineligible....In nations where the pool of candidates is small, this restriction has been devastating." In how many countries has he observed this devastation?

For Dulles, rejection of *HV* isn't important enough to disqualify one from a crucial teaching post. He thinks everyone should respect the "intelligence and sincerity of those with whom they differ on *HV*." But shouldn't intelligent dissenters wake up and admit the grave harm they've done to the Body of Christ? I wonder what the bishops thought about the Dulles Dallas talk, and what they said. Too bad Bishop Austin Vaughan was ill and therefore not present.

Many a good theologian would dispute Dulles's assertion that dissent to *HV* is morally legitimate and "would solve a problem." It bordered on the diabolical for him to say that the theological dissent to *HV* was itself a manifestation of the popular conviction that contraception was tolerable and sometimes necessary. (Remember, he said he'd make no judgments about the morality of *HV*!)

"ALIENATION": WHOSE FAULT?

"The more the hierarchy insists on adherence to *HV*," Father Dulles pontificated, "the more alienated do the majority of the faithful feel." Why is that, Father? And whose fault? As a perceptive layman observed, Dulles should've said, "The more the hierarchy insists on *HV*, the more alienated do the majority of dissenters feel."

Besides, when have the U.S. bishops ever insisted on adherence to *HV*? I can count on one hand the prelates who've spoken out openly for *HV* in the last five years. (If you've heard any bishops explaining or defending *HV*, please send me their names.)

Isn't it strange that our bishops have chosen not to celebrate the twenty-fifth anniversary of this prophetic encyclical? In my opinion, *HV* will go down in history as the most important one of all, or surely at least a pivotal one, because it dealt with basic morality, marital love, sexuality, parental rights, marriage and the family, demography, the origins of human life, and God's very plan for humanity.

"As long as the overwhelming majority of lay people are at odds with the hierarchy on the question of birth control, the basis of marriage and family life will be gravely inhibited," Dulles opined. How can the laity be "at odds with the hierarchy" on birth control when the hierarchy hasn't spoken out?

A shrewd layman writes, "Have dioceses required pre-Cana couples to study the encyclical? Have there been diocesan-sponsored workshops for CCD and Catholic school teachers? Has the National Catholic Education Association made 'Living the Message of *HV*' a theme for its annual meeting? No, no, and no" (*Religious Life*, April 1993, p. 7).

Father John Morrissey, a professor at St. Vincent de Paul Major Seminary in Florida, has proclaimed: "The pope needs a refresher course in moral theology, especially in the area of contraception."

DISSENTER "EDUCATES" THE POPE

Worse still is what goes on in seminaries. Let me cite just one example. Father John Morrissey, professor of moral theology and social doctrine at St. Vincent de Paul Major

Seminary in Boynton Beach, Florida, spoke at Epiphany Church in Miami on 14 January 1993. He accepted the French hierarchy's declaration that, to save all of the values of marriage, couples may morally contracept. Liberally quoting the counterfeit-Catholic theologian Charles Curran, Father Morrissey proclaimed, "The pope needs a refresher course in moral theology, especially in the area of contraception" (what arrogance!). *HV* is "non-authoritative," he decreed; abstinence is "unrealistic." Citing rebel bishops, he said, "If it's good enough for the bishops, it's good enough for me." (Morrissey would've followed the English hierarchy out of the Church in the sixteenth century.)

This Florida theologian, who evidently thinks he's more competent than the Vicar of Christ, recited virtually every false argument of the dissident theologians and even those that Pope Paul VI specifically refuted in *HV*. (Send me $2 for six pages of notes on his talk!) He admitted that "most doctors regard IUDs as abortifacients," but said nothing about the abortifacient nature of the Pill. And what about the many other abortifacients? No wonder I wasn't allowed to lecture at that seminary (I'm "too rigid")! Shouldn't Miami Archbishop Edward McCarthy correct Father Morrissey?

Tragically, Morrissey isn't alone; his views are taught in most U.S. and European seminaries. That's why good bishops (and there are more than you may think) are careful to send their future priests to good seminaries, e.g., Mount St. Mary's (Maryland), St. Joseph's (New York), and St. Charles Borromeo (Philadelphia).

But back to the Dallas Dulles: Numbers don't decide morality. For example, it's been a constant teaching of the Church, from the Fathers through St. Thomas Aquinas to Pope John Paul II's *Centesimus Annus*, that no one has a right to superfluous goods or luxuries when others lack necessities—food, medical care, shelter, and a reasonable education. Having seen the poverty of humanity as few human beings have, I can say flatly that 95 percent of Americans—and 95 percent of all people in the West—don't obey this teaching of the Church. Is it, therefore, erroneous? By Dulles's reasoning, it should be.

Besides, I don't know a single Catholic who's left the Church because of *HV*. How could he, when he doesn't know what *HV* teaches? I've never seen one authentic study proving *HV* is a significant cause of people's leaving.

Another gem from Dulles: "Priests are placed in a difficult position as teachers, preachers, and confessors....This is demoralizing for priests and confusing for the laity." It shouldn't be difficult for obedient priests who know their theology, remain loyal to the pope, and haven't had wild Jesuit, Redemptorist, SVD, or Benedictine theologians to miseducate them.

CATHOLIC TRUTH SATISFIES SOULS

I've observed the Catholic Church functioning in eighty-eight countries of the world over the last forty-six years. I want to tell Father Dulles that any priest who's loyal to the teachings of the Church and who preaches them intelligently is *always* successful with most parishioners or students. Essentially, it's the priests who fail to preach against contraception/sterilization (and often against abortion) who are destroying the parishes.

Who is so naive as to think that the children of contracepting parents today—already deprived of a truly Catholic education in most instances—are going to practice their faith in the next generation? These young "Catholics" are already falling away by the millions. And why don't more bishops, priests, and religious see that contraception has led to abortion in every country?

Dulles complained about strained relations between bishops and theologians in which "otherwise qualified theologians who dissent to *HV* find themselves excluded and shunned by the Church authorities while scholars who continue to work cordially with the hierarchy are sometimes portrayed as sycophantic court theologians." Oh? By whom? If a theologian dissents openly from an enormously important teaching such as that embodied in *HV*, is he really qualified? Why should any bishop employ or listen to him?

The Fordham theologian then asserted that the "prevailing climate of dissent" is linked to "many other negative phenomena," from declining Mass attendance and waning financial support for the Church to defections from the priesthood and the lack of new vocations.

I attribute the declining Mass attendance to the many bishops, priests, and religious who for a generation haven't taught the faith fully. There are few Catholics, if any, who'd blame their absence from Mass on *HV*, which many have never even heard of!

(I once met a bishop who admitted he'd never read *HV*. To his credit, he let HLI do a weekend conference on natural fertility regulation, humbly sat through the whole thing, and told me later how much he'd learned. Good man.)

And hasn't ecumenist Dulles noticed that religious orders such as Opus Dei, the Legionaries of Christ, the Nashville Dominicans, the Daughters of St. Paul, Mother Teresa's Missionaries of Charity, and others—all of whom are loyal to the Holy See—have many vocations? I've never forgotten my professor of pastoral theology telling our seminary class, "Teach your people to pray and they will pay." I've never known this formula to fail!

Another Dulles Dallas dogma: "Those who are strongly convinced by the arguments for or against contraception should recognize the extreme difficulty of the question and should therefore respect the intelligence and sincerity of those with whom they differ." But Moses didn't act that way, nor did any other prophet—nor Jesus Himself.

If Dulles would accept the teaching of the Church and the repeated admonitions of the pope, the matter would be settled. In that case, one side is obviously very wrong, and although we must always respect persons, we must never fail charitably to point out their errors.

According to Father Dulles, "In making appointments to sensitive positions, such as seminary professorships, the hierarchy must take account of the candidates' general [!] fidelity to Catholic doctrine."

IS GENERAL LOYALTY ENOUGH?

"In making appointments to sensitive positions, such as seminary professorships, the hierarchy must take account of the candidates' general [!] fidelity to Catholic doctrine. *Humanae Vitae* should not be made the sole litmus test, but theologians who aggressively attack the encyclical would seem to disqualify themselves," says Father Dulles.

Would Dulles let himself be operated on by a doctor who was *generally* competent? Would he fly with a pilot who was *generally* qualified? He seems to favor "pick-and-choose" theologians who've produced legions of "pick-and-choose" Catholics.

Dulles warns that overzealous efforts to uproot evil in the Church can destroy much good. Is that why the clergy are so timid about teaching Catholic sexual ethics? Why orthodox pastors feel abandoned by their bishops? Why "papal" priests are persecuted? Why prolife activists know that no help is coming from the chancery?

Nature abhors a vacuum, and in the silence of the pulpits another message on sexuality is shaping our culture and our flock: the message of the ubiquitous Planned Parenthood (PP) and its cohorts. Silence is often not golden but craven. Surely the clergy's abdication of their responsibility to teach the fullness of moral truth exacts a high price. Can we expect the sex mess and the abortion holocaust to end if our spiritual leaders choose to follow Dulles's advice about a "respectful silence" and "general fidelity"?

Clearly, he and his kind are a big part of the problem. Instead of seeing the obvious link between dissent from *HV* and the global sexual meltdown, and then renouncing dissent, Dulles merely calls for a truce between the magisterium and the rebels—a mutual toleration. But there's no common ground between truth and error, good and evil, chastity and lust, the marital embrace and contraception. It won't do, twenty-five years after *HV*, simply to say, "Let's all be nice and quiet now."

Finally, I can hardly stand the hypocrisy. Against a widespread "syndrome of permissiveness" in almost all areas of sexuality and procreation, proclaimed Dulles, "every opportunity should be used to promote common witness among all who oppose a merely hedonistic or recreational view of sex and who seek to discern the true meaning of sexuality in the framework of God's creative designs." This, from a dissenter! Does Dulles still not see that one very real cause of this "merely hedonistic or recreational view of sex" is he himself and too many other theologians like him?

Again, I lay the "syndrome of permissiveness" squarely at the feet of the rebel theologians and those bishops who allowed them to rebel. Remember, a few years ago the vast majority of theologians in the Catholic Theological Society of America voted against the Holy See and for the rebel leader, Charles Curran.

A CONSPIRACY OF SILENCE

I'm dismayed that bishops have declared no public demurral to Dulles's disingenuous and dissent-driven discourse at Dallas. When bishops join in the conspiracy of silence surrounding *HV*, then we can understand why so many parish priests refuse to preach on grave moral issues such as contraception, sterilization, abortifacients, and surgical abortion.

We can understand why at most 1 percent of our 100,000 U.S. Catholic doctors refuse to prescribe contraceptives and abortifacients, or to perform or make referrals for sterilizations. We can understand why there's almost no difference between Catholics and the general population in the prevalence of contraception and sterilization; and why we see so many Catholic women at abortion mills, often accompanied by their Catholic boyfriends, mothers, fathers, grandparents, uncles, or aunts.

We can understand why Catholic youth fornicate as much as their non-Catholic peers; why so many Catholic marriages are on the rocks; why so few young men and women think religious life, priesthood, and celibacy are desirable or even possible; why Mass attendance is at an all-time low; and why concerned U.S. Catholics were given virtually no ways to help when the doors of Russia opened to a new evangelization.

Let us pray that Father Dulles, his ideological kindred,

and those who follow them come to see the truth about *HV* and the damage wrought by dissent. Let us pray that our bishops summon the courage to lead rather than to follow. Let us beg God to deliver us from the confused ecclesiology of faith-destroying dissidents such as Dulles, who need to read Cardinal Joseph Ratzinger's famous talk on the proper role of theologians in the Church. Please pray for all of our theologians and bishops.

> ***Cardinal Roger Mahony is trying to destroy Human Life International. Stand by. Pray!***

H.L.I. IN MORTAL DANGER!

Cardinal Roger Mahony is trying to destroy HLI. Stand by. Pray!

COURAGEOUS COLLEGIANS FIGHT FOR LIFE

Although there are prolife groups on campuses across the nation, two organizations work on many campuses: American Collegians for Life (ACL) and Collegians Activated to Liberate Life (CALL).

Since 1987, ACL has grown to more than 300 prolife campus groups throughout the USA. ACL's primary mission is to help form statewide networks of local college prolife groups. These networks, in turn, can organize statewide projects to change the minds and hearts of students and the broader community.

ACL operates in many states, including California, Wisconsin, New Jersey, Maryland, Texas, Ohio, and Pennsylvania. HLI, thanks to your generosity, has donated thousands of dollars' worth of equipment, videos, and literature to ACL.

Every January, before the March for Life, ACL holds a national prolife leadership conference in Washington, D.C.

For more information on ACL's vital work, write to American Collegians for Life, P.O. Box 1112, Washington, D.C., 20013.

Inspired by one of the world's great prolife priests, Father Charles Fiore, Collegians Activated to Liberate Life (CALL) is a campus-founded network with offices in Madison, Wisconsin, and contacts throughout the Midwest. Since September 1992, a full-time staff of seven has been visiting colleges to mobilize students into a driving force for life.

CALL brings collegians together several times each semester for regional rallies, weekend projects, rescues, and leadership-planning sessions. It aids struggling college groups and starts up new groups where none exist. Staff members take a year off from their studies, getting funding from supporters. They learn the many valuable skills needed in prolife work.

WHY WON'T NOTRE DAME'S PRESIDENT JOIN PROLIFE PRAYERS?

CALL held "Agape in Action," an alternative spring-break project at the University of Notre Dame, 14-16 March 1993. The school's administration originally gave them permission to hold all their activities on campus but later withdrew it, and so various churches in the city opened their arms to them. The administration forbade the Notre Dame prolife club to take part in these off-campus events.

Students and seminarians from several states held demonstrations in the mornings, heard talks by nationally known prolife leaders in the afternoons, and went to rallies in the evenings. Both Father Matthew Habiger and I spoke to the CALL students in South Bend.

Father Edward Malloy, CSC, president of Notre Dame, refused to meet with members of CALL until after they had held a seven-hour sit-in in the hall outside his office. He refused to come pray with them at an abortion mill located just three blocks from Our Lady's campus. Likewise, he refused to commit himself to doing so during the coming year.

From these prolife students, HLI has learned there are

abortion mills within blocks of secular universities, target-
ing young women and their babies. The same is true at
Notre Dame and at St. Mary's College, where a girl threw
a newborn baby into a garbage can a few years ago.
There's no apparent effort on the part of the university or
St. Mary's to prevent abortions there. A lawyer who's a
Notre Dame alumnus is part owner and legal defender of a
downtown South Bend abortion mill that CALL picketed.

For more information on the work of these great young
people, write to CALL, 1605 Monroe Street, Suite 107,
Madison, Wisconsin 53711, or phone 608/238-5262. Both of
these college prolife groups deserve your generous support.

A SUGGESTION FOR OUR BISHOPS

Proaborts, feminists, and homosexuals promote their
causes by staging huge demonstrations in Washington,
D.C. Why don't Catholics ever do that, apart from joining
Nellie Gray's March for Life each January 22?

Surely the bishops could manage to get five million of
our fifty-four million Catholics into Washington, tying up
the whole city, overloading the transportation system,
praying the rosary, and letting Slick Willie, Hillary, and
Gory Al & Co. know we want preborn babies protected.
Prolife Baptists, evangelicals, Jews, and others would
surely swell the tide of humanity. Once for all, let's show
our antilife government and media, and the nation, that
we Christians are not political pygmies.

H.L.I. WEEKEND IN NOVA SCOTIA

HLI sponsored a highly successful strategy weekend at
Antigonish, 14-16 May 1993. More than 250 participants
gave their rapt attention to speakers, bought every audio-
and videotape of the talks, pored over displays of literature, and expressed great appreciation for the conference.

Ramona MacDonnell, RN, director of HLI's branch in
Antigonish, coordinated the event in conjunction with
Theresa Bell, executive director of HLI-Canada in Ottawa.
Many volunteers made the event run smoothly. Topics
were chosen for their direct interest to Nova Scotians.

Father Matthew spoke on *HV* and on "Chastity

Formation *v.* Chastity Education." Dr. William Coulson's topics were "The Self-Esteem Movement and Youth Suicide" and "A Psychological Evaluation of Sex Education." Monsignor Michael Wrenn, the banquet speaker, explained "Catechisms and Controversies" and "Dissent and Theology."

Father Joe Hattie, OMI, who works in the Archdiocese of Vancouver, addressed "Informed Conscience and NFP." Terese Ferri, a lawyer from Cold Lake, Alberta, with her husband and eleven children, covered "Home Schooling." Bishop Colin Campbell preached at the conference's Saturday-morning Mass.

A strategy weekend provides local prolife activists with many tools to advance the sacredness of all human life. HLI presents the Catholic moral teaching, analysis of social trends, and suggestions on how to deal with specific problems.

A strategy weekend provides local prolife activists with many tools to advance the sacredness of all human life. Local people know the problems confronting the family, young people, marriages, schools, parishes, and the culture. And only they can find ways to exert a positive influence upon the local community.

HLI's most important service is to present the moral teaching of the Catholic Church, clear-headed analysis of what's taking place in society, and, based on its international experience, suggestions for effective ways to deal with problems.

HLI will hold its second Canadian strategy weekend this year at Edmonton, Alberta, 1-3 October. There'll also be a special four-hour basic-training session for prolife/pro-family trainers by expert Brian Clowes. The purpose of these sessions is to help Canadians recruit and train more prolife workers and leaders.

It's safe to say that eastern Canada will be talking

about the Antigonish conference for months to come. HLI is alive and well in Canada. Please pray for the Canadian bishops as they make plans to work more closely with all the prolife groups in advancing the prolife/profamily movement.

Letters

"Doing the most important work on earth"—a man like Pope John Paul II would never say that to Father Paul Marx unless it were the absolute truth.

In looking at the photo of the aborted child I can't help being moved to dry tears—*dry*, because of anger at my fellow men, who have so much and care so little. They even make grisly jokes: "You make 'em, we scrape 'em; no fetus can beat us."

My interest is deeply personal. In high school I had a girlfriend. We loved each other, but her parents were well-to-do, and my background was almost poverty-stricken. She aborted the life she had within her. I cannot begin to describe how that abortion forever changed her life, my life, and (of course) the life of the baby who is now dead. I have never recovered from that incident of more than eleven years ago. Oh, if only I could turn back time!

You keep on, Father Marx! Don't stop, Padre, for truly you *are* "doing the most important work on earth"—saving Love.

Vicente

(Note: Because of the personal nature of this letter, we are withholding the author's full name and address—*Ed.*)

I am a prolife girl from Poland, and I took part in the HLI conference in March, in Holland. I'd like to thank you very much for the invitation that enabled me to go there.

I have a very pleasant memory of the congress and hope to participate in similar prolife meetings in the future. I met many wonderful people from different countries of the world, and, to tell you the truth, I wish I were together with all of you again!

I am trying to gather some young people, here in Krakow, who would help me to organize various actions to fight for the right to life for everybody. I must tell you that the conference was a big stimulus for me to wake up and become much more active in what I am doing for the unborn. I am confident that God will help and bless me and my friends in our great prolife work.

Anka Dybowska
Krakow, Poland

I am writing to you to request additional materials, especially studies, which would help to convince skeptical OB/GYN's that increased contraceptive use leads to increased abortions.

This has suddenly become important to me and my wife personally. We are expecting our fourth child, and in talking to her obstetrician we decided to be more confrontational about his practice of prescribing birth-control devices. He is Catholic, and, like all of the other thirteen Catholic OB's in Springfield (as of October 1992, at least), he bases his medical practice on contraceptive/abortifacient birth-control methods. It is really distressing to us that of all these Catholic doctors, none practices Catholic medicine. None of them perform or refer for abortions and so call themselves prolife, but their practices are nonetheless causing abortions through chemical abortifacients and contraceptive failures that lead patients to get abortions elsewhere. They are closing their eyes to this, of course. We feel trapped.

Our doctor admits he knows virtually nothing of natural family planning, which he claims has a 25 percent failure rate. When I left him material on NFP's effectiveness in the 98-99 percent rate, he shrugged it off, saying that most patients are too uneducated or "stupid" to use it. He shrugs off the moral problem of chemical abortion from the Pill and Norplant, saying, "The intent is not to abort, but to prevent ovulation." "Good intent" is his moral rationale, although even this nonabortive intent (contraception) is condemned by the Church! Against 2,000 years of the finest theological minds that have condemned contraception, he sums up his reason for rejecting the

Church's teaching by saying, "I believe people should have a *choice.*"

I honestly believe he is too blind to see his own reliance on proabortion rhetoric. I am amazed at the arrogance of those who dismiss the Church's conclusions without ever seriously considering or reading the reasons the Church arrived at these conclusions. Catholic OB's will spend a great deal of time learning about Norplant to increase their income—but no time at all learning about NFP.

One of my main points with him was that contraceptive use increases abortion rates. He was extremely skeptical, yet I think it was a point that bothered him somewhat. That is why I want to document it to the hilt. One of the few modern studies I have is limited to teens and is only suggestive. It is a 1984 study published in *Family Planning Perspectives*, which found that the earlier teenage girls are started on the Pill, the more likely they are to become pregnant before marriage.

Our "Catholic" doctors pretend they aren't involved in abortion, but they're up to their knees in it. In some respects, I can hardly blame them when they are not being challenged to take the lead on this issue by priests or bishops. The link between increased contraception use and abortion is one we have to document irrefutably. The abortionists believe it, too.

We plan to gather a list of NFP practitioners and other Christians who oppose abortifacient birth-control methods and take out a signature ad in the diocesan newspaper saying that all these women want to switch to a practice that champions moral medicine.

David C. Reardon
Elliott Institute for Social
Sciences Research
Springfield, Illinois

*"If you had 48 international branches, your desk
would be a mess, too!"*

**Cold and snow can't stop prolife missionaries—or Fr. Marx's secretary,
Brenda Bonk**

Mission to Europe

No. 103   July 1993

I**n June, three staff members** and I made a twelve-day mission journey to France, Switzerland, and Poland with the goal of working more actively in Europe. Once-Christian Europe is now mission territory: The typical European woman has only 1.6 children in her married lifetime, with Italian women having 1.3, fewer than any other women in the world (U.S. women have 2.0).

We also hoped to enhance HLI's work in Poland as a base for spreading the Gospel of Life in the fifteen states freed from the former USSR.

LIMPING PROLIFERS IN DYING FRANCE

This "eldest daughter of the Church" has been called— unjustly—"the sewer of Europe." But certainly, no other "Catholic" European country has less prolife activity than France.

We were told there was much prolife literature around, but we couldn't find it. We were told there were some 30-40 prolife groups, too, but they don't seem very active and surely aren't united in a national movement. We were told again and again that French prolifers were tired and exhausted—but from what?

Nor do the country's bishops have a specific, organized, national program to defend preborn children. HLI has kept an eye on France for years, wanting to help. In fact, I spoke there several times in the early '70s.

France's demographic decay began with the massive practice of contraception after World War I. Pope Pius XI's encyclical *Casti Connubii* was written largely for the benefit of the French, who were heavy users of condoms and withdrawal.

When Hitler quickly overran France in World War II, Marshal Pétain, the French commander, moaned that had the mothers of France done their duty, he could have called on one million young Frenchmen to defend the fatherland. But when nations play with sex and when selfish parents use contraceptives, the nation's future and the Church's future are always in danger.

In 1970, Parliament legalized contraception. In 1975, it passed a trial abortion law allowing baby-killing in the first ten weeks of life for virtually any reason; in 1980, this was finalized. With the evil genius of Simone Veil as health minister, the feminists and the International Planned Parenthood Federation (IPPF) infiltrators had planned their destructive work carefully.

Today the government reports about 200,000 abortions per year, 20 percent of them induced with the RU-486 abortion pill. But everyone knows there are very many more, as shown by the birthrate, which is only about 1.7 children per family.

According to French law, baby-killings must be performed in "clinics" or hospitals in which abortions don't exceed 30 percent of the business.

The French prolife movement was united in the beginning, but it splintered badly in the late 1970s, thanks to Dr. Emmanuel Tremblay, a devotee of the notorious Club of Life, the now-jailed Lyndon Larouche, and the radical Union for New Politics.

Allegedly, the architects of this mayhem were connected with the Soviet KGB. The motivation? The best answer you get is that the Reds and their friends wanted to divide and weaken the nation and the West.

SILENT PULPITS AND PERSECUTED PROLIFERS

The pioneering, national baby-saving program of Mme. Genevieve Poullot—F.E.A. Sécours aux Futures Mères—has been remarkable. The famed geneticist Dr. Jerome Lejeune and his wife are associated with this work.

Tremblay and his cohorts criticized Dr. Lejeune brutally; the great German prolifer, the Lutheran Dr. Siegfried Ernst, got the same treatment. They called me a

"Nazi" and "weak on euthanasia," even though I wrote one of the first anti-"mercy"-killing publications, *The Mercy Killers* (1971), which is still in print.

It seems that no one is doing more in France today than Claire and Henri Fontana and their group, *La Trêve de Dieu* (the truce of God) . Inspired by Joan Andrews and the great rescuer Father James Morrow, head of HLI's branch in Scotland, the Fontanas began their rescue work in 1990; at one time, some 500 people were involved.

Last January 30 the French government tried to snuff out the fledgling rescue effort by passing a law saying rescuers and picketers couldn't confront abortion mills and hospitals. There were virtually no protests against the law, which hasn't been tested. The rescue movement is quiet for the moment, except for some clandestine efforts here and there. A prominent French cardinal, however, has a statement ready to be published in defense of the rescuers.

In 1986, some 5,000 souls took part in a huge profamily congress in Paris, organized by Venezuela's Christine de Vollmer, the USA's Mercedes Wilson, and France's Angela de Malherbe. A French bishop actually wrote an article against it! The hierarchy opposed it until Pope John Paul II intervened to assure Paris's Cardinal Jean Marie Lustiger that the congress was indeed truly Catholic. His Eminence then offered the final Mass and preached. Unfortunately, there was little follow-up.

Not a single practicing French Catholic whom I asked had ever heard contraception mentioned from the pulpit.

In no other country have the followers of the late Archbishop Marcel Lefebvre made greater inroads, in part because, some say, the bishops are "hibernating." When the pope told Ugandans that chastity, not condoms, was the only way to prevent AIDS, the anti-Catholic French press labeled him "a murderer." Strangely, no French bishop came forth to defend the Vicar of Christ.

Nationally, only 4 to 7 percent of France's Catholics go
to Mass weekly. Some 25 percent of French couples are on
the anti-baby Pill, 20 percent use the abortifacient IUD,
and about 15 percent think the condom is king. Fewer
than 3 percent practice natural birth regulation (NBR).

Not a single practicing French Catholic whom I asked
had ever heard contraception mentioned from the pulpit,
and most had never heard abortion condemned. *Humanae
Vitae* is virtually ignored. When that pivotal, prophetic
encyclical appeared in 1968, the French bishops, like the
German, presented their people with a subtle dissent.
Cornered, one good French pastor said that if he preached
on contraception he'd divide his parish. Adults and especially students have been known to walk out of talks where
speakers mentioned contraception or abortion unfavorably.

THE DEVASTATED VINEYARD

Several French prolife leaders, however, have assured me
there are some bishops who understand the situation but
have no idea how to begin teaching sexual morality again.
Countless young couples "live together," as in the rest of
Europe. Several priests told me that a great many girls are
pregnant at marriage.

Some years ago the Socialists in Parliament legalized
homosexual acts. Today there are at least 1,000 male prostitutes in Paris alone. Prostitution and pornography are
widespread.

I've visited eighty-nine countries, but only in France
have I found the "survivor's syndrome." By a certain age,
one of every two French women has aborted at least one
child. Her surviving children often know this and therefore
feel threatened, insecure, and depressed.

The syndrome also shows itself in unique teenage
problems. French mothers cry often over their abortions;
they confess them again and again. Therefore, as our first
concrete effort under the leadership of an old friend, Dr.
Marie Peeters (an associate of Dr. Lejeune), we'll sponsor a
daylong conference for priests in Paris in November. We
hope to feature the world's authority on post-abortion syndrome, Dr. Philip Ney of Canada.

Prime Minister Edouard Balladur is a Catholic who allegedly attends Mass regularly, but he has appointed pro-aborts to key cabinet positions. One is the notorious feminist Simone Veil, the architect of the abortion law, as minister of social affairs. Prolife Catholics expect very little from the conservative government recently swept into office, chiefly because it's preoccupied with the 11 percent who are unemployed and with the immigration problem, to the dismay of François Mitterand's Socialists.

French "Catholic" politicians are mostly like the pro-abort Knights of Columbus in Congress and other U.S. "Catholic" politicians. A notable exception in Parliament is Deputy Christine Boutin, who's a delight to talk to. She, like our representatives Henry Hyde, Chris Smith, and Bob Dornan, speaks out fearlessly for the preborn babies. Parliament rejected her bill to reduce the number of abortions by fostering adoptions. Parliament is now considering a dangerous bill on bioethics; thank God, the deputies defeated a bill to kill newborn babies with severe physical defects.

All of Europe—in fact, the entire West—is finally learning that babies are the only future any nation has. Only tiny Malta still has a replacement-level birthrate!

On TV, you've seen German "skinheads" and neo-Nazis attacking foreigners, particularly the Moslem Turks, who number 1.8 million. France has similar problems with her 3.6 million aliens, 60 percent of whom are non-European. Of course, millions more are already French citizens.

The quarreling national assembly has already voted to reverse a law granting French citizenship to anyone born in France, and has passed a law requiring foreigners to remain in the country for at least two years before bringing in relatives under reunification programs. In the future, don't expect a Turk or an Algerian—and surely not a Frenchman—to be there to carry your bags in Paris!

HOW CATHOLIC IS THE CHURCH?

The Mason Mitterand's Socialists tried to take over the Catholic school system some years ago. This attempt brought more than a million people into the streets of

Paris, and the government backed off. Priests, however, told me that Catholics wanted mainly to preserve their schools so they'd have a choice. They also said private schools were better overall than public schools, so the real motivation was hardly spiritual.

The French religious climate is hard to assess. Seminaries teach a questionable theology; the great Cardinal Lustiger pulled his seminarians out of the regional seminary in Paris and started his own. He sends his seminarians to Brussels for their philosophy studies. Still, France, a nation of 60 million, has 1,000 ordinations yearly (although the 38 million Poles have 1,100).

Religious vocations have declined notably, but French-founded religious communities in Africa are flourishing. Good parents insist that French Catholic schools don't teach the Faith, a problem universal in the West. Perhaps a good sign for the future: the French have bought about one million copies of the new universal *Catechism*.

There are good programs here and there, unique attempts at revival, such as the Parisian parish that runs a restaurant! Parish volunteers manage it as an outreach, with a small chapel on the second floor. The restaurant is in the middle of a pornography/prostitution area harboring the infamous Moulin Rouge nakedness peddlers.

Young people, hungry for the truth, are responding. One couple-team has taught NBR to 400 married twosomes. The ecumenical Taize community flourishes, as do small new religious communities here and there.

In this milieu, HLI will sponsor a weekend prolife/profamily seminar in Paris with French leaders, for anyone who'll come. We've been warned that France is "a nation of minefields" when it comes to organizing such an event, but we shall go forward prayerfully to do what we can, with God's help and that of good, believing French people such as the Fontanas.

Before the weekend conference, we'll sponsor a ten-day pilgrimage/tour, as we did in Ireland last year; it'll center on Lourdes. HLI is still supplying the excellent prolife center in Lourdes that lawyer J. B. Grenouilleau established years ago. By the way, he organized a life chain in Paris last year; only 240 people took part.

DANGER: *COP*ULATION EXPLOSION!

France is Europe's largest agricultural producer, which explains the difficulties France is creating with international trade laws. In fact, as they say in Europe, there are mountains of cheese and butter, an overabundance of other stored foods, and "lakes of wine" unsold, just as in the rest of the wealthy West—while fanatical propagandists such as Lester Brown and Paul Erlich keep screaming about "overpopulation" and the depletion of Mother Earth's resources. (Funny thing: no one ever warns people against over*cop*ulation.)

It's precisely these fanatics whom our bimonthly *Population Research Institute (PRI) Review* refutes and exposes; *PRI* seems to be the only organized group doing so anywhere in the world. (Time for a commercial: send HLI $25 for a subscription to *PRI Review*; and/or send $25 for ten back issues, a unique, eye-opening resource.)

PRI Review has exposed the depopulation activities of UNICEF worldwide, and it finally got the Holy See (and hopefully the deceived Knights of Columbus—see *Report No. 93*) to recognize what a dangerous antilife organization this is. UNICEF is tied in with the imperialistic, global depopulation program, as PRI's research has proven.

Like IPPF and its foundress, Margaret Sanger, UNICEF loves babies—but wants millions fewer of them. Of course, it also does much that's commendable. But UNICEF could do the good things without carrying out the antilife/antifamily programs that are financed by so many unwitting U.S. donors, including Catholics.

H.L.I.–SWITZERLAND IN ACTION

Thanks to the great prolife gynecologist/ researcher/leader Dr. Rudolf Ehmann, HLI runs a center in Lucerne. This nation of 6.4 million people has 1.4 million foreign workers, mostly men. The president of HLI-Switzerland is the tireless Petra Graf-Spiess, who works closely with Dr. Ehmann (she's giving a good prolife example by carrying her fourth child).

The Swiss have a well-organized, well-financed right-to-life movement, *Ja zum Leben*. Like our National Right to Life Committee, it works only on the tip of the antilife/antifamily juggernaut, i.e., abortion and euthanasia. The group's able leaders are Mr. and Mrs. Ramon Granges. I spoke for them many times in the 1970s.

The much-persecuted Dr. Ehmann, by the way, is the only Swiss gynecologist known to be totally prolife. He wrote our new booklet, *Abortifacient Contraception: The Pharmaceutical Holocaust*, which details the scientific evidence that the Pill, the IUD, the Norplant implant, the injectable Depo Provera, and the Morning-after Pill are abortifacients. We're now spreading this revealing booklet all over the world, with our friends' help.

There are many ways to save helpless preborn babies; informing people worldwide about these abortifacients is something to be proud of. HLI supporters have confronted many a Catholic doctor with the evidence in this booklet, only to get a "don't bother me" reaction or a devil-may-care shrug of the shoulders.

Millions of dollars are being spent in the search for a simple abortifacient that a woman would take routinely every morning.

U.N. DEATH POTIONS COMING

Under the guidance of the UN's World Health organization (WHO) in Geneva, millions of dollars are being spent in the search for a simple abortifacient that a woman would take routinely every morning. The goal is a potion that wouldn't be too hard on her health but would cause early, microscopic abortions; she'd never even know whether she had been pregnant.

This early, at-home, bathroom abortion is the future. What good will antiabortion laws be then? Shouldn't we be preparing for this horror now with a national program on chastity, true love, preparation for marriage, family spirituality and committed celibacy? Phone or write your bishop and ask him to help HLI's new project for collecting and publishing the office addresses and phone numbers of truly prolife doctors, those who refuse to perform abortions, to refer mothers to abortionists, or to prescribe abortifacient pills and devices.

In 1984, Swiss voters rejected a referendum aimed at protecting all citizens from conception 'till natural death. Lawmakers eventually dismantled almost all legal protection for preborn babies. Now they're considering a bill for absolute abortion-on-demand, like the USA's FOCA (Freedom of Choice Act). Dr. Ehmann thinks it'll pass.

On 17 May 1992, the government banned human gene-pool manipulation, embryo donation, and surrogate motherhood. *In vitro* fertilization is legal; donating an embryo, ovum, or sperm is forbidden.

Like their father, Satan, the pro-aborts never quit 'til they get everything—never mind that they destroy young people, the family, the Church, and society in the process. This seems to be what they want, although I've never been able to fathom fully the real motivation behind this devilish death movement.

The Masons, by the way, have always been very strong in Switzerland, as in France. IPPF, which has been working in beautiful Switzerland for years, is now fine-tuning its organization for the final onslaught.

H.L.I. ACCUSED OF BISHOP-BASHING— AND KILLING!

Swiss sources told me HLI is being blamed for organizing the killing of abortionist Daniel Gunn in Florida! When you do God's work, people accuse you of all sorts of things.

Even a Prince of the Church, Cardinal Roger Mahony, is attacking us. He seems to want to destroy HLI, judging from his letters to fellow cardinals and others. He says we've done nothing but bash bishops for 20 years!

More than once, we've invited Cardinal Mahony to send a trusted priest to look over the letters of commendation and the requests for help, that HLI receives from cardinals, archbishops, bishops, religious superiors, missionaries, priests, nuns, and others all over the world. He has steadfastly spurned our offer to open our files to him to give him an idea of the global dimensions of the world's largest pro-life/profamily apostolate. Please pray for him often.

(More on Switzerland in a later issue.)

CONDOM HOAX EXPOSED

We'll soon distribute our new four-minute video, *Safe Sex? Not!*, around the world. We're much indebted to the Demers family for producing this timely video (you can get your copy from HLI for $10). (And have you read our eye-opening new AIDS pamphlet, Dr. Stanley Monteith's *To Deceive a Nation: AIDs Update 1993*? Send HLI $2 .)

The sperm is the smallest cell in the human body, as the ovum is the largest. The tiny sperm measures three microns; the cell bearing the AIDs virus measures .1 micron, which means that the HIV cell is thirty times smaller. Yet the pores in condoms are 100 to 300 microns wide! C. M. Roland, editor of *Rubber Chemistry and Technology*, has pointed out that no condom can trap all sperm cells; obviously, no condom can trap all of the much-smaller HIV cells, either. That's the message of *Safe Sex? Not!*

THE LATEST NEWS FROM POLAND

This was my fifth journey to the most Catholic country on earth. Poland has made astonishing progress economically and politically, yet a great deal still needs to be done. The Communists, who now call themselves "Socialists," still have much influence in the government. Before the party lost power officially, the Reds wormed themselves into control of media and high positions in industry.

They never succeeded in collectivizing the farms, but industry was another story; today only about 25 percent is in private hands. A recent attempt to speed up the pace of privatization brought down the government, which had to deal with too many splintering political parties. The unemployment rate is 20 percent, and the middle class is shrinking. This is one reason 1.36 million Poles aged 25 to 49 left the country in 1992 alone.

Out of 38 million Poles, 36 million are Catholics, most of whom attend Mass regularly. The Church is still in a dominant position, even though her authority and influence is eroding ever so gradually because of a massive influx of the West's worst: Masonry, pornography, New Age religion, raw sex, and the devilish influence of IPPF, radical feminism, deadly affluence, and other evils.

The Masons are particularly vicious. They attack the Church relentlessly, calling Her intolerant, medieval, totalitarian, and sexist. (Sound familiar?)

Poland has more seminarians than any country in the world: 9,000. Last year the Poles ordained 1,100 priests. About 5,000 priests and religious serve in the mission fields. Some of them labor in countries formerly imprisoned by the USSR. Others are in Africa. Sixty secular priests toil in England, 120 in France, and many in Germany. Each year some 200 Polish priests and religious enter the foreign missions. Today Poland is the only source of missionaries in the West.

Polish seminarians know nothing of the intellectual nonsense in Western seminaries—thank God! You see Poland's numerous nuns everywhere, in habit. The Franciscans are producing an excellent monthly magazine, *Promyk Jutrzenski*, emphasizing prolife/profamily themes. If you asked me which of the eighty-nine countries I've visited is healthiest spiritually and morally, all things considered, I'd say Poland.

H.L.I.'S WORK EXPANDS

That's why HLI established a large center in Gdansk with a $100,000 annual budget. And we just bought a 1,400-square-foot house (fully furnished) in Gdansk from a prolife widow, for $61,000.

The Solidarity movement began in Gdansk. It eventually toppled European Communism with the help of our Polish pope, Our Lady of Fatima, and our friends' rosaries and sacrifices. From Gdansk we'll launch our efforts into the former USSR. One of our first tasks in former captive nations will be to explain the origins of human life; the people have little awareness that abortion is baby-killing. We've begun translating crucial prolife and religious literature, I'll tell you much more about Russia and the

East in my September *Report.*

Our center in Gdansk will supply the best prolife/pro-family literature and videos to the newly formed Polish Federation for Life and, above all, the nations of the former USSR, particularly Russia, Ukraine, Belarus and Georgia. we've hired Ewa Kowalewska, an editor, as executive director; she speaks Russian and other Slavic languages fluently. A secretary, a translator, and part-time help will work with her in a modern office with the latest equipment. The monthly labor cost will be $1,200.

A prolife publishing firm will cheaply print for HLI in Poznan in central Poland. Dr. Pawel Wosicki, a totally committed prolifer, will be our printer; help will come from our well-established branch in Katowice, headed by psychologist Andrzej Winkler and his colleagues; we've been working with Andrzej for years. By the way, he's Poland's foremost alcohol/drug counselor. You may remember him from his talks at our world conference in Santa Clara two years ago.

Someone has rightly said that the newly freed Slavic peoples are so hungry for God that whoever gets there first with the most will convert them. Many sects have moved in, armed with lots of money and social services. In Ukraine there are 6,000 Catholic parishes, but only 2,500 have a priest; the others are waiting. Some parishes still have priests from the Orthodox Church. HLI already has a fully functioning office in Ukraine, thanks to our friends.

As you read this, I'm traveling in Russia and other Eastern countries, working with Dr. Antun Lisec of Croatia. Despite the incredible harm done by eighty years of satanic Communism, the people of the East are surprisingly hungry for religious truth. There are now 500 seminarians, with more enrolling each year. Some 350 seminarians are enrolled in Lvov, Ukraine, alone. The opportunities for HLI are mind-boggling.

POLES BATTLE ABORTION

In 1956, Poland's Red government imposed abortion-on-demand. Since then, abortionists have killed an estimated 18 million polish babies. After the Red regime fell, resistance to abortion began immediately.

(Five years before, HLI had planted many seeds.) T h e national Polish Federation for Life is now being born with our help, encouragement, and guidance.

A year ago members of the Sejm (parliament) introduced a bill to outlaw all abortions. Because the Sejm is made up of many parties and riddled with feminists, Communists, and the dastardly IPPF (the last funded largely by foreign money), the bill was amended to allow abortions for cases of rape, incest, serious health risks to the mother, and severe fetal defects (certified by two doctors). Ominously, the bill also calls for sex "education" and the distribution of contraceptives.

IPPF has already sponsored two courses in universities to train teachers in its pornographic sex "education" (sex preparation). The good thing about the very inadequate new abortion law is that it requires abortions to be performed in hospitals only and therefore to be recorded.

Thanks to the work of prolifers, the bishops' best efforts, and the strong appeals the pope has made in Poland, the Poles now at least have a law, which they hope to improve greatly in the next session of the Sejm. Prolifers are now working to elect more prolife lawmakers in the upcoming election.

Offices that arrange for Polish mothers to abort in other countries have already sprung up on the borders.

Meanwhile, the number of abortions has declined considerably. But offices that arrange for Polish mothers to abort in other countries have already sprung up on the borders. Many Polish doctors refuse to kill preborn babies, especially now that the Polish Medical Association has declared abortion unethical. Pregnant mothers feel more comfortable in public.

UNDOING THE REDS' LEGACY

Now that the Church is free, she has reestablished the Catholic school system and other institutions run by the many nuns. Things are looking up, although the obstacles and problems are daunting.

One out of three marriages in the cities ends in divorce, and one of six in the country. Alcoholism is an enormous problem, with several million confirmed alcoholics. But there are only 120 actual cases of AIDS and only 200 people infected with HIV. Leaders told me that creeping affluence is eroding spiritual values, confirming Ben Franklin's observation, "A remedy for luxury has never been found."

One thing is certain: HLI faces an enormous challenge and opportunity in Poland. Into the battle for the preborn babies and the family we'll throw as much personnel and financing as our benefactors' prayers and generosity make possible. We must save this vital, pivotal, vocation-rich Catholic nation.

We're making plans to launch our Mary Corps in the former USSR. Many HLI supporters have shown great interest in this apostolate; we rely on Our Lady of Fatima to lead and guide us to moral/spiritual success in the East.

The Poles have much going for themselves, thanks to Cardinal Stefan Wyszynski, whose ingenious parish catechetical program saved the Catholic Church, to the utter frustration of the godless Reds. Thanks to the former cardinal of Krakow (now Pope John Paul II), today almost every parish has a family-counseling center that also teaches marriage preparation and natural birth regulation. The Responsible Parenthood Society also serves families, through fourteen flourishing branches. And virtually every Polish diocese is building a haven for "lonely girls," mostly snatched from the abortionists.

Because Moscow redrew the map after World War II, there are many Poles in the countries of the former USSR; it'll be easy for HLI to work with them. A major problem, though, is the resistance of the Russian Orthodox Church, which complains that Rome is proselytizing and which drags its feet in giving up the churches that used to belong to the Catholic Church. The Reds turned over all Catholic churches to the Orthodox Church after the latter became largely a tool of the Kremlin—a sad story revealed in the now-open archives of the KGB. Many Russians know this, are unhappy about it, and join the Catholic Church.

So now, as never before, HLI will be busy in Gdansk in the north, Poznan in the middle, and Katowice in the south, without neglecting Warsaw, the capital. From our new center we'll pour our energy, videos, and publications into the Eastern countries, under the guidance of our Polish staff and Dr. Lisec, who's been preparing the way. Please pray!

UPDATE: SOCIETY OF THE DIVINE WORD (S.V.D.) MISSIONARIES

In *Report No. 99* we exposed the serious errors in Father Karl Peschke's widely used seminary text, *Christian Ethics*, published by the SVDs. We've held out several olive branches to the SVDs, but they still have given us no assurance that they accept the Church's teaching on contraception and *Humanae Vitae*.

From all parts of the world we've received evidence of the errors spread by Father Peschke. For example, in the Philippines' *Daily Inquirer* (24 January 1993), a letter quotes his book at length to justify opposing the "official Church opinion" on contraception. Please don't give money to the SVDs until they fully support the Church's teaching on sexual morality. Meanwhile, please pray for their conversion.

REBELS PLOT AGAINST NEW CATECHISM

After the first draft came out in the 1980s, certain famous Jesuits sponsored a seminar at Georgetown University to plan ways to counter it. The venture cost some $70,000; Harper & Row published the proceedings.

Since that time, for almost seven years, the Modernist theologians have plotted to destroy the influence of the *Catechism of the Catholic Church*. They want no official, binding statement of the truths taught by Christ's Church.

Thus, under the auspices of the department of theology of the Pontifical Catholic University of America, owned and controlled by the U.S. bishops, rebel theologians held a four-day meeting in June, doing their best to destroy the *Catechism*. The scandalous report of this meeting went out through the nation's Catholic papers via the bishops' Catholic News Service.

At the gathering, Father Gerald Sloyan, a dissenter from *Humanae Vitae* who has taught at Catholic University, Temple University and Minnesota's St. John's University, summarized his view of the *Catechism*:

> It is marvelously informative in some matters but woefully deficient in others; hence, its use cries out at many points for nuance, supplementation and correction [!].
>
> In the short run, adaptations [!] of it should be attempted only by people who know as much theology as the authors. It cannot be promoted as a dependable book for use as it stands because of the uneven quality of its statements. In brief, it requires a second, revised edition very soon.

There you have it! Bill Marshner of our staff attended the meeting and wrote a critique, which I'll send you for an offering of $2 to HLI.

With typical German subtlety, the president of the German hierarchy conveyed the message: Don't take the **Catechism** *too seriously.*

BEWARE THE "INTERPRETERS"!

Of course, the rebel National Conference of Catechetical Leadership has published a ridiculous report, "Implementing the *Catechism of the Catholic Church*."

The general pitch of the Modernist "interpreters" is:

The *Catechism* is meant for bishops and theologians and must be interpreted and adapted for individual countries and regions! The attack is worldwide.

In announcing the *Catechism* in Leipzig, Bishop Karl Lehmann, president of the German hierarchy, observed astonishingly that the *Catechism* needs to be understood and judged in the light of new theological and hermeneutical developments. In other words, with typical German subtlety, he conveyed the message: Don't take the *Catechism* too seriously.

Many "noted" German theologians, intellectuals, and scholars supported him, including Germany's Monsignor Johannes Gründel, the counterpart of our own Father Charles Curran. For Monsignor Gründel and the German bishops, who dissented from *Humanae Vitae*, to accept the *Catechism* as the official, undisputed teaching of the Catholic Church would be to admit they've taught false doctrine for twenty-five years.

Just as strange, at a meeting of the Catholic Academy of Bavaria, Vienna's Dominican Auxiliary Bishop Christopher Schönborn, whom the pope appointed as secretary of the commission responsible for the *Catechism*, made waffling statements about *Humanae Vitae*, after saying he could take no responsibility for the moral section of the *Catechism*!

Meanwhile, His Holiness and Vatican officials insist that the *Catechism* is the authentic, authoritative, and official teaching of the Church for Catholics everywhere; it's not a pick-and-choose document. And so, on 5 June 1993, the Pontiff told visiting U.S. bishops:

> The *Catechism* is truly God's timely gift to the whole Church and to every Christian—an authoritative guide to sound and vibrant preaching, an invaluable resource for parish adult-formation programs, a basic text for upper grades of Catholic high schools [N.B.], colleges, and universities.

As England's great rescue priest, Father James Morrow, has said, "Read the *Cathecism*, not the commentaries." And please ignore the strange "Implementing the *Catechism of the Catholic Church*" from the Washington, DC-based national Conference of Catechetical Leadership.

Replicate of Original Letters

FAX: 0091 4869 32096.

Office: 32096, 32197   PHONE:
Residence: 32297, 32097   Office 47
      Residence 96, 97

Reg. No. 1 126 / 80 T C L S & C S Reg. Act of 1955

POST BOX 11
PEERMADE–685 531
IDUKKI DT., KERALA
INDIA

Ref: PDS/93/0160.

Date 6-2-1993.

Very Rev. Fr. Paul Marx, OSB., PhD
President & Founder, HLI
Human Life International
7845 Airpark Road
Suite E
Gaithersburg, Maryland 20879
U. S. A.

Dear Very reverend Fr. Paul,

I thank you very much for your literature on 12th World
Conference on Love, Life & the Family.

Through our Community Health Department we are propagating
Prolife Programme in 72 villages. It would be very good
of you to give us permission to translate some of your
important books and booklets of prolife. We will be
very much grateful to you if you can bless us also with
some money for our attempt. Please also send us some
Mass Stipends

It will be a big assistance for those priests who are
involved in this programme.

Looking forward to hearing from you,

Yours sincerely,

PAID
3-25-93
#16360 $ 100.

Fr. Mathew Arackal.

Ave Maria +

JOHN ALBERT.
DICKOYA ESTATE,
DICKOYA,
SRI LANKA.
6th December, 1992.

Rev. Fr. Paul Marx, O.S.B., Phd.,
Human Life International,
7845 Airpark Road, Suite E,
Gaithersburg, Maryland 20879,
U. S. A.

Dear Rev. Father,

I thank you very much for all your goodself's thoughtfulness &
kindness for sending me a valuable & important parcel of Books
together with the Video Casette "Candlelight Conflict".

I will be giving these books to three Parish Libraries here in
different parts of the Country as a Christmas present from your
goodself, of which the Rev. Fathers & Parishoners will be so glad of
am sure. The Video Casette your goodself sent is very important,
a good Catholic friend of mine has promised me to spare his
Video 'Deck' - Video Casette Player, on Sundays for a few hours to
show these kind of Video Casettes on our estate owned Television
set to the poor estate workers and surrounding people here.
I myself, my good friend, Our Parish Priest and all the poor people
here are so happy about this, all of us are so grateful to your
goodself about this. I have told all here about your kindness and
in return every body have promised to pray for your goodself and
your Apostolate.

I do not like it very much, and I feel so sorry to trouble your goodself
always, but I cannot help my self as there's no one else to ask this
kind of help from. When your goodself has a chance of sending us
a parcel next, and if there is any possibility for your goodself we would
be so happy to have the following Video Casettes please if you could,
which we happened to see in a Catalog of "Ignatius Press" of 15 Oakland
Ave; Harrison NY 10528, sent to me by my poor friend in U.S.A. Mr. Phil F.
Meade of 10 Hagy Pl, Pittsburgh. PA. 15232., and we state them here after
choosing them according to their prices (Low Priced ones) and according to
the place in preference: (1) "Miracles: Lourdes, Fatima, Guadalupe & Knock."
(2) "AIDS: What you Haven't Been told" or "No Second Chance" (3) "The Gates
of Hell" & (4) "Meet the Abortion Providers". If there is any possibility only
to send please, and it would not mind as per your possibility and preference even please, or the One " Jesus of Nazareth."   P.T.O -
                                                        (over)

 විවෘත කිරීමට මෙතැනින් කපන්න. திறப்பதற்கு இங்கே வெட்டுங்கள் To open slit here

ගුවන් ලියුම வான் கடிதம்
AEROGRAMME

Temple of the Tooth
Kandy

8.00

ඉලංකාව ශ්‍රී ලංකා SRI LANKA

REV. FR. PAUL MARX, O.S.B.,
HUMAN LIFE INTERNATIONAL,
7845 AIRPARK ROAD,
SUITE E,
GAITHERSBURG,   MARYLAND 20879,
U. S. A.

AIRLANKA
Taking Sri Lanka to the World

දෙවන නැවීම இரண்டாவது மடிப்பு Second fold

Cultural Pageant

යවන්න அனுப்புவர் Sender

SRI LANKA

JOHN ALBERT,
DICKOYA ESTATE,
DICKOYA,   SRI LANKA.

කිසිවක් අඩංගු නොෙවීය යුතුය No enclosures permitted
உள்ளடக்கல் அனுமதிக்கப்படமாட்டாது

Other than the Casettes like 'Abortion' or 'Aids' we requested for religious
ones as we cannot get them at all here for any rate only please. When-
or if sending please send only one of each please, as the Customs -
Officials here may tax me. and which I would not be able to afford.
If one of each they may not. they tried to tax me for the books too for
which a known Priest helped me by telling them that these are for free
distribution etc. We are not troubling your goodself that you must. but
only if there's any possibility please, as these will be very worthy for poor
us. Assuring your goodself our prayers & for your Apostolate, I remain
God Bless!
Yours sincerely in Christ!

John Albert.

MAY THE HOLY TRIUNE GOD LIVE IN OUR HEARTS!

St. Paul's Rectory

P.O. Box 3285
Accra, Ghana, Africa

3 June, 1993

Reverend and Dear Father In The Love Of The Hearts Of Jesus and
Mary,

According to the letter of your confrere: Fr. Habiger, O.S.B.
which I just received with "Special Report 100" you were of my
age on May 8th!!!!! CONGRATULATIONS, and I hope May 8th proved
to be "Happy Birthday" for ou!

My belated "Birthday Gift" is a Holy Mass for all that you
need and desire in the line of God's graces and blessings , first,
for yourself, and then for your worldwide missionary apostolate
on behalf of the unborn!

My 73rd birthday was March 28th, as you may have taken notice
in my March 15th newsletter.

At the moment, life here is extremely hectic! Every second is
"explosive"!

Since the divisions of ecclesiastical territory of Ghana by
the Pope last November, complications especially for me in what
was the Interdiocesan Tribunal since 1983, is now hamstrung and
whilst marriage cases keep pouring in not only from Ghana from
the three Archdioceses and 8 dioceses, but also from abroad
because of Ghanaians who have migrated elsewhere, I am rather
bewildered at the moment!

Archbishop Andoh was just named a Consultor of the Propaganda
in Rome, and was called there on May 7th. He is also the Moderator
at the moment of the Interdiocesan Tribunl ,but cannot get free
for that. He is obliged to return to Rome for his Pallium as

BY AIR MAIL

GHANA P&T

AÉROGRAMME

AIR LETTER

Rev. Father Paul Marx,O.S.B.
Human Life International
7845 Airpark Road, Suite E.
Gaithersburg, MD. 20879
U.S.A.

AN AIR LETTER SHOULD NOT CONTAIN ANY
ENCLOSURE: IF IT DOES IT WILL BE SURCHARGED
OR SENT BY ORDINARY MAIL

Sender's name and address

Rev. A.Kretschmer,S.V.D.
Box 3285
Accra,Ghana,Africa

Archbishop onf June 29. Then he will be "enstooled" as a "Paramount Chief" in
Holy Spirit Cathedral on July 15th as Metropolitan Archbishop of the Metropolitan Archdiocese of Accra.To finalize our First Centenary of Evagelization of
the Accra territory:Jan.31,1893-Jan. 31,1993, on Aug. 22 Card. Tomoko is expected to come as the Papal Legate for the close of the Centenary.

The Ghana Hierarchy has proposed to Pope John Paul II that since he promised
to end the "Special African Synod" to be held in Rome next year instead of
Africa because of political upheavals, that he come again to Ghana to end the
Synod here! What Providence has in store for me is fortunately a mystery!!!!

Begging for your prayers and with the assurance of mine in return and my
missionary blessing on your world-mission, fraternally,

[signature]

Niech przeżywanie Tajemnicy
Bożego Narodzenia
stanie się źródłem nowych mocy,
radości i pokoju.

Życzę również Drogiemu Ojcu,
obfitych Łask Bożych -
w Nowym 1993 Roku - zapewniam
również o wdzięcznej pamięci
modlitewnej -

+ *Alexander Kaszkiewicz* *[signature]*

Bp Alexander Kaszkiewicz

Grodno, BOŻE NARODZENIE 1992r.

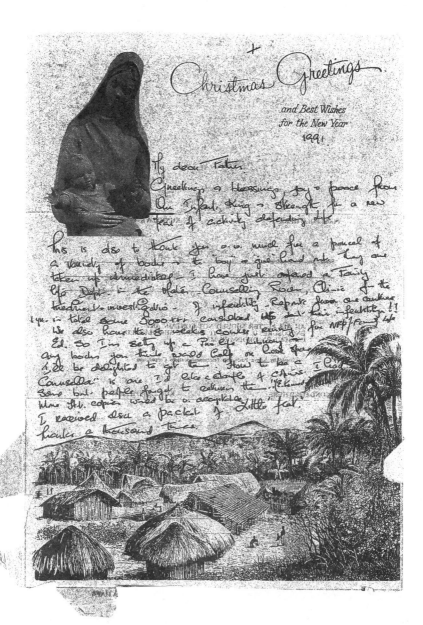

Christmas Greetings

and Best Wishes
for the New Year
1991

My dear Father

Greetings & Blessings joy & peace from
Our Infant King — Strength for a new
year of activity defending life.

This is also to thank you so much for a parcel of
a variety of books & toys & girls hand out. They are
taken up immediately. I have just opened a Family
Life Dept. in the older Counselling Room Clinic of the
medical investigation. & infertility Reports from our centres
I ye in total some 5000++ consulted life and their infertility !!
We also have the 8 weeks course running for NFP/Family Life
Ed. So I'm setting up a Pro Life Library —
any books you think would help on Love sharing etc
I'd be delighted to get them. How to be a
Counsellor is one I'd also adopt & advise. I had
some but people forget to return them. If/when
some A.V. copies would be acceptable.
I received also a packet of "Little" feat.
Thanks a thousand times

Again I would like to thank you & staff for keeping us
so well informed – I assure you we use every bit of
the information we get. I'll send you a letter we sent
in reply to those who want abortion legalised by Std:
Pot. You met Dr. Kwiu in Rome? I believe it was a
good meeting. It was wonderful to get the Pro-Lifers
together & pool their experience.
So Father God bless you your work & staff &
thanks again to your kindness. Renewed wishes
... Sincerely
Sr. Sbanillaw

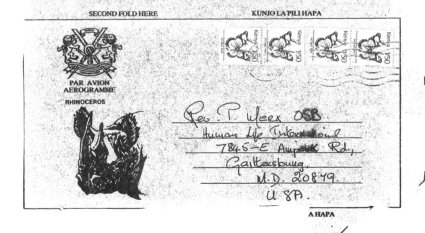

TO OPEN SLIT HERE   KUFUNGUA KATA HAPA

Sender's name and address   Sr. Sbanillaw
Box 30325
Nairobi Kenya

AN AIR LETTER SHOULD NOT CONTAIN ANY
ENCLOSURE; IF IT DOES IT WILL BE SURCHARGED
OR SENT BY ORDINARY MAIL.

Issued by Kenya Posts and Telecommunications Corporation

SECOND FOLD HERE   KUNJO LA PILI HAPA

PAR AVION
AEROGRAMME

RHINOCEROS

Kenya 1/50   Kenya 1/50   Kenya 1/50   Kenya 1/50

Rev. P. Weex OSB.
Human Life International
7845-E Airpark Rd.,
Gaithersburg,
M.D. 20849.
U.S.A.

A HAPA

May   our

CHRIST   FAMILIES

be the   both

CENTER   NATURAL

of our   and

HEARTS   SUPER-

and of   NATURAL

CHRISTMAS CRIB, GOOD SHEPHERD CONVENT, CHUNCHON,   SO. KOREA

Thank You for the video tapes. They
are really precious!
   May you be filled with the Holy Spirit
to accomplish the work the Lord has entrusted
to you to save babies.
   You are in our prayers.
      United in Him,
         Sr. Joanna Le, RGS.

Christmas, 1992

Dear Fr. Paul Marx,

Loving greetings for Christmas. As we kneel at the crib to worship and thank our Lord for the many blessings of this past year we remember our friends and loved ones. We thank God for them and ask Him to bless each and all.

This year, in addition to our work in Mary's Home, we took over the administration of the Chunchon Girls' Vocational School. It is a school and dormitory for girls coming from poor or difficult circumstances. Sixty students are enrolled for each of the two 6-month courses being offered in hair science, dressmaking and machine embroidery. Because the aim of the school is to help the girls to lead good lives, the Sisters revised the curriculum so that the first hour of the day is devoted to moral guidance with classes in moral values, Bible study, and Korean culture. Beginning in September term, the Sisters implemented the Korean version of teen-STAR, a pro-chastity program for youth. Unbeknown to the Sisters, one of the girls who enrolled in the March term was pregnant. She planned to quietly have an abortion. But because of the instruction at the Vocational School and in spite of opposition from her family, she came to Mary's Home.

In Mary's Home, the Sisters, besides all of their regular work, now go out to give Pro-Life presentation. They also have a monthly day of prayer with women who have had an abortion(s). The women find this very helpful.

Sisters Rose Virginia   Much love from us all.

Martina, Sr. Mary Rita   In Jesus, our Good Shepherd
Sr. Ma. Virginia Kim

Joanna   Good Shepherd Sisters
Sr. M. Bonaventure   Sr. Stella

Sister Monica   Francisca, Magdalena, Regina.   Euphrasia

194 Soksa Dong, Chunchon, 200-180, South Korea
Tel. (0361) 261-4618; FAX (361) 261-3209

Cardinal Newman Catechist Centre

✝ National Resource Centre ✝ Non-profit Catholic Bookshop ✝ Specialists in Family Catechetics

Venerable John Henry Cardinal
Newman
Cor ad cor loquitur

Newman Centre
1 Chetwynd Road
Merrylands NSW 2160
Australia
Fax (02)637-3351
Phone (02)637-9406

17th June, 1993

Dear Father Marx,

Thank you ever so much for all the wonderful material you are sending and I do read much of it and only wish I could share it more. But even the future of our Newsletter is in doubt now that I am appointed acting chaplain to a big hospital on the other side of Sydney, and can only visit the Newman Centre once a week.

No, I have not forgotten "Humanae Vitae" and thanks to your encouragement I was preparing a new edition in two sizes, A5 and A6 (this page is A4, A5 is half of it, and A6 is a quarter of it). That rough photocopy reduction which you liked was very labour-intensive to produce so we wanted our energies to produce something worthwhile. For instance, I was replacing "fecund" with fertile or fruitful, and "fecundation" with "fertilization". There were also the overly strict translations of the conditions which justified using NFP: "grave motives", "serious causes", which did not reflect the latin words "seriis causis", "justis rationibus", respectively. "Serius, a, um" means serious in the sense of earnest, not "grave" in contrast to "just" as we use it in canon law.

Well, all this is on the back-burner, as is Newsletter no. 120 (I can't even send you 118 and 119 with this, because they are 90 miles away and I can't leave my post).

NEWMAN CENTRE PUBLICATIONS — *Catholic Family Catechism, Heart Speaks to Heart, Confirmation Kit for Home Preparation, Bush Boys: An Outdoor Adventure & The ABC of Camping, Cuthbert Joins the Bush Boys, Why We Believe, Reasoning Things Out, Catholic Thinking.*
DISTRIBUTORS — *Faith & Life Series* (1-8), *Divine Master Series* (9-12), *St. Joseph Picture Books.*

My legs are recovering from the thrombosis but I've no longer the physical and mental energy to overcome the obstacles: lack of Time, Space and, while doing its Hospital, privacy in the presbytery.

You perhaps do not realise that the Newman Centre is run on a shoe string, and that the staff are not my secretaries. They are fully engaged in selling books, and I have no secretarial help whatever for my own projects. The Newsletters are an exception in that Marie McNulty usually does the pre-sorting for the Post Office (which gets us a concession rate of postage within Australia), but I prepare the text and usually print them.

If and when I get the text of HV finalized, and get my bishop's approval, I'll at least send you a copy you could print yourselves. But as for a 1000, I am daunted at the labour-intensity of it.

Another project shelved for the time being was a new edition of the Credo of the People of God, for its 25th anniversary, too, on 30th June.

Another again was to do something with the Minority Report of the Birth Control Commission, "leaked" to The Tablet in 1967. It has material not in HV which is most relevant today.

But the reality is that I can't ever be sure of getting out the next newsletter....

Yours sincerely in Our Lord,

James Tierney

The Rev. B.J.N. TIERNEY

P.S. Enclosed cards have just arrived from Milan.

P.P.S. National Shrine of the Little Flower, Canada (Monsignor Blanc) has just print my "Catholic Family Catechism Apostles' Edition Pocket Size":

Catholic Association of Medical Practitioners

c/o The Secretary,
Dept. of Prev. & Soc. Medicine,
University, College Hospital,
Ibadan, Nigeria.

Monday 25.07.92.

Rev Paul Marx, OSB, PhD,
Human Life International
7845 Airpark Road, Suite E,
Gaithersburg, M.D. 20879,
U.S.A.

Dear Fr Marx,

Grace and peace be with you!

We are in reciept of your letter of the 16th of July, and write
to thank you for it, especially for the cheque enclosed which we
are in the process of cashing. We pray the Good Lord to sustain
you, and the HLI.

The enclosed letter to Mr L. Adekoya informs you as well where we are
with the plans for the symposium and we would not need to repeat it.
So, once again, stay well, thank you; and please, remain blessed.

Yours sincerely in the course of truth,

Dr D.I. Ogar
Secretary General

Index

Dedek, J. 163, 166
Demers family 322
Depo-Provera 5, 36, 74, 137, 185, 187, 218, 261, 320
Dewey 279
Dignity 41-43
dissident theology and practice 10, 28-29, 37, 41-46, 51-56,
  59-67, 75, 78, 80-82, 95-96, 110-115, 135-141, 153-
  154, 163-175, 181-185, 188-189, 214-221, 227-245,
  257-263, 273, 284-285, 293-304, 307
Dominica, S. 77
Dominicans 110-112, 113-115, 154, 241-244
Donceel, J. 163, 168
Döpfner, Cardinal Julius 141
Dornan, Representative Bob 317
Dowd, John F. 100
Dowling, Bishop Owen 181
Downey, Father James 223
drugs 25-27, 324
Duffy, Bishop Joseph 93
Dulles, Father Avery 293-304
Dunn, Pat 189
Dunning, Sister Mary E. 111
Durocher, Sister Lucille 210
Dutch Cathechism 138
Dybowska, Anka 309-310
Eclipse of Reason 17
Ehmann, Dr. Rudolph 270, 319-321
England/British 25, 89, 91, 106, 164, 173, 174, 179-180,
  186, 212, 249, 261-262, 273, 323
environmentalism 43, 45, 183, 219
Erlich, Paul 319
Ernst, Dr. Siegfried 314
Espitia, Hilda 134
European Community (EC) 92, 94, 255
European Economic Community (EEC) 39, 91, 199
euthanasia xv, 6, 8, 15, 32-33, 39, 72, 86, 95, 118, 130,
  135, 137-138, 185, 200, 260, 263, 271-272, 284, 315,
  320
Ezeanya, Archbishop Stephen N. 47
Familiaris Consortio 59, 69, 108, 121